Cybersecurity and Third-Party Risk

Third Party Threat Hunting

Gregory C. Rasner

WILEY

I dedicate this book to two women in my life who made this book possible. First is my mom, who emphasized a love of reading and education that gave me the capacity to write. Second is my wife, who has been my biggest fan, encouraged me to write the book, and put up with the hours of me sitting at my desk writing it. And to my father, who taught me the qualities of a great business leader, father, and husband.

(ISC)²®

(ISC)² books published by Wiley provide aspiring and experienced cybersecurity professionals with unique insights and advice for delivering on (ISC)²'s vision of inspiring a safe and secure world.

(ISC)² is an international nonprofit membership association focused on inspiring a safe and secure cyber world. Best known for the acclaimed Certified Information Systems Security Professional (CISSP) certification, (ISC)² offers a portfolio of credentials that are part of a holistic, programmatic approach to security. (ISC)²'s membership is made up of certified cyber, information, software and infrastructure security professionals who are making a difference and helping to advance the industry.

About the Author

Gregory **C. Rasner** has worked as a cybersecurity and IT leader in Finance, Biotech, Technology, and Software fields. He holds a BA from Claremont McKenna College along with certifications: CISSP, CCNA, CIPM, ITIL. Along with the book *Cybersecurity and Third-Party Risk* published by Wiley, he has written several online articles for major publications, and is a frequent speaker at forums and conferences on related topics. He has five kids and a wife who is also a cybersecurity professional. Rasner was in the USMC and has held leadership roles in several veterans organizations. Greg was instrumental in establishing the cybersecurity program at Johnston Community College, is a board member on the Technology Advisory Board, and teaches part-time at JCC as well. Fun for him is camping and traveling with his family.

About the Technical Editor

Narendra Patlolla is a senior information security leader. He is currently head of cybersecurity architecture at Arthur J Gallagher & Co. With over 20 years of progressive experience in the industry and cybersecurity discipline, Patlolla previously held key leadership roles at multiple Fortune 500 enterprises, where he established identity and security architecture programs and gained extensive experience in implementing multiple vendor and bespoke solutions. He has managed large security programs across multiple industry verticals (insurance, financial services, technology, healthcare, and marketing services).

Narendra holds a B.S in mechanical engineering, M.S in computer information technology, and M.B.A in finance and management. He is also a Certified Information Security Manager (CISM), a Certified Information Systems Security Professional (CISSP), and a Certified Open Group Architecture Framework (TOGAF) architect. Narendra is a member of the IDSA Executive Advisory Board.

Acknowledgments

First, I acknowledge God's gifts and blessings to me to be able to write this book. Second, to my Technical Editor, Narendra Patlolla, for such a great job at making the work better. Next are my colleagues and friends who have been so critical to what I learned in leadership, cybersecurity, and operations: John Stewart, Edna Conway, Michelle Guel, Oisin Mac Alasdair, Mark Sullivan, Steve Scott, Ed Goff, Christina Bray, James Claypool, David Quinlan, Ikenna Iloabuchi, Alexander Mulnick, Noah Shindler, Vincent Lau, KC Udoh, Karen Heflin, and many others who have helped me learn and lead. Lastly, the Wiley team, Jim Minatel, Pete Gaughan, and Jan Lynn, who were awesome.

Contents

Foreword

After a recent cybersecurity breach shook both U.S. government agencies and corporations and was proclaimed the worst ever, many colleagues asked me if this was my "I told you so" moment. While I could have gloated a bit, I instead reminded them and anyone else who would listen that the next one is right around the corner if third-party risk is not front and center in the security discussion.

As an executive at Cisco and Microsoft, I have built new organizations delivering trust, transparency, cybersecurity, compliance, risk management, sustainability and value-chain transformation. I have been invited to provide testimony to U.S. Presidential Commissions on cybersecurity and currently serve on the executive committee of the Department of Homeland Security's Information and Communications Technology Supply Chain Risk Management Task Force. In addition, I have authored NATO directives and contributed my input to numerous government and industry bodies. In all cases, third-party risk is my primary concern and focus.

There are no easy answers when it comes to third-party security and risk. We all operate in a hyper-connected world and third-party ecosystems continue to expand. When one considers

IT/OT convergence, the proliferation of IoT/IIoT, expanding global supply chains, and the accelerated move to a platform economy, it is obvious that the threat surface for both private and public sector organizations continues to grow. So how do we as security and risk professionals tackle this mounting challenge?

Greg's book, *Cybersecurity and Third-Party Risk*, is both timely and necessary. As colleagues at Cisco, Greg and I pondered and identified solutions to the very issues he raises throughout this book. Readers can leverage his clear risk identification and practical guidance to build sustainable and effective third-party risk programs. As the book points out, third-party risk is nothing new and is not going away. But let's be clear: The message is not one of fear, and the book clearly establishes what we can and must continue to do to meaningfully address this critical risk.

Cybersecurity and Third-Party Risk should be added to the bookshelves of all security and risk professionals, regardless of the industry in which they operate. It will serve as a guide to developing a foundational third-party security program as you address the growing third-party risk at your organization. Consider yourself fortunate to have access to both Greg's expertise and his thoughtful and comprehensive approach to a challenge we must all consider a priority.

Edna Conway
Vice President, Chief Security &
Risk Officer, Azure
Microsoft

Introduction

Third-party risk (or supply-chain security) are not new disciplines, and there have been frameworks, regulatory directives, professional certifications, and organizations that all attest to its maturity. Cybersecurity could be considered more mature, since it has been around in some form since computing came of age in the 1970s. Nowadays, it's even more complex in terms of frameworks, disciplines, certifications, regulatory guidance and directives, and avenues of study. Why do the surveys, time after time, indicate that well over 50 percent of organizations do not perform any type of Third-Party Risk Management (TPRM), and even fewer have anything other than an ad hoc cybersecurity due diligence program for vendors? Reasons for this lack of attention and collaboration can be found in hundreds, if not thousands, of breaches and security incidents that were the result of poor third-party oversight and a lack of any due diligence and due care for the vendors' cybersecurity.

This book is designed to provide a detailed look into the problems and risks, then give specific examples of how to create a robust and active Cybersecurity Third-Party Risk Management program. It begins by covering the basics of the due diligence processes and the vendor lifecycle, with models and illustrations on how to create these basic but necessary steps. Then it goes more in depth about the next parts in the creation of a mature program: cyber legal language, offshore vendors, connectivity security, software security, and use of a predictive reporting dashboard.

The book is designed to not only help you build a program, but to take an existing program from one of compliance checkbox work to an active threat-hunting practice. Many programs that do currently exist are designed and run as an obligation to "check a box" for a regulator or an internal auditor. Yet, no one has ever secured their network or data by doing *only* what the regulators told them to do. Security is an ongoing activity that requires its application in third-party risk to be equally active and ongoing. Its activities and results should emulate a cyber operations or threat operations team that focuses its efforts on reducing cybersecurity threats externally at the suppliers. Get away from checking boxes and filling out remote questionnaires and take a risk-based approach that engages your highest risk and/or most critical third parties in conversations to build trust and collaboration to lower risk for both your organization and the vendor.

Who Will Benefit Most from This Book

A superset of cybersecurity, third-party risk, and executive leadership will benefit the most from reading this book. On the cybersecurity side, analysts to senior leadership will be able to take their information security knowledge and experience to perform the hands-on work and management of third-party risk, while third-party risk professionals will better understand and appreciate the need to include a more robust cybersecurity risk domain. Executive and senior leadership in business who are not focused on cybersecurity or third-party risk will gain an understanding of the risk, practice, and frameworks, and how to lower their risk for a cybersecurity event at their vendors.

Looking Ahead in This Book

This book is divided into two sections. Section 1, titled "The Basics," lays the case for the need of a robust and active Cybersecurity Third-Party Risk Management program as well as the necessary and basic due diligence activities and processes needed. These are not basic as in "simple," but in terms that they are the foundation necessary to building a mature program, which is covered in Section 2, titled "Next Steps." This section details what comes next, after you have built the basic foundation. This "Next Steps" section describes cyber legal language, cloud security, software security, connectivity security, offshore vendors, and how to build predictive reporting that focuses on the highest risk vendors.

Chapter 1 opens with a detailed description of risk by using examples of the SolarWinds and other supply-chain attacks, which happened in late 2020, as prime examples of how the threat actors have evolved both in their identity and tactics. Examples are also provided in a long list of companies who have lost their data due to a vendor that did not take due care with their data. Chapter 2 provides some basics on cybersecurity. This book does not require the reader to be a cybersecurity or third-party risk expert, but it does require that a few concepts are defined and frameworks are covered for both topics to ensure all readers are at a set level. Chapter 3 delves into how the COVID-19 pandemic affected the security landscape and how quickly the attackers adapted to new opportunities. What happens when the pandemic is over and how it will change behaviors and business in ways that will become the new normal will mean a continued increase in cybercriminal activity.

Chapter 4 is an in-depth look at Third-Party Risk Management (TPRM) and is included to provide a set level for the readers as well as to tie the cybersecurity and TPRM concepts together, as both domains are aimed at identifying and managing risk. Chapters 5 through 9 cover the vendor lifecycle of intake, ongoing security, and offboarding due diligence activities Chapter 5 reviews the activities and requirements for vetting and performing security assessments of new vendors or services from existing suppliers. Chapter 6 describes ongoing cybersecurity due diligence activities such as remote assessments. Chapter 7 is then devoted to the important complex topic of on-site assessments, which are essential due diligence processes for the physical validation of security controls at a vendor site and the gold standard for assurance.

Chapter 8 covers the Continuous Monitoring (CM) program and how it is a crucial security control for vendors for the times in between the point-in-time assessments. Building a robust CM program means taking a set of tools and internal data to engage vendors on potential real threats that they may be unaware of and reducing risk collaboratively. Chapter 9, the last chapter on the vendor lifecycle, discusses offboarding. Many firms overlook this part of the lifecycle, so this chapter covers the critical steps and due diligence that must be done to ensure there's no risk to the data or connectivity from a vendor.

Section 2 begins with Chapter 10, which discusses the large topic of the cloud. The shared responsibility model is discussed and how it affects the security controls that your vendor is responsible for and what they have outsourced to the Cloud Service Provider (CSP). Cybersecurity, offshore vendors, cloud and privacy legal language and process is covered in Chapter 11; and then Chapter 12 details in depth the possible ways to test and perform due diligence on third-party software. Connectivity to a vendor is a unique risk that opens a whole organization's network and data to an attacker traversing from the vendor or exploiting the hardware they use to connect, and is discussed in Chapter 13. Chapter 14 contains details on how to manage offshore vendor risk, while Chapter 15 wraps up with ways to take all the data collected with the due diligence and other cybersecurity activities to become more predictive for risks and produce reports.

Special Features

The notes found sprinkled throughout this book are designed to provide an example or expansion on topics that bring the topic (either in the chapter or the book as a whole) into a real-world illustration or in-depth analysis. Tips are added in the book to deliver information to the reader on how to improve a process or activity (or a common pitfall to avoid), while definitions help the reader to understand the concepts involved.

What Is the Risk?

On December 10, 2020, ESET researchers announce they have found that a chat software called Able Desktop (Able)—part of a widely used business management suite in Mongolia including 430 Mongolian government agencies—was exploited to deliver the HyperBro backdoor, the Korplug RAT (remote access trojan), and another RAT named Tmanger. They also found and identified a connection with the ShadowPad backdoor, used by at least five threat actors in the exploit. Two installers were infected with the trojan and the compromised Able update system was installed with the malicious software. Evidence shows that the Able system had been compromised since June 2020, while the malware-infected installers were delivered as far back as May 2018.

The post explains that HyperbBro is commonly attributed to the cybercriminal group named "LuckyMouse," a Chinese-speaking threat actor known for highly targeted cyberattacks. Primarily active in South East and Central Asia, many of their attacks have a political aim. Tmanger is attributed to TA428, also a Chinese *Advanced Persistent Threat* (APT) group. Because these two applications are used normally by different APTs and are now together in one attack, the ESET team theorizes that LuckyMouse and TA428 are sharing data and weapons; they are also likely the subgroup of a larger APT. Given the region and threat actors, it is considered to be a political attack that had been planned as early as May 2018, yet not carried out in earnest until two years later.

Advanced Persistent Threat (APT) is the term given to state actors (i.e., government run or authorized hackers) or large cybercriminal syndicates that have a lot of time and patience to perform very stealthy, large-scale attacks aimed at political or economic goals.

The SolarWinds Supply-Chain Attack

On December 13, 2020, FireEye, a global leader in cybersecurity, publishes on its website the first details about the SolarWinds Supply-Chain Attack, a global intrusion campaign inserting a trojan into the SolarWinds Orion business software updates to distribute the malware. FireEye names the malware "Sunburst." After the attackers successfully hacked into FireEye, their activity demonstrated lateral movement and data exfiltration. "The actors behind this campaign gained access to numerous public and private organizations around the world. . . . This campaign may have begun as early as Spring 2020 and is currently ongoing. . . . The campaign is the work of a highly skilled actor and the operation was conducted with significant operational security," as explained in the Summary from FireEye's website on December 13th.

The attackers added a .dll file (a configuration file) called SolarWinds.Orion.Core.BusinessLayer.dll to the Orion product, which had been digitally signed and enabled backdoor communications over HTTP (i.e., normal, unencrypted web traffic), to other servers. The Sunburst malware is suspected to have lain quietly for two weeks, while it performed some reconnaissance via executing commands that led to file transfers and to controlling the victim's servers (i.e., reboots, disabling services). Using a native product within Orion, the Orion Improvement Program (OIP), Sunburst blended in with the program's normal functions expertly. It even had the capability to sniff out the antivirus and cybersecurity forensic tools being used, likely to learn how to better go undetected.

"As much as anything, this attack provides a moment of reckoning. It requires that we look with clear eyes at the growing threats we face and commit to more effective and collaborative leadership by the government and the tech sector in the United

States to spearhead a strong and coordinated global cybersecurity response," according to Brad Smith, President of Microsoft (December 17, 2020) as posted on his blog about the SolarWinds attack. This attack was used to steal valuable intellectual property from the top-tier security company FireEye. As of the time of this writing, it has been confirmed to have affected dozens of U.S. cabinet-level agencies. Due to the pervasiveness of the SolarWinds product across the world, more breaches will be discovered in the following days, weeks, months, and years to come. Some may never be discovered (or admitted); however, there will be international victims. It is a coup for the suspected perpetrators, thought to be a state actor who used a supply side attack, exploiting the weakness of a popular network and monitoring tool, SolarWinds, to circumvent the tight defenses of the intended victims.

On December 18th, Microsoft released information identifying more than 40 government agencies, higher learning institutions, Non-Governmental Organizations (NGOs), and information technology companies that were infiltrated, with four-fifths of them being U.S.-based, and nearly half of those being tech companies. On his blog, Brad Smith said

> This is not "espionage as usual," even in the digital age. Instead, it represents an act of recklessness that created a serious technological vulnerability for the United States and the world. While the most recent attack appears to reflect a particular focus on the United States and many other democracies, it also provides a powerful reminder that people in virtually every country are at risk and need protection irrespective of the governments they live under.

One act of recklessness that he refers to is that this pervasive software, SolarWinds Orion, was clearly not performing its own due diligence and due care to protect itself and its customers, and this product is used by nearly everyone. Further recklessness was that all the customers of SolarWinds were not performing at expectations for cybersecurity's best practice.

If customers had performed some key cybersecurity assessment on a third-party software maker like SolarWinds, this attack could have been detected. Were intake questions asked about the type of data to which SolarWinds had access and where that data might go or be stored? Depending on a company's solution type, asking questions about how the secure software development lifecycle is managed and audited is considered to be appropriate.

With the hardware device, what was SolarWind's supply chain security for the hardware parts and assembly? For the company that had ventured to perform an on-site cybersecurity physical validation of SolarWinds, was any evidence produced on how they performed external security scans (which might have detected the default password on their download page "SolarWinds123")? Who performed these external scans? The company? Or did they hire an outside firm and were the results viewable? Often, such companies will not share these results, so you must negotiate to at least see the Table of Contents, who performed such security scans, and when.

Final question: Had SolarWinds remediated all the findings in the external security scan? While this is not the first time a breach has occurred, the scale of the SolarWinds breach will dwarf all others.

The VGCA Supply-Chain Attack

On December 17, 2020, ESET Research announced it had detected a large supply-chain attack against the digital signing authority of the government of Vietnam (ca.gov.vn), the website for the Vietnam Government Certification Authority (VGCA), which is part of the Government Cipher Committee under the Ministry of Information and Communication. Vietnam has made the digital leap, and almost anyone in the country who requires a government service, product, or approval is required to use a digital signature. These e-signatures have the same authority and enforceability as a traditional paper document autograph according to government decree.

The VGCA also develops and makes available for download a toolkit to automate the process of e-signatures. This toolkit is widely used by the government, private companies, and individuals. VGCA's website was hacked as early as July 23rd, and no later than August 16, 2020. The compromised toolkits contained malware known as PhantomNet, and SManager ESET confirms that the files were downloaded from the VGCA website directly, and not the result of a redirect from another location. While these infected files were not signed with proper digital certificates, it appears that prior files were not correctly signed either. This may have led to users not rejecting the improper digital certificates of the trojan-infected files because they behaved the same before the malware was added.

When an infected file was downloaded and run, the correct VGCA program ran along with the malware. This masqueraded the trojan to the end user because they saw the normal program running correctly, being unaware of the trojan or unlikely to look for it because the program appeared to be running normally. The file eToken.exe extracted a Windows cabinet file (.cab), which was used as an archive file to support compression and maintain archive integrity. The file 7z.cab was the file that contained a backdoor for the attackers to exploit. The attackers went to great lengths to ensure that the backdoor ran, regardless of the user's privileges on the device.

If the 7z.cab file was able to run as an administrator on the machine, the program wrote the backdoor to c:\Windows\

appatch\netapi32.dll, which then registered it as a service to ensure it kept running after any reboot. On a device that only allowed the file to run as a normal user, the install placed it in a temporary directory, but the program scheduled a task to ensure its persistence. ESET named this backdoor PhantomNet. They mentioned that the victim list included the Philippines, but no evidence was found of a delivery mechanism.

The trojan was determined to be a simple program, and according to the sophistication of the attack, it is likely there were other more malicious plugins added to exploit the backdoor. When the victim's web configuration was determined, then it reached out to a command and control (C&C) server to get instructions. Communications with the C&C servers was done over HTTPS (secure, encrypted web traffic), and the attackers went to the trouble of preventing the interception of traffic (i.e., man-in-the-middle attack on their own data) by using their own certificates.

Data analysis indicates that the malware was used for lateral movement. Once inside the computer, it enabled the attacker to move around the network for other data. The malware collected and transferred information about the computer, user accounts, and victim. In the post-attack forensics, no data was discovered nor was the goal of the attack.

ESET wrote on its website:

Conclusion: With the compromise of Able Desktop, the attack on WIZVERA VeraPort by Lazarus and the recent supply-chain attack on SolarWinds Orion, we see that supply-chain attacks are a quite common compromise vector for cyberespionage groups. In this specific case, they compromised the website of a Vietnamese certificate authority, in which users are likely to have a high level of trust. Supply-chain attacks are typically hard to find, as the malicious code is generally hidden among a lot of legitimate code, making its discovery significantly more difficult.

The Zyxel Backdoor Attack

On January 2, 2020, Zyxel (networking device maker) announced over 100,000 of their firewalls, VPN gateways, and access point controllers (i.e., Wi-Fi controllers) contained a hardcoded administrator backdoor account, which gives root-level access (i.e., a super administrator that can do anything on the device) on both the secure shell (SSH) and web administrator portal. This is on top of a previous similar incident with Zyxel in 2016, where they had a backdoor that allowed any user to escalate their account to root-level account privileges. This backdoor is still being exploited by botnets to this day, four years later.

A *hardcoded backdoor root account* is one that cannot be underestimated in how critical the security flaw is. When an account is built within the code of a product, it cannot be removed unless the code itself is changed or updated by the manufacturer. Additionally, the root account is what is referred to as a "super user," which has privileges as an administrator. The products affected the manufacturers Advanced Threat Protection (i.e., firewall), Unified Security Gateway (i.e., hybrid firewall/virtual private network [VPN] gateway), USG FLEX (i.e., hybrid firewall/VPN gateway), VPN, and NXC (i.e., Wi-Fi access point controller) series. These devices formed the perimeter and internal security control points for thousands of companies worldwide. The attacker's ability to exploit these network devices most assuredly gives them lateral access into the victim's network. At the time of this backdoor announcement, Zyxel offered patches for all of the products except for the NXC series; it is not producing a patch for another four months.

Zyxel Patch Release

The expected patch release is April 2021. Until then, the only option for organizations is to unplug and replace the devices to ensure security posture.

The hardcoded user account "zyfwp" and password "PrOw!N_fXp" were stored in visible plaintext (i.e., unencrypted or obfuscated). Dutch researchers reported that the password was clearly visible in the code binaries. Apparently the account had the root-level access to install firmware updates. In the previous 2016 incident, a hacker would've needed to already have a user account on the device to exploit it and to become a super user. In that instance, the root account is directly accessible on HTTPS (port 443) connection to the device.

According to Zyxel's website, "A hardcoded credential vulnerability was identified in the 'zyfwp' user account in some Zyxel firewalls and AP controllers. The account was designed to deliver automatic firmware updates to connected access points through FTP." A search on Shodan (a search engine that can find computers and devices connected to the internet) shows nearly 30,000 of these devices deployed in Russia; 5,000 in Taiwan, Germany, and Finland; with nearly 3,000 in the United States.

Other Supply-Chain Attacks

Starting in early December 2020 and into early 2021 (January 2), there were four major third-party (supply-chain) attacks and vulnerabilities announced in the span of 20 days. These attacks or vulnerabilities went on for months or longer. Evidence in the

SolarWinds and Vietnam attacks pointed to advanced persistent threats launching into the weaponization of the supply chain. In two of the cases, the attacks were directed at nearly a whole country (Vietnam through the VGCA, and Mongolia through the Able Desktop). In three of the instances, the attackers were all APTs and were stealthy enough to remain undetected for months or longer. These attackers have seen what they can do with the weakest links—vendors—to get to a wide range of targets.

Chief Information Security Officers (CISOs) at Fortune 500 companies have spent billions of dollars in the last decade securing their networks from such breaches. Some great tools have been implemented, like Intrusion Detection/Prevention Systems (IDS, IPS), Cloud Access Security Broker (CASB), Privileged Access Manager (PAM), Security Information and Event Management (SIEM), and Security Operations Centers (also referred to as Cyber Fusion Centers) have been built to track and eliminate threats. However, the level of breaches in 2020 continued to increase exponentially. The number of third-party breach instances grew because every company is some other company's vendor. As the number of these breaches increased, it meant another vendor with hundreds, thousands, or millions of customers became a victim as well.

Public law enforcement is also sounding the alarm. On December 8, 2020, at the American Bankers Association (ABA) Financial Crimes Enforcement Conference, FBI Director Christopher Wray stated, "The financial sector has the most robust cybersecurity of any industry," which is why cybercriminals try third-party channels. Banks can also be affected by ransomware targeting third parties, a threat that Wray said "may be somewhat underestimated by a lot of people." While he specifically called out financial firms, the same could be said of many other sectors, including aerospace, energy, technology, biotech, and others, which generally have excellent security on their own company's assets. Most of the victims of the SolarWinds attack have been in the technology and government sectors, which typically have had good-to-excellent security. In those cases, hackers will target the weakest link, attacking vendors who take security less seriously.

Hundreds of examples like this have occurred over the last decade, across the world, and in every industry: Ticketmaster, Capital One, Tesla, Under Armor, Boeing, PayPal, Chubb, nearly every major worldwide automaker, Sears, Best Buy, Entercom, and T-Mobile. In the case of FireEye or a customer of Zyxel, these companies lost protected data as a result of a third (or fourth) party. No one in the public realm remembers that third party; they simply remember the company they trusted with their data who let them down. Such breaches cost these companies large amounts of money, which directly affected consumers, and extensively damaged the companies' reputations. In areas where there was a heavy regulatory presence, the breached firms were often left holding fines as well. In August 2020, the Office of the Comptroller of the Currency (OCC) assessed an $80 million civil penalty against Capital One for failure to establish effective risk assessment processes prior to migrating significant information technology operations to its public cloud environment. It is expected to cost Capital One up to $150 million, and it cost the company's CISO his job at the firm.

Problem Scope

The secret is out: If you want to attain protected data as a hacker, you do not attack a big company or organization that likely has good security. You go after a third party that more likely does not. Companies have created the equivalent of how to deter car thieves: Ensure that your car looks difficult enough to break into so that thieves move onto the automobile with its doors unlocked and keys in the ignition. When a burglar sees a car with a car alarm, they know that they can look and eventually find a target that isn't so well protected. Exploiting the weakest link is not new. A bank robber could go to the bank to steal money, but a softer target would likely be the courier service as it brings the money into and out of the bank.

To date, cybersecurity and third-party risk teams have not often collaborated or understood the common threat, instead focusing their security on their own silos. In most regulated industries, this has led to the typical rush to the bottom to meet the regulatory requirements; meaning, rather than create a security program that secures their data and network, they do just enough to keep the regulators happy. Regulators are never considered to be on the leading edge. Whether it is in financial fraud or cybercrime, they simply do not lead in best practices for any field. However, it is not their responsibility. Regulations are typically designed to limit the behavior of a company that may cause financial or bodily harm. The most highly regulated industries, such as energy, biotechnology, finance, telecommunications, aerospace, and many others, have robust Third-Party Risk Management and cybersecurity teams. However, if these industries rely on doing what the regulators require of them, they are not going to be performing their best practices.

The most successful companies at preventing their systems from being compromised go beyond what a regulator or regulation mandates them to do for compliance. The regulations and their enforcers get involved after something bad has already occurred. Sarbanes-Oxley (SOX) was a financial regulation designed to lower the risk of financial fraud by publicly traded companies after the damage done by the tech bubble crash in the early 2000s. The Dodd-Frank Wall Street Reform and Consumer Protection Act was passed in 2010 after the financial meltdown leading to the Great Recession. These widespread changes in regulation occurred as a reaction to the excesses and missteps that lawmakers felt led to the meltdown. Nearly every regulation passed is due to a previous misstep, not in anticipation of the next misstep or mistake

Being reliant on the government to set the standard for what to do and how to do it is a recipe for disaster. This is not to say, however, that regulations are without their merit when enforced correctly. The argument here is not about whether there should be regulations, but more about if organizations should be advised to view those regulations as the bare minimum to perform. In the case of cybersecurity and third-party risk, regulations provide some excellent guidance on what is important for organizations. However, if a cybersecurity or third-party risk team only relies on regulators for the best practical procedures to follow, there's a high likelihood their companies will be hacked. In fact, the likelihood is that they will be hacked quite a bit faster than those companies that view regulatory requirements as their starting point.

To illustrate the point, we can look at the Payment Card Industry Security Standard (PCI-DSS), which is the payment card standard (using credit and debit cards), to guarantee consumer financial data protection. PCI-DSS has very specific recommendations and is regularly updated for how to secure networks, protect user data, require strong access controls, perform network security tests, and regularly review information security policies. PCI-DSS is tested regularly, and its standards are considered rigorous. It is not regulated by the government; instead, it's a group of companies that standardized their practices. Meaning, private companies collaborated to create what is nationally viewed as a success in security.

Third-party risk, or what another company is doing to lower risk to your company, might seem like it places a CISO and the cybersecurity organization at a disadvantage because they cannot control what goes on at another entity. However, that is a myth.

While a third party cannot be directly controlled, there are ways to direct and monitor their behavior and choices to greatly reduce your risk. Anyone who has ever been taught risk or worked as a risk professional knows the mantra: Risk can never be zero. In fact, anything is possible. Regardless of whether your company is using all the fancy technology and expensive software, or employing hundreds of cybersecurity professionals hunting for vulnerabilities, there still is a chance, or risk, of a breach.

The goal is reduce risk to a level that is commensurate with your company's effort to reduce it, based upon its risk appetite. This risk reduction effort of a third party requires a change in a company's cybersecurity approach and attitude. As we dive into the numbers, it will become apparent that not enough companies perform the required due diligence. Out of those that do, some do not perform it at the level necessary to reduce the risk. Often, risk reduction is performed as a compliance effort, and merely viewed as a checkbox to complete in order to keep regulators and auditors at bay. This attitude of "ignoring the risk" or "doing it as 'checkbox' security" has caused cybersecurity Third-Party Risk Management (TPRM) to be absent from adequate attention and activity.

Compliance Does Not Equal Security

Compliance is not security, yet security is an important piece of compliance. By definition, *being compliant* is when your organization meets the minimum requirements for specific regulations at a specific moment in time. If we look at many of the companies on the recently breached list, it's likely all were meeting their regulatory obligations for compliance in their respective industries. In the case of Target when its payment system was hacked, it had just completed a certification of its PCI-DSS. Most regulations are simply a form of deterrence (of things like insider trading or dumping chemicals into a river). Regulations discourage bad behavior either by people or companies.

Security is an ongoing activity—a continuously occurring activity and not one that occurs at a point in time. Compliance activities are performed as a checklist by internal or external auditors to verify that a company's team is following regulations. It's is an important activity that helps prevent bad acts. Employees and companies see these checks being performed, then are discouraged from doing bad things, such as ill-gotten gains via insider trading or killing fish by dumping chemicals. Security has the dubious distinction of being sure data is not lost. Once data is lost, it cannot be retrieved—it is gone forever into the Dark Web or other places. The deterrent must come from the company's cybersecurity efforts, not the government regulators.

A company can be 100-percent compliant and also be 100-percent owned by hackers. For example, you can drive a car with seatbelts, an automatic brake system (ABS), collision detection and avoidance, blind spot detection, and more, all turned on. Say your car is up to current safety regulations, you, the driver, are all buckled up and sober. There should be no accidents or injuries. Yet, another driver who doesn't always pay attention to the safety warnings fails to perform their best practices while driving, resulting in a collision with injuries. You, a driver, were 100-percent compliant, yet another driver was not.

Another difference in compliance activities is the timing of each action. Compliance activities are done at a certain point in time for what is present in terms of controls and checks. Another third party (i.e., auditors, regulators) or an internal team ensures that the company they're working with satisfies a set of requirements that allows it to continue to perform business. When all conditions have been satisfied, the compliance activity is finished. Security, however, is never finished. It is continually monitored, reviewed, and improved.

Third-Party Breach Examples

Throughout many chapters in this book, you will find case study sections where we dive into some of these breaches. However, it is important to understand the scope and history of how often third-party incidents occur. Many public breaches attributed to a particular company are, in fact, the result of a third party. One of the most well-known examples is the Target breach. In fact, it was Target's Heating, Ventilation, and Air Conditioning (HVAC) provider that was breached to get access to Target's data.

Following are a few examples of the major third-party breaches to show how easily they cross over any boundary (i.e., geographic, sectors, sizes):

- **Target (2013):** The data of 70 million customers and 40 million credit/debit card information records was leaked by HVAC company Fazio Mechanical Services.
- **Lowe's (2014):** Millions of drivers' records were exposed by SafetyFirst, a vendor that stored the exposed data in an online database.
- **JP Morgan Chase & Co (2014):** Contact information for 76 million consumers and 7 million small businesses was exposed by a third-party website used to sponsor a foot race.
- **Sam's Club, Costco, CVS, RiteAid, Walmart Canada, Tesco (2015):** Millions of customer data records were hacked at PNI Digital Media, which is used for online photo ordering and printing.
- **T-Mobile (2015):** A total of 15 million personally identifiable information (PII) records were leaked by Experian, a customer credit assessment company.
- **Forever 21 and Hyatt Hotels (2017):** An unknown number of credit card data records were released due to its POS system.

- **Uber (2017):** Coding site GitHub's misconfiguration caused data for 57 million users to be exposed.
- **Equifax (2017):** Highly confidential data for 143 million consumers was released due to an undisclosed third-party tool used to build web applications.
- **Verizon (2017):** The restricted data of 14 million customers was exposed by customer analytics provider NICE Systems.
- **Hard Rock Hotels & Casinos (2017):** Sabre Corp, a travel reservation service, was exploited, causing a leak of credit card data for an undisclosed number of customers at 11 of its properties.
- **ShadowPad (2017):** A server management software (made by NetSarang) used by hundreds of multinational and large companies worldwide exposed a still unknown number of protected data records.
- **Republican National Committee (2017):** The PII for 200 million registered Republican voters was leaked via the third-party Deep Root.
- **BevMo (2018):** Online payment provider NCR Corporation was breached for over 14,000 BevMo customers.
- **Nordstrom (2018):** A third-party tool that managed the direct deposit permitted the personal information about Nordstrom's employees to be leaked.
- **Ontario Cannabis Store (2018):** Canada Post, an online tracking tool, allowed the loss of the store's customer data.
- **SuperMicro (2018):** A flaw present in the microchips used by major companies, such as Apple and Amazon, caused an unknown amount of data to be leaked.
- **Facebook (2018):** Any platform that shared login credentials with Facebook resulted in the exposure of 50 million user accounts.

- **The Conservative Party (UK) (2018):** CrowdComms, a conference application used by the Conservative Party, was the party responsible for the loss of protected data about Ministers of Parliament (MP), conference attendees, and journalists.
- **British Airways (2018):** An undisclosed third-party misconfiguration of JavaScript caused the financial and personal information of over 300,000 customers to be released.
- **University of Louisville (2018):** Health Fitness, a fitness vendor, released employee names, employee IDs, and physicians' names.
- **Washoe County School District (2018):** District teachers' emails, usernames, and passwords were exposed by an instructional tool provided by Edmodo.
- **MedCall Healthcare Advisers (2018):** Over 150 businesses were affected by this third-party breach, with 7 GB of medical information data being exfiltrated.
- **GoDaddy (2018):** Sensitive records for over 30,000 servers were released by a misconfigured Amazon S3 bucket.
- **Air Canada (2018):** An undisclosed mobile application provider caused the loss of customer data.
- **Fiserv (2018):** This financial third-party website provider was the reason that hundreds of banks had the records for their customers exposed.
- **Ticketmaster (2018):** Inbeta, a provider of Ticketmaster's website application, caused a leak of customer data.
- **Universal Music Group (2018):** Cloud-storage provider Agilisium caused the loss of internal File Transfer Protocol (FTP) credentials, Amazon Web Services (AWS) secret keys and passwords, along with internal root passwords for structured query language (SQL) databases.

- **Chili's Grill & Bar (2018):** Chili's POS system was breached, causing the loss of an undisclosed number of credit card data records.

- **Best Buy, Sears, Kmart, and Delta (2018):** An online chat provider used by these firms lost over a million customer records in total.

- **Applebee's (2018):** 160 restaurants and their customer data were released by the chain's POS system.

- **Western Union (2018):** Private data about transactions was released by an undisclosed vendor who performed off-site cloud storage.

- **Ascension (2019):** A misconfigured server at a third party exposed millions of bank loan and mortgage documents.

- **Amadeus (2019):** The online booking systems for over 140 airlines worldwide had a critical flaw that allowed hackers to get access to the flight reservation systems.

- **Adverline (2019):** A third party to online European sellers had malicious code injected, exfiltrating credit card information.

- **Click2Gov (2019):** An online payment tool used by many U.S. and Canadian municipalities was compromised, releasing information on citizens in St. John in Canada and Hanover County in Virginia.

- **BankersLife (2019):** Breached third party allowed the information about Humana's customers to leak.

- **BenefitMall (2019):** A third-party administrator for Highmark BCBS, Aetna, Humana, and United Health caused a leak of customer data.

- **Quest Diagnostics (2019):** From August 2018 to March 2019, a hacker gained access to Quest's data at a billing collections vendor called American Medical Collection Agency (AMCA). A total of 11.9 million records were exposed.

- **Suprema (2019):** A firm offering biometric security software exposed 27.8 million unencrypted records for over 6,000 firms, including U.K. Metro Police, Power World Gyms, and Global Village.

- **LensCrafters, Target, EyeMed (2020):** Luxottica, a breached online appointment application provider, caused the loss of thousands of protected health information (PHI) records.

- **Insurance companies in Texas and Colorado (2020):** Insurance carriers were impacted by a breach at Vertafore, which provides software to insurance companies.

- **First Federal Community Bank, Bank of Swainsboro, First Bank & Trust, Rio Bank (2020):** ABS, a bank software provider, released the PII for the banks' customers.

- **Hotels.com and Expedia (2020):** Channel manager vendor, Prestige Software, was breached, exposing names, credit card information, and reservation details.

- **Australian Stock Exchange (2020):** An undisclosed amount of protected data was exfiltrated from the media-monitoring vendor Insentia.

- **Google (2020):** A law firm known as Fragomen, Del Rey, Bernsen & Loewy disclosed information that Google used for the I-9 process (i.e., proof of ability to work in the United States).

- **City of Odessa (2020):** Click2Gov, a frequently breached vendor, leaked details on how Odessa residents paid their utility bills.

- **Tribune Media and Times Media Group (2020):** Marketing company, View Media, was breached, releasing information about 38 million U.S. residents.

- **Buffalo, NY, area hospitals; FeedMore; and Phipps Conservatory (2020):** Blackbaud, a data management vendor, released the names, medical services numbers, dates of patient services, and a list of donors.

- **Rochester YMCA (2020):** An undisclosed software vendor was breached for the names, addresses, and gift history of donors.

- **SEI Investments (2020):** MJ Brunner, a third-party software provider to SEI Investments, was breached, affecting customers at dozens of investment banks.

- **Bank of America (2020):** Caused by an unnamed third-party merchant, Paycheck Protection Plan (PPP) application business details, including Social Security numbers (SSNs), emails, addresses, and more, were released.

- **Citrix (2020):** An undisclosed vendor disclosed Citrix's customer data, which was exposed on the Dark Web.

- **Marriott (2020):** A Russian franchise operator was the reason for the second breach at this hotel chain in just two years. This time over 5 million records were compromised.

- **T-Mobile (2020):** An email vendor's breach was the reason that thousands of customer names, addresses, phone numbers, emails, rate plans, and more were exposed. This is the second public breach for T-Mobile, with the last one occurring in 2015.

- **Radio.com (2020):** Its cloud-hosting provider misconfigured their instance, which resulted in its customers' PII being made public.

- **Chubb (2020):** A third-party service provider released internal sensitive data about Chubb.

- **General Electric (2020):** Canon, which was used by GE for business processes, was breached, resulting in information on past and current GE employees and sensitive data being released.

- **Amazon, eBay, Shopify, Stripe, PayPal (2020):** A third-party application breach was the reason for the release of over 8 million records on sales information, customer names, emails, mailing addresses, and credit card information including the last four digits of account numbers.

- **SpaceX, Tesla, Boeing, Lockheed Martin (2020):** Viser, a parts manufacturer, released partial schematics for a missile antenna and other restricted internal data.

- **Carson City (2020):** Click2Gov caused the release of residents' names, addresses, email, debit/credit cards, card security codes (CVV), and bank account and routing numbers.

- **Idaho Central Credit Union (2020):** A mortgage portal provider was hacked, releasing customer banking information.

- **Nedbank (2020):** Nearly 2 million customer PII records were released by Computer Facilities (Pty) Ltd., a marketing and promotional firm.

- **Mitsubishi (2020):** A large amount of internal restricted data was exfiltrated via an undisclosed vendor in China.

- **P&N Bank (2020):** A third-party customer relationship manager (CRM) hosting company caused the loss of nearly 100,000 customer records.

- **Ubiquiti Inc (2021):** A maker of Internet of Things devices, it lost an undisclosed amount of customer names, email addresses, passwords, addresses and phone numbers due to a third-party cloud provider.

- **Bonobos (2021):** This men's clothing retailer had the data for over 7 million customers (addresses, phones numbers, account info, partial credit card information) stolen from its cloud data provider.

- **US Cellular (2021):** The fourth largest wireless carrier in the U.S. exposed the private data of almost 5 million customers from its CRM software.

According to a Ponemon Institute survey in 2019, 60 percent of the companies surveyed admitted to not performing adequate cybersecurity vetting of their third parties. Thirty-three percent replied they had no or an ad-hoc cybersecurity vetting process. Fifty-nine percent admitted being affected by a third-party breach in the previous year. In that same survey, the companies also admitted to sharing their data on average with and requiring protection from a whopping 588 third parties. Following those numbers, this means *over half* the companies admitted to not performing their cybersecurity due diligence on nearly 600 third parties. Note, these statistics are pre-COVID-19 pandemic. However, post pandemic, the cyber-attack increase was over 800 percent, according to the FBI as of May 2020. Prior to the pandemic, the problem was pronounced, with the breaches listed including Capital One, Home Depot, and others. However, the lack of due diligence and programs to review the cybersecurity of third parties by so many firms led to an explosion of breaches. And, as everyone is someone else's third party (i.e., every company is selling to someone and using vendors to assist in that effort), the problem was magnified to a boiling point.

Third-Party Risk Management

Third-Party Risk Management (TPRM) as a discipline is not very old. In the financial sector, it was not mandated by the Office of the Comptroller of the Currency (OCC) until 2013, when it regulated that all banks must manage the risk of all their third parties. OCC 2013-29 defined "third party" as any entity a company does business with, including vendors, suppliers, partners, affiliates, brokers, manufacturers, and agents. Third parties can include upstream (i.e., vendors) and downstream (i.e., resellers) and non-contractual parties. Other regulated sectors have seen similar requirements, often indirectly via privacy regulations. For example, General Data Protection Regulation (GDPR) or the California Privacy Rights Act (CPRA) require many companies subject to these regulations to perform due diligence on vendors who have access to their customer data. This may not lead to a full-blown risk management division or group, but someone will be required to perform some oversight in an organized process, lest they get subjected to the extreme financial penalties both regulations require.

Other risk domains exist in TPRM: strategic, reputation, operational, transaction, and compliance domains. Why is the focus in this book on the cybersecurity domain exclusively? That is where the money is. While there are financial and reputational risks for the other domains, none of them provide the level of risk to a firm such as the risk of information security. As described previously, there are number of breaches that can be directly attributed to a cybersecurity breach at a vendor. It is not that these other domains aren't important, but none of them have the impact that a cybersecurity risk poses to a firm, financially or reputationally. Perform an internet search on the other domains, and you will struggle to find results. A similar search on cybersecurity breaches produces more results than one can list in a single page. Like any organization with more than one domain, if one of those domains presents a higher risk for practitioners, and evidence shows that Information Security does, then that domain needs more research, resources, and results.

While TRPM organizations struggle to keep up with the level of breaches and incidents with vendors, evidence shows most cybersecurity organizations are not taking a lead in this domain, and that TPRM groups do not have the expertise to address this gap. According to the Ponemon Institute "Data Risk in the Third-Party Ecosystem" study (2018), only 40 percent perform any cybersecurity due diligence. Sixty percent perform none or only ad-hoc cybersecurity reviews. The evidence indicates that a large percent of the 40 percent (i.e., those that perform some cybersecurity due diligence) do not do enough (as evidenced by the level of breaches/incidents). TPRM organizations must begin focusing more on the Information Security domain, and either directly bring cybersecurity experts into their organizations or partner with cybersecurity teams to address the gap. Doing so will also require that a cybersecurity team is able to understand the problem with third parties and address the risk.

While the fines and publicity for failure to follow TPRM guidelines are not as big, instances of regulators acting can be found:

- In 2020, the OCC assessed an $85 million civil money penalty against USAA for failure to implement and maintain an effective risk management compliance.
- In 2020, the OCC assessed a $60 million civil money penalty against Morgan Stanley for not properly decommissioning some Wealth Management business data centers.
- In 2020, the OCC assessed a $400 million civil money penalty against Citibank for failures in enterprise risk management.
- In 2020, the Federal Reserve announced an enforcement action against Citigroup Inc., requiring that the firm correct several longstanding deficiencies.
- In 2020, the OCC assessed an $80 million civil money penalty against Capital One for not establishing an effective risk assessment process, which led to the breach in its public cloud.
- In 2013, the U.S. Security and Exchange Commission (SEC) lowered the burden of proof for proxy disclosure enhancements on risk management inadequacy from fraud to simply negligence. This means that boards of directors and senior

management of publicly traded companies can no longer claim they had no knowledge about a risk.

- In 2019, the SEC and Commodities Futures Trading Commission (CFTC) charged Options Clearing Corp. with failing to establish and maintain adequate risk management policies, forcing the organization to pay a $20 million penalty.

Cybersecurity and Third-Party Risk

Cybersecurity as a field is also very young, though it is older than TPRM. Cybersecurity is often thought to have begun after the first cyberattack was thwarted in 1986 in the Soviet Union, when Marcus Hess hacked into 400 military servers and the Pentagon. Intending to sell the information to the KGB, Hess was foiled by American Clifford Stoll.

In the 1970s, several attacks occurred on the early internet. For example, Bob Thomas created the first computer worm named Creeper, which traveled between early APRANET terminals with the message "I'M THE CREEPER: CATCH ME IF YOU CAN." Also, in the same decade, Ray Tomlinson created the worm, Reaper, the first antivirus software that could find copies of Creeper and delete them. However, the one that finally illustrated the need for information security at the doorstep of the novice IT industry was the Morris Worm.

The Morris Worm

In 1988, Robert Morris, like all curious computer scientists, wondered "how big is the internet"? And like all good curious computer scientists, he decided to write a program to find out the answer of "how big?" The answer was found by his worm, which traveled through networks like wildfire,

(Continued)

(Continued)

invaded Unix terminals, and crossed domains faster than a speeding bullet. His worm was so good at replicating that it would infect the same computer multiple times, and each additional infection would continually slow the computer down to the point of damaging it. Robert Morris was charged under crimes covered by the Computer Fraud and Abuse Act. Enacted in 1986, this act was an amendment to the first federal computer crime law and addressed hacking. This act continues to be updated, but only as recently as 2008, which reaffirms our earlier point that regulators are not considered to be at the cutting edge, and that good cybersecurity programs should not be designed to meet regulations. Such programs should exceed these regulations in order to have any hope of being successful. If we consider the 1970s as the start of cybersecurity, it is only within the last 20 years that companies have had Chief Information Security Officers (CISOs) and divisions, groups, or teams who reported directly to them.

Cybersecurity, like any other discipline, has developed several frameworks, associations, testing accreditors, credentials, and subdisciplines over those 20+ years. ISC2, ISACA, and EC-Council, are just three of the credential/testing accreditors. CISSP, CIPM, CISM, CompTIA Security+, and countless other managerial, technical, and administrative certifications are also available. For the purposes of demonstration on the complexity of the cybersecurity subject matter, we use the Certified Information Systems Security Professional (CISSP) as the best example. This certification is still the gold standard in the industry, and can be proven by study after study indicating that the demand vastly outstrips the supply of certificate holders of CISSP.

Within infosec, they have developed clear subdomains (citing the CISSP 8 domains):

- Security and Risk Management
- Asset Security
- Security Architecture and Engineering
- Communications and Network Security
- Identity and Access Management
- Security Assessment and Testing
- Security Operations
- Software Development Security

Further subdomains can be found within these cybersecurity domains. For example, let's look at the Security and Risk Management domain:

- Security and Risk Management Domain: It comprises 15 percent of the CISSP exam and is the largest domain found in CISSP. The latest editions of the study guides for this exam detail the following:
  - The Confidentiality, Integrity and Availability of information
  - Security governance principles
  - Compliance requirements
  - Legal and regulatory issues relating to information security
  - IT policies and procedures
  - Risk-based management concepts

This information is in Chapter 1 "Security and Risk Management" in the *CISSP All-in-One-Exam, 8th Edition* by Shon Harris. Notice there is one bullet on risk-based management concepts.

Within those study guides, none of them have more than two pages on "Supplier Management" or "Vendor Risk Management Process," depending on how it is listed in the index. The focus of these guides is on the management of a process and compliance language, such as service-level agreements (SLAs), legal concerns, and privacy regulations. Supplier management is viewed as something belonging to a process team, which certainly some of the work will be, but it misses the opportunity to take an aggressive approach, such as in a Security Operations domain.

However, this is not the responsibility of the CISSP body of knowledge or necessarily any other cybersecurity certification. These guides are designed to give frameworks and a library of information that the cybersecurity profession can then use to manage the risk. Hundreds of specialties and job roles exist in cybersecurity and except for job-specific certifications, the study guides and exams are not prescribing how cyber organizations run their operations and programs. In this case, the cybersecurity industry has been largely focused on securing internal networks. TPRM professionals have spent the last 10 years growing their profession. The gap has been widening over time, but the COVID-19 pandemic made the problem more pronounced. The approach for this domain must evolve into a field of its own, mimicking cybersecurity operations more than cyber Governance, Risk and Compliance (GRC).

Cybersecurity operations teams have been developing at an ever-increasing pace in the last 10 years, especially after the Sony Pictures hack in 2014, which showed that a foe like a state actor with determination and nearly unlimited resources (unlike a script kiddie or even criminal hackers) can get into any company and disclose such deeply embarrassing details. There are firewall and router certifications for ethical hacking and for security that focus solely on finding or preventing the bad actors. However, none of them spend any amount of time on learning how to secure company data at the third parties. Indeed, this is an area for improvement as the cybersecurity professionals begin to learn how to perform at a higher level on third-party risk.

Business or Technology Risk and Cybersecurity Risk

Many companies of larger size have departments or groups that are designed to manage and report risk for the whole company. These teams are very important as centralized groups for risk management at big organizations. Often, these teams perform the process and compliance work for third-party risk, including the cybersecurity domain.

While these professionals are trained and certified in how to evaluate risk within an organization, the issue of evaluating cybersecurity risk produces better results when performed by trained and certified cybersecurity professionals. The cybersecurity domain is very complex, as illustrated in the section titled "Cybersecurity and Third-Party Risk." Even within the field, there are numerous specialty fields and certifications along with a fast-changing environment. Expecting a generalist risk professional to opine on controls for information security topics might produce adequate, but not necessarily accurate, data.

In cases where a risk organization consists of general risk professionals who don't have the specialty training and experience of cybersecurity professionals, it is optimal if these professionals, like the TPRM team, collaborate with the cybersecurity teams at their company for that level of expertise.

Cybersecurity Third-Party Risk as a Force Multiplier

Military science uses a term called *force multiplier*, which refers to a combination of circumstances that gives personnel the ability to amplify their normal capabilities to achieve greater goals. In modern times, the Global Positioning System (GPS) has been a force multiplier, as it enabled more personnel to be moved at a faster pace due to the capabilities added from the technology. In the U.S. Special Forces, a lot of time is spent on creating and training local fighter forces as a form of a force multiplier. The small force of a 12-man unit can go out and lead a unit of 100–200 local fighters. The force multiplier here is the U.S. Special Forces troops growing in strength from 12 to 200. A cybersecurity team, partnering with TPRM, can be a force multiplier to strengthen the risk management of third parties.

As understood, the cybersecurity field is complex and full of certifications, specialties, technical details, and domains. This complexity can be simplified for a TPRM team when a specialized team of cybersecurity professionals are able to execute on an active threat hunting mentality in reference to third parties. The whole TPRM and business risk teams do not have to be experts in information security, but they can use the force multiplier effect of a few good cybersecurity special forces. These special forces are trained to monitor security controls at vendors, to ensure that enemy forces are reined in by contractual obligations, to constantly watch for new threats, and to partner with vendors to train their local forces to better fight the enemy directly. The collaboration and teamwork between the cyber and TPRM professionals continually sharing and updating reference documents multiplies the strengths of both teams.

TPRM must grow its strength in cybersecurity. Cybersecurity must increase its own research, resources, and results on third-party risk. For those in business and cybersecurity as well as TPRM, this is an opportunity to exponentially grow cybersecurity across industries. If the TPRM process grew its cybersecurity with a force multiplier approach, and cybersecurity research and resources were focused more on third-party risk, we would more broadly adopt what is required: a rethink of cybersecurity and third-party risk. This adoption would include a practice around vendor risk management that places cybersecurity at the forefront, and a cybersecurity team that uses the same resources as cyber operations threat analysts.

The earlier statistic that stated the average company is connected with 600 vendors with PII becomes the exponential part. As more companies adopt a cybersecurity and third-party risk approach and are able to partner with these vendors, across multiple industries, we get real security change across all the third parties. It's a simple math equation: It becomes a multiplier for better corporate information security across the globe.

Conclusion

The evidence of the risk exists: At the end of 2020, in one month there were three nation-state APT attacks that exploited weaknesses in supply chain cybersecurity. Two of them were aimed at two countries: Mongolia and Vietnam. The damage and scope of the SolarWinds Orion exploit is not yet known as more victims are being uncovered, but it does include big names in technology and major government systems globally. The advanced persistent actors (i.e., hackers) are clearly targeting and weaponizing the supply chain. They have discovered that third-party cybersecurity is the weakest link to their actual targets.

The investment that CISOs and cybersecurity professionals have made in the last 20 years has been proven effective in many ways. Most companies and governments that know they will be a target (due to size, money, power) have beefed up their own cybersecurity. But behind these medium and large organizations are thousands or millions of smaller companies that are focused on selling, not securing, their data. Cybersecurity can lean into this area more forcefully, trying and implementing new capabilities learned from other cyber domains and leadership. The need is to take Cybersecurity Third-Party Risk from a compliance-driven effort to an active always learning, always searching for risk approach in order to lower risk from vendors.

2

Cybersecurity Basics

While this book does not require the reader to be either a risk expert or cybersecurity expert, given there will be terminology and process discussions on some cybersecurity topics, some time spent on the terminology and the subject matter is warranted.

Cybersecurity has three main pillars: Confidentiality, Integrity and Availability (CIA):

- **Confidentiality:** Prescribes only authorized users and systems should be able to access or modify data.
- **Integrity:** Data should be maintained in a correct state and cannot be improperly modified.
- **Availability:** Authorized users should be able to access data when needed.

This is called the CIA Triad as shown in Figure 2.1.

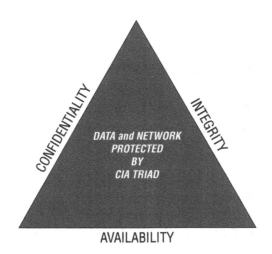

FIGURE 2.1   The CIA Triad

These pillars are designed to break down the complexities of cybersecurity to determine how to best make decisions. For example:

- Does the vendor store our data in ways that make it more secure?
- Will this product ensure the integrity of our data in the cloud?
- Can the vendor ensure that the data will be available when required to those who need it?

Because this book is mainly focused on third parties, references will be aligned with that focus in mind. It is *not* about what security your organization is performing, but what is going on at the third party, both with the specific services they provide and also how they secure their own enterprise. We include several examples of how a vendor's connection is used to target a company, and how their company-wide cyber controls directly impact the ability to protect a company's data and any connection to your network (both intermittent and persistent).

Cybersecurity Basics for Third-Party Risk

Some terminology and a few foundational cybersecurity principles are required for a discussion on vendor risk management. Many of these concepts and components of cybersecurity are reviewed throughout this book. The reader isn't expected to be a cybersecurity expert; however, it's easier to grasp risk, priority, and actions if you have a basic understanding of them. You should keep the following bolded terms, which have simplified explanations, in mind.

Encryption is the process of taking plaintext, like a text message or email, and scrambling it into an unreadable format called *cipher text*. This text helps protect the confidentiality of data, either stored on computer systems or transmitted through a network like the internet. This capability is at the core of most discussions for securing data. There are subcategories in this area, such as synchronous and asynchronous encryption, but for this book, the discussions revolve mostly around the level of encryption. Advanced Encryption Standard (AES) is the type of encryption most often used by the U.S. government, among others. Most organizations typically leverage the AES-128 or AES-256 level of encryption for their enterprise. The trade-off of higher encryption levels is speed—the higher the number, the more processing power it takes to decrypt—thus, the higher the number, the better.

Another area of encryption to focus on is the three states of encryption. Data consists of three states: at-rest, in-motion, and in-use. *At-rest* is as it sounds, meaning when the data is in a database or file. *In-motion* refers to when data is traveling over a network or the internet. When a process is using the data, as in the CPU or memory, it is considered to be *in-use*. In all three states, it is important to have the data encrypted. As you engage vendors on how they protect the data, ensure that your discussion involves all three states.

In recent years, a new mantra has been born: "Identity is the new perimeter." This statement refers to how millions of people, especially after the rush to remote work during the COVID-19 pandemic, are now connecting to work and school away from those places. Their identities, which are used to connect users to organizations, work, or school, and how that access is managed, which is known as *access management*, is very important when protecting the enterprise (and the data that resides internally at the vendor). It requires entities to focus on several areas for third-party risk.

First, we cover the access process, which includes three steps: identity, authorization, and access. The identity phase is where a user types in their name and password and the system confirms their identity. Next, the authorization step confirms what access the user has—what that user is permitted to see and do. Lastly, the correct level of access is provided. Once these three steps are completed, the user is permitted to access the data and resources they have authorization to view.

The most common type of access in corporate environments, role-based access (RBAC), includes predefined job roles with a specific set of access privileges. This implementation is demonstrated by the difference between two examples of types of roles. For example, a human resources (HR) manager will likely have access to payroll and personnel files. However, if they try to log in to a finance server, it will not permit them to connect because they do not have a role in the finance department. If the HR manager requires entry into that server, they must submit a business reason to the access management team for needing access to that server.

Exposed Credentials

The ongoing explosion of exposed credentials makes understanding and prioritizing risk difficult. In 2020, Digital Shadows published a study with some illustrative statistics:

- Over 15 billion credentials have been exposed and are for sale on the internet.
- The number of credentials for sale has increased by 300 percent since 2018.

- Normal consumer accounts are sold for an average of $15/account.
- Financial accounts are valued at $70/account.
- Domain administrator accounts are sold for a premium of $3,149/account.

The differences in cost and the number of accounts are part of the problem. As the study states, there are more accounts for sale than people on Earth. The vast majority of accounts for sale are normal user accounts. However, so many of them are for sale that it is difficult to defend against them. Multi-factor authentication (MFA) and other services are the best defense for this type of standard user account. MFA is explained in more detail later.

Administrator or elevated account access is where the money and the risk is at its highest. The challenge there is determining from the Dark Web which are valid privileged accounts and which are actually standard user accounts. Again, MFA and Privileged Access Manager (PAM) systems are the best defense.

Single Sign-On (SSO) is a mechanism that limits the number of times a user has to submit their identity for access verification. In most larger organizations, users are required to interact with multiple systems. Their SSO enables them to log in once and gives them permission to gain access without reentering their credentials. The different systems pass this credential permission between them silently and provide access to other systems and services without referencing the credentials.

Multi-factor authentication (MFA), also referred to as two-factor authentication (2FA), refers to when there is more than one login step required. (Note, two or more factors can be involved in this authentication.) There are four main types of MFA:

1. Things you know, like your password or PIN.
2. Things you have, such as an employee badge or security token (physical and soft).
3. Things you can refer to, such as biometric items like your fingerprints, retinas, or voice.
4. Where you are based—your location. Most systems leverage this in the background, so the end user may be unaware of this check. Note, this MFA type is not used as often, but if you are based in the United States and someone attempts to use your login in South America, the system is attuned to this difference and would take appropriate action, such as prompt for additional verification or deny access.

MFA is an important security feature and should be pushed to all account types. At a minimum, MFA must be used for all privileged and elevated accounts. Privileged accounts are those with elevated access and permissions to do things that present a higher risk, such as system administrators, senior executives, and data owners. This important feature ensures that only the authorized user gains data access.

Least-privilege is a principle where a user has only the privileges (i.e., access) they need to complete the task or job at hand. For example, a database user who only needs access to be able to view data records should not have permission to perform deletions or change any users' rights to the database. Least-privilege is important for ensuring that the Confidentiality, Integrity and Availability is kept for the data.

As part of the security hygiene, **patch management** is an important component. It's the process of distributing and applying updates to software and hardware. This process is vital to fixing errors and vulnerabilities. Vendors must focus on what their processes are and how they prioritize them as security vulnerabilities are identified and categorized (high to lower priority), tested, and deployed into production.

An **Intrusion Detection System (IDS)** is hardware or software that monitors network traffic and computer systems looking for anomalous behavior or known threats. The IDS alerts security personnel, which is why this system is called a detection system—it takes no other action except to detect and alert. While there are several IDS types, what your vendor uses is generally not an issue. The disadvantage of an IDS is that it doesn't take any actions, it merely alerts; if it detects suspicious network traffic, it does not stop the traffic. The general rule of thumb is that most companies do not buy an IDS as a standalone product but as part of a suite or bundled product. This system doesn't take action against the suspicious traffic, but leaves it in place within the enterprise notifying Security so it can be monitored.

An **Intrusion Prevention System (IPS)** is software or hardware that can both detect and prevent known threats. These systems can also just alert, depending on how their thresholds are configured. These systems continuously evolve, and in recent years, have advanced. Network access controls and firewalls are now available with this feature.

Firewalls inspect network traffic and block or allow traffic based upon rules. Available as hardware and software, these devices have highly evolved from their early days and can now read and inspect encrypted traffic. These Next-Generation Firewalls (NGFW) can look deep into the data within the network traffic as it passes by, and can provide options to take action, stopping anything that meets its malicious criteria.

An **IP address** is a string of numbers that identifies a unique computer or network. These unique numbers allow communications within private networks or over the internet. Think of an IP address as an address found on a mailed letter. As the email (or traffic) is passed along on the network, the provided IP address indicates where the email must go in order to get to the intended recipient. IP addresses have three numbers in four sets: 192.168.1.1 or 10.102.201.32 and billions of combinations.

Ports are physical or logical openings that allow connectivity for a specific program or application. An example of a physical port could be to plug in a mouse or a USB stick. On the logical side, an example is normal internet browsing that occurs over port 80. If you are connecting to a secure site, such as your bank, you would connect over port 443. These ports are there so that each side of the connection knows exactly which port to use when communicating. Similar to the IP address, a port enables the traffic to arrive at the intended computer or network; the port specifies which "room" to go to for the conversation.

A **domain name server (DNS)** is a system of computers that translate human-friendly names (www.rasner.com) to an IP address, simply because IP addresses can evolve and virtually no one wants to memorize one. Whenever a user types in a website address, a DNS server helps translate it into the correct IP address to ensure that the target resource (i.e., a website, database server, printer, etc.) is found.

Network access control is a method used to restrict access to network resources by ensuring that devices (i.e., laptops, mobile devices, computers, servers, printers, etc.) comply with security policies. It is also known by its protocol name of 802.1x, and is viewed as an essential tool for limiting network access to those devices that meet security criteria and are allowed to connect to a network.

Out of band communications refers to devices that are not the primary connectivity device. For example, many vendors will use a router or VPN concentrator as hardware devices to connect to a customer's network. Some will want to place a modem or an alternate device for connecting to that network if the router is offline. These devices can be problematic for connectivity as they are usually not connected to any monitoring or logging system; hence, they can be a used as a backdoor by hackers.

A shared responsibility model for cloud security is adhered to by Cloud Service Provider (CSPs) and refers to how different solutions shift the responsibility from the CSP to the customer. In a traditional data center owned by a company, that company is responsible for its technology's delivery. When deploying to the cloud, the level of responsibility increases for the customer as they shift from Infrastructure as a Service (IaaS) to Platform as a Service (PaaS). The IaaS model requires the customer to perform more of the security and maintenance than in the PaaS model.

Personally Identifiable Information (PII) is data that is used alone or with other data and enables a viewer to identify an individual. Thousands of combinations of information are possible that make up data PII, but typically it contains name, Social Security numbers, financial info, drivers' licenses, physical address, phone numbers, or more.

Personal Health Information (PHI) is PII that pertains to an individual's medical information, such as smoking status, any illnesses, medications, and other very confidential medical data. PHI is considered more sensitive than PII and as such, requires more security.

Data classification is when data is analyzed and organized into categories based upon its sensitivity to the sorting organization. There are often three or four classes of data for most companies, but there should only be one category that is labeled as public and one labeled private or sensitive.

For the purposes of this book and how cybersecurity third-party risk approaches this topic, the *cloud* is defined as any location not inside your own data center, server closet, or laptop hard drive (if you are a small-business owner). The cloud could be located in a CSP, such as AWS, Google, or Azure, at a co-location facility provider, or at a data center managed by the vendor directly.

Advanced Persistent Threat (APT) is considered a more superior threat actor because hackers use continuous, clandestine, and advanced techniques to gain access, remain stealthy for longer periods of time, and often leave undetected or with little evidence left behind for forensics. APTs are starting to utilize the supply chain cyber weaknesses.

Cybersecurity Frameworks

The information security field has been around long enough for more than a few standards to be written. Security frameworks are a collection of government cybersecurity policies and guidelines, and best practices set in place protect information systems. They often have specific instructions for organizations to handle PII to lower the risk of a breach or damage. Dozens of them exist globally, but you must be aware of a few top useful ones to understand their scope and focus. Cybersecurity frameworks provide defined structures for people, process, and technology that a company uses as a reference to secure their networks, data, and systems from cyber threats. Some are regulatory guidance (e.g., New York Department of Financial Services [NYDFS] or the Health Insurance Portability and Accountability Act [HIPAA]), which provide a framework's structure. Some companies adopt a framework that is aligned with their industry (e.g., Control Objectives for Information and Related Technologies [COBIT] and Finance, or HIPPA and healthcare providers).

National Institute of Standards and Technology Cybersecurity Framework (NIST-CSF) was created in response to the U.S. Presidential Executive Order 13636, whose purpose was to enhance the security of the country's critical infrastructure. While aimed at critical infrastructure such as power and water delivery, many private companies have adopted it. NIST-CSF contains the following five functions that manage the risk to data and systems security: Identify, Protect, Detect, Respond, and Recover. This is shown in Figure 2.2.

The Identify function focuses on identifying physical and software assets as a basis for managing assets. It defines what an organization's supply chain risk management strategy is, according to its priorities, constraints, risk tolerance, and assumptions that support the risk-based decisions managing their supply chain risks.

The Protect function provides security controls to ensure the security and integrity of an organization's infrastructure systems. Through identity and access management (IAM), an organization seeks to limit and contain any possible damage, thus protecting both its physical and logical access. A data protection program must be aligned with the organization's risk strategy and appetite, and its data protection must align with the cybersecurity core principles of Confidentiality, Integrity and

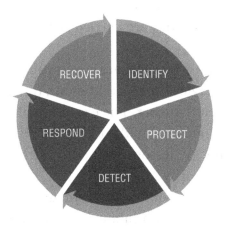

FIGURE 2.2 The NIST Cybersecurity Framework

Availability. Its goals are to defend the organization's resources with a patch and vulnerability management programs, and to assist the staff in safeguarding its data and assets with awareness and training in best practices on the safe handling of protected information.

The Detect function is as it sounds—it refers to the activity taken to discover indications of a security incident. This detection must be timely. Monitoring capabilities must be continuously implemented in order to find and identify anomalous events to catch malicious or suspicious behavior. When we think of an organization's cyber operations teams defending against hackers, we typically think of them as being in detection mode. Some of the capabilities used to detect are Security Information and Event Management (SIEM), Data Loss Prevention (DLP), Intrusion Detection Systems (IDS), Intrusion Prevention Systems (IPS), and the other tools, which are focused on this detection activity.

The Respond function ensures that correct actions are taken when a cybersecurity event is detected. Such activity ensures that cyber Incident Response plans are executed according to an organization's previously established processes. All work done to analyze and support recovery work is performed in a timely manner, and corrective activities are carried out to contain the incident and close the issue.

The Recover function acknowledges any impact, then prioritizes the restoration of services or capabilities in a timely manner to further reduce the event's impact. The execution of a recovery plan as it's designed and implemented ensures the restoration of an organization's systems. A "lessons learned" meeting, or what may be known as a post-mortem on the incident, must occur to determine if any changes are required in the organization's existing plans. Communications—both inbound and outbound—are coordinated during and post recovery from the event.

What is important about this framework is that it prepares a cybersecurity organization for the inevitable: the breach. Risk is never a zero game, and eventually the vulnerability and threat actors align perfectly. The adoption of this cybersecurity framework forces an organization to best prepare to protect its data, but also for when an event does occur. An organization must have recognized plans in order to limit an attack's impact.

The **ISO 27001 cybersecurity framework** is an international standard that states a risk-based process requires an adopting organization to incorporate measures for detecting security threats to information systems. ISO 27001 has a total of 114 controls that are categorized into 14 categories (with the number of controls):

- Information Security Policies (2 controls)
- Information Security Organization (7 controls)
- Human Resources Security (6 controls)
- Asset Management (10 controls)
- Access Controls (14 controls)
- Cryptography (2 controls)
- Physical and Environmental Security (15 controls)
- Operations Security (14 controls)
- Communications Security (7 controls)
- Systems Acquisition, Development, and Maintenance (13 controls)
- Supplier Relationships (5 controls)
- Information Security Incident Management (7 controls)
- Business Continuity Management (4 controls)
- Compliance (8 controls)

Organizations are not required to implement all 114 controls listed. The framework provides an outline for the controls that can be referred back to when performing a gap analysis and risk assessment compared to the ISO 27001. The downside is that the controls are not described in depth. To compensate for this lack of detail, organizations turn to the supplementary ISO 27002, which provides a lot of specificity to the cybersecurity controls. In ISO 27002, each control is given a page to explain how it operates and how to carry out the control.

NIST 800-53 was created to enable government agencies to have effective cybersecurity controls. This framework specifically describes the requirements for federal government agencies to protect data and information systems. It has over 900 security requirements, which makes it very complex for an organization to implement. The number of requirements and the mandates required to enforce the compliance are focused primarily on any company whose systems interact with a federal agency information system. Also because of this complexity, unless the company is required to follow NIST 800-53, most private companies will adhere to NIST-CSF.

The **New York Department of Financial Services (NYDFS)** framework is a cybersecurity framework that covers nearly any entity performing financial services through the state of New York. The framework originates from NYDFS Cybersecurity Regulation (23 NYCRR 500) and "is designed to promote the protection of customer information as well as the information technology systems or regulated entities." It requires companies to conduct risk assessments and to implement a program with security controls that detects and responds to cyber events.

The covered entity, a financial institution, must implement the following six items:

1. A risk assessment must be conducted periodically to assess the Confidentiality, Integrity and Availability of information systems and protected data.

2. An audit trail must record and respond to security incidents and be maintained for five years.

3. Limits on data retention must be set in place to ensure that data is disposed of properly when no longer needed.

4. Access Privileges must be implemented and limited to protected data, and access records must be periodically reviewed.

5. An Incident Response plan must be published to ensure that cybersecurity events are clearly communicated, roles and responsibilities are clear, and remediation takes place.

6. Notices to the superintendent (the superintendent is the organization that oversees the regulation) must be provided within 72 hours after a "material" cybersecurity event is detected.

NYDFS is similar to the General Data Protection Regulation (GDPR) and the California Privacy Protection, which have outsized power due to their economic size. Much of the world's finance flows through New York, and so many world finance companies are subjected to this framework. More importantly for this book, the NYDFS has a part that requires covered entities (i.e., those subject to the regulation) to perform due diligence on their third parties at regular intervals.

The **Federal Information Systems Management Act (FISMA)** is a framework for federal agencies. This standard defines a set of security requirements that the agencies use to improve their cybersecurity. The benchmark requires that third parties to an agency conform to their information security requirements. It contains nine steps for securing government data, operations, and assets:

1. Defining the information categories for security levels

2. Understanding the minimum security controls for protecting data

3. Refining controls through risk assessments

4. Documenting controls and developing security plans

5. Implementing the required security controls

6. Evaluating the effectiveness of implemented controls

7. Establishing security risks for federal resources and data

8. Authorizing the use of secure information systems

9. Continuously monitoring the implemented controls

Several other frameworks are worth describing in high-level detail. The **Australian Signals Directorate (ASD) Essential 8** contains controls and strategies that are a part of the ASD Strategies to Mitigate Cyber Security Incidents. Based upon experience of the Australian government, these controls are considered by them to be the cybersecurity baseline in that country. If implemented correctly, the country reports it can mitigate up to 85 percent of most common cyberattacks.

The **Control Objectives for Information and Related Technology (COBIT)** framework is a high-level framework for identifying and mitigating risk. COBIT is primarily used in the finance space to adhere to Sarbanes-Oxley (SOX). SOX is also known as the Public Company Accounting Reform and Investor Protection Act. Developed by information technology (IT) governance professionals to lower risk, it has evolved to align to business goals.

The **Ten Steps to Cybersecurity** framework is an initiative of the United Kingdom's Department of Business to provide senior leaders with a cybersecurity overview. This framework acknowledges the urgency of giving executives knowledge about information security issues and risks that impact businesses, along with controls to mitigate them. It provides in business English (i.e., non-technical, non-jargon) an explanation in wider terms of the numerous cybersecurity risks, defenses, mitigations, and resolutions.

The **Technical Committee on Cyber Security (TC CYBER)** framework was developed to improve the telecommunication security in the European Union (EU). It contains a series of requirements for improving privacy for companies and individuals. The focus is to confirm that EU residents and citizens have a high level of privacy protection when communicating on all the various mediums in the zone. Although it's focused on the EU, it has been adopted by other countries worldwide.

These cybersecurity frameworks are important in third-party risk due diligence work. When engaging with vendors about security due diligence, one of the first questions to ask is what cybersecurity framework they adhere to. Their answer will provide valuable information about how their organization performs its own security activities. Many of the frameworks or standards have similar themes and controls because cybersecurity does not vary industry to industry. However, what is often different is its focus or scope. Understanding which industry a vendor is in or the one you are subject to, can establish which framework is best used or a required fit.

Due Care and Due Diligence

Two of the concepts discussed often in this book, as well as in cybersecurity and third-party risk, is due care and due diligence. *Due care* is using a reasonable effort to protect the interests of a company. For due care with vendors, it is ensuring they develop and formalize security policies, standards, baselines, and procedures to ensure the security of their environment. *Due diligence* is performing a reasonable exam and investigation before taking action. The opposite of due diligence is the *ad-hoc process*. An ad-hoc process is one that is not predefined but is essentially done without guidance. In this book, performing due diligence refers to the efforts of researching the risks of third parties. Due diligence is performing the necessary research to understand risk, while due care is performing the actions identified as needed from due diligence.

Internal Security Standards versus External Security Standards

We delve into the policies and legal documentation pertaining to cybersecurity and third-party risk in later chapters. However, it is worth noting a problem often misunderstood: Why are standards or policies for vendors often more strict than internal corporate standards? Many complain that it doesn't seem fair or is a case of "do as I say, not as I do," or worse, that it is being hypocritical.

The answer is explained in this analogy: Say you have a hard drive in your house that contains sensitive data, which is likely a 100-percent accurate statement as nearly every reader of this book surely has a home computer containing sensitive data. This sensitive data, such as electronic bank statements or downloaded documents, is known as PII. Do you specifically lock that up when you leave your home? Not likely; you likely lock your door and turn on your security alarm, which is secure enough.

Let's say you'll be on a vacation while your house is going through a major renovation and while that is going on, you don't want to leave your computer where contractors have access (which is good vendor risk management, by the way). Your trusted neighbor offers to store it in his home while you are away. (He is your neighbor and friend but not family.) Before he receives the computer, you decide to encrypt the hard drive, install a basic input/output system (BIOS) password (i.e., what a user will see when the computer is first starting up), as well as ensure that your Windows account password is complex. (Please stop using your dog's name plus your birth year!) Again, you feel you're taking the proper due care to secure your data before it's given to a third party.

As you drop off your laptop at your neighbors' house, you ask where he plans on storing it. Surprised, because he had not thought about it, your neighbor casually replies, "Over there on that shelf." This idea makes you uncomfortable for two reasons: First, he does not seem to appreciate how much you value this data. Second, storing it on an open shelf, where people you do not know can walk by and view it, leads me back to the problem with the strangers (i.e., the contractors) in your home. You then bribe him with a promise to bring him back a nice bottle of rum from your trip, in exchange for him storing it in his safe.

In your own home, you did not encrypt the data (not recommending this, just making a point) or have the best access rights administration. In addition, your data never was locked up when it was in your home. When you decided to move the data outside of your area of control, not only did you increase the security on it, but you required your neighbor to place it in a safe. He probably thinks you are ungrateful and demanding, but the thought of the rum is enough to make the extra work worth the effort. Your risk of a data leak is vastly reduced, as the only people who have access to it have the safe's combination. If there is a data breach, the list of culprits likely will not be lengthy.

(Continued)

(Continued)

A vendor has a business relationship with a company—it's business, nothing personal. As a company paying for a service or product, there is nothing wrong with requiring certain risk reduction behaviors that your company does not require internally. Most often the internal and external standards are the same; however, in some areas, such as encryption or access management, they can diverge. For example, internally a company could have a standard of AES-128 encryption; however, that same company would require a standard of AES-256 or equivalent externally from others. They want the assurance that their data is kept even more secure when housed outside their environment.

Cybercrime and Cybersecurity

The breaches and security incidents described in this book are primarily caused by cybercriminals and other bad actors. *Breaches* occur when an unauthorized individual gains access to a network and exposes sensitive data. *Cybercrime* is when such individuals use computers or the internet to perform criminal activities. The following outlines several types of cybercrime:

- **Email and internet fraud:** A fraudster sends an email enticing the user to a financial gain by offering a scheme, such as you will receive $10,000 or more if you send a portion of that amount to release it.
- **Identity fraud:** This cybercrime occurs when a cyber bad actor uses stolen identity data to commit a crime (e.g., when they apply for a credit card using a stolen identity).

- **Financial and payment card data theft:** Just as it sounds, this cybercrime is the stealing of credit/debit card numbers or nefarious direct access to bank accounts.

- **Theft and sale of protected corporate data:** While the focus is often on PII, there are other types of sensitive data at nearly every company that can be stolen and sold by bad actors, including internal price lists, computer/network information, financial data, and intellectual property.

- **Ransomware:** This cybercrime includes encrypting (i.e., making it unavailable to read) the target's data—ranging from a single desktop to whole server farms—and demanding money to unlock the encryption.

- **Crypto jacking:** This cybercrime is stealing your computer's processing power to "mine" for cryptocurrency and does not include targeting data.

- **Cyberespionage:** Whether done by a state actor (i.e., country), cybercriminals, or a competitor, this cybercrime involves spying on a firm using electronic means (i.e., computer).

The types of bad actors and their motivations can vary just as widely. While the vast majority are out for financial reward, a few other drivers exist:

- **Cybercriminal:** The modern-day equivalent of the bank robbers, cybercriminals are electronic thieves. Most often, they deploy ransomware, phishing attacks, spear phishing, fake documentation, or denial-of-service attacks. The Home Depot attack in 2014 was the work of cybercriminals to steal payment card information.

- **Nation-state:** Many nations have dedicated, highly skilled hackers who're paid to hack and perform espionage.

However, some countries are more like cybercriminals, using their resources to become electronic bank robbers, and are known as Advanced Persistent Threats (APTs) because these organizations have nearly unlimited resources and time to focus on their target. Examples include the Sony attack by North Korean hackers in 2014; and Stuxnet (in 2009) whose origin hasn't been confirmed but largely thought to be a collaboration between Israeli and U.S. intelligence services to damage and delay the Iranian nuclear plans. Stuxnet is largely considered the first occurrence of cyberwarfare.

- **Disgruntled employee:** The insider threat is often not appreciated by business. We like to trust our employees and colleagues; however, there are some who will steal company data or property. For example, in 2018, a Tesla employee sabotaged the computer systems and sent proprietary data to outside parties.

- **Professional hacking group:** Usually this group consists of a loose confederation of highly skilled hackers who pool their resources to target for a political purpose, financial gain, or on behalf of cybercriminals. This group can also be referred to as APT due their resources and commitment. In 2020, the Philippine Long Distance Telephone (PLDT) company had its customer service Twitter account hacked by the Anonymous Philippines group. The group changed the profile name to "PLDT Doesn't Care." The first tweet by the hackers was aggressive: "As the pandemic arises, Filipinos need fast internet to communicate with their loved ones. Do your job. The corrupt fear us, the honest support us, the heroic join us. We are Anonymous. We are Legion. We do not forgive. We do not forget. Expect us."

- **Hacktivist:** Driven by political or social causes, this bad actor typically steals embarrassing information to cause reputational damage. The 2012 WikiLeaks' leaking of declassified information from the U.S. State Department and other countries is an example of hacktivism.

- **Botnet masters:** These malware creators create bots, which are an automated collection of internet-connected devices that an attacker has compromised. These bots are leveraged by the creator to steal data or compromise systems. The botnet Mirai is a prime example. In 2016, the creators of this botnet software launched an attack on a security service company and at its peak infected over 6 million devices.

- **Script kiddies:** These generally unsophisticated hackers use off-the-shelf tools to gain access mostly for bragging rights, but sometimes for financial gain. In 2015, a 15-year-old was arrested for hacking into the U.K. telecom carrier Talk-Talk Group PLC. While the attack was not sophisticated, it exploited an easy SQL injection method to gain access to a database.

Types of Cyberattacks

A cyberattack is defined as a malicious and deliberate attempt by someone to breach the systems of another. Various types of cyberattacks exist, including the following:

- **Phishing:** Nearly 100 percent of email users have received phishing emails. Posing as legitimate emails, these fake emails are used to encourage the email recipient to click a link, download a file, or even call a number so that the attacker can steal credentials or data, plant malware, or contact them for another malicious intent. One of the most concerning successful phishing examples is also a third-party one as well: In January of 2019, there was a report of how Russian state threat actors had gained access to the U.S. power grid. They didn't accomplish this by attacking the hardened sites at the power infrastructure operators, but at their suppliers. A phishing campaign targeted the vendors for the power grid operators, taking advantage of the trust relationship they had with the intended target.

Phishing types can include the following:

- **Spear phishing:** This type is targeted at a specific individual, and isn't a typical mass email campaign to thousands of targets. Often, these specific targets are researched on LinkedIn and other company websites before being phished. There are only so many ways an email address is created (e.g., grasner@ or greg.rasner@ or Gregory .rasner@ and so on). If an attacker can focus on one (or a few targets) who likely has privileged access (i.e., IT Admin, HR Sys Admin, etc.), then they only have to try a few dozen options before they likely get it right.

- **Whale phishing:** Where do you go to get the best data? To the top! Whale phishing is when attackers target the big fish, such as C-level or very senior IT/security staff. This phishing type takes a little more finesse than the first two types as many firms are also likely to focus their countermeasures at this team of privileged access users. However, the extra effort can have a larger reward as the attacker gets a level of elevated access that takes a lot longer to attain (and more likely to discover) in a typical security breach.

- **Vishing:** Rather than email, this type is performed over the telephone and involves social engineering to convince the target it is a legitimate call. The goal is to attain enough information from the call for the attackers to get their target's credentials directly from the call or gain enough information to make guessing it a lot easier.

- **Botnets:** This cyberattack type is when a network of private computers are infected with malicious software and controlled as a group without the owner's knowledge (e.g., to send spam messages). Kraken, a botnet first discovered in 2008 and on pace to be one of the most successful, has infected over 10 percent of Fortune 500 systems and sends over 500,000 spam emails a day!

- **Man-in-the-middle (MitM) attack:** Otherwise known as eavesdropping attacks, MitM attacks occur when an attacker is able to insert themselves into a two-way conversation. When successful, the attacker is then able to filter and steal data from the connection. The most common attack type is via an unsecure, or weakly secured, Wi-Fi access point; or by installing malware to redirect traffic to a bad actor.

- **Denial-of-service (DoS) or distributed denial-of-service (DDoS):** A DoS attack overwhelms or floods a system or network to the point that it makes it unavailable. A DDoS is a case where multiple attackers are performing a DoS. One of the biggest examples of DDoS attack occurred in February 2020 when Amazon Web Services mitigated the biggest such attack recorded to date.

- **Brute-force:** When an attacker systematically submits numerous passwords or passphrases until the correct one is found. In 2016, Alibaba was the victim of a successful brute-force attack that resulted in the loss of 21 million account data records.

- **Malware:** A term used to describe malicious software and includes worms, ransomware, viruses, spyware/adware, and trojans:

  - **Worm:** A standalone program that replicates itself to spread to other computers. The most famous worm is the Morris Worm (see Chapter 1).

  - **Ransomware:** A type of malware that uses encryption to remove a data owner's access so that the attacker can hold the data hostage until the data's owner pays the ransom. There has been a large growth of ransomware, and most cyber intelligence sources anticipate this growth to continue as a threat in 2021 and beyond. Wanna-Cry was the biggest ransomware event so far, with over 250,000 systems affected, in 150 countries, with an average of $300,000 paid per system, and over 176 types of encryption used.

  - **Virus:** A type of malicious code (or program) written to alter the way a computer operates, and designed to spread from one computer to another. The Mydoom virus is the biggest known virus to date, with an estimated $38 billion damages in 2014.

  - **Spyware/adware:** These include the annoying pop-up advertisements on search engines, which redirect your search. Some arrive as browser add-ons purporting to help save money or time. Other instances include being placed as malware on a system or as spyware performing key logging (i.e., the action of recording the keys struck on a keyboard). CoolWebSearch is a browser add-on that took advantage of security vulnerabilities in Internet Explorer to hijack it, change settings, and send the browsing history to the software publishers.

- **Trojan:** The most common type of cyberattack, it typically arrives in the form of a legitimate-looking email asking the reader to perform an update or click a link for something. The malware is then unknowingly downloaded into the target's computer; hence, the name Trojan. Storm Worm, in 2007, is a well-known type of trojan horse attack. It tricked victims into clicking an email link to an article that downloaded trojan malware. It affected over 1.5 million systems, and is estimated to have cost $10 billion in damages.

Analysis of a Breach

Now that we've covered all the types of cybercrimes, bad actors, and breach threats, let's discuss how a breach is typically carried out. It can be broken down into five main steps: research, intrusion, lateral movement, privilege escalation, and exfiltration. CEO John Chambers once said, "There are two types of companies: Those that have been hacked, and those who don't know yet that they have been hacked."

Phase 1: Research   This phase can begin months before detection. For most attackers, it begins by finding out as much as possible about their target. Searches on LinkedIn and company websites for possible phishing targets are common. Their reconnaissance may include researching who the third parties and affiliates are, locating buildings and Wi-Fi networks, and discovering information on security systems and any entry points. Like any good attacker, knowing where the target stores its valuables and how they protect them are key components of planning a hack. Once all this intelligence is gathered, the type of tools and methodology can then be determined, and their intrusion can begin.

Phase 2: Intrusion   As in the research phase, intrusion can take months before discovery. This phase involves the attacker being focused on breaking into the perimeter of the target, with a persistent foothold being their ultimate goal. Whether they used a phishing campaign to steal credentials or used hacking tools to crack into the network, attackers usually are able to do this and remain nearly invisible to the victim. Once they are inside the network, the attacker will work to ensure their access is long term in the anticipation of revisiting on a regular basis.

The five steps to a breach are shown in Figure 2.3 below.

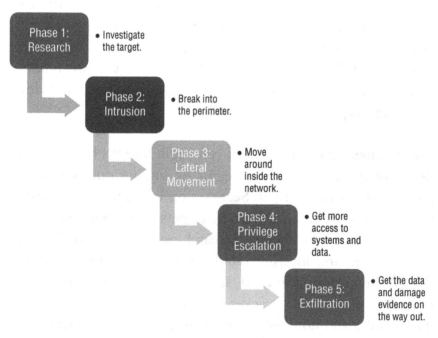

FIGURE 2.3   The Five Steps to a Breach

Phase 3: Lateral Movement After the access becomes more persistent (the attacker has a solid foothold in the target network), the attacker's goal is to find and access more systems within the network. They will search files, databases, password files, sensitive data locations, and network mapping for this work. Most often, the attacker is impersonating an authorized user, so detection is difficult without robust countermeasures such as SIEM and IDS/IPS. This phase generally takes place months or weeks prior to detection.

Phase 4: Privilege Escalation The majority or totality of sensitive information in most company networks is (or should be) protected behind layers of defense that require special access rights. In cases where these user accounts have elevated access, such as in the case of administrators or data owners, this is called *Privileged Access*. This type of access allows the attacker to get at the data needed, so they must find a way to escalate their initial access. Once this access is obtained, then the attacker will go after their internal targets: sensitive company documents, PII, mail servers, document systems, and other areas.

Phase 5: Exfiltration In this final phase, the attacker is in the home stretch. They have attained the intel necessary, broken into the network, looked around for the stuff to steal, gained access to those systems, and are now ready to steal it. They steal the data, sometimes damaging critical systems used to track their movements and disrupt operations. Some destroy any evidence with a ransomware attack at this point. Some linger in the network, if they think they are not detected, waiting for new opportunities to exploit their access. Once they have reached this stage, it is very difficult to stop the attack and the cost to the company increases the longer it goes undetected.

The Third-Party Breach Timeline: Target

The discussion of the five phases for a breach can be best demonstrated by using Target as an actual example. In December 2013, it was announced that around 70 million payment card data records for Target's shoppers had been stolen through the point-of-sale (POS) system. In addition, over 11 GB of data was exfiltrated. The anatomy of how it occurred illustrates both the vulnerability of third parties and how an attacker goes through the five phases.

Research: HVAC vendors were likely targeted as this third party is used as a backdoor to gain access. An internet search could have produced information about how Target works with its vendors and likely would've shown vendor portals. Also easily found is the Microsoft study done on how Target uses its virtualization software, the MS Domain Name Server (DNS), its software for managing system configurations (Systems Center Configuration Manager [SCCM]), and other important intel about internal systems.

Analysis then shows a phishing email was sent to Target's HVAC vendor, Fazio Mechanical, with malware that was a password-stealing bot. It is suspected that this software sent stolen credentials to the attackers.

Intrusion: Using the stolen credentials from Fazio Mechanical, attackers logged in to Target's systems via a vendor portal. Because they stole valid credentials, no alarms were sent. This type of credential from the vendor gave them the continuous access to make repeated attempts at the next steps for the breach.

Lateral Movement: Using the valid user credentials and a solid beachhead (i.e., a foothold within the target network), they now could leverage much of their research into what type of systems the target had running internally to the attacker's advantage. Along with their tools for hacking, knowing that they had

SCCM and Microsoft's DNS, among other products, would have given them an advantage in looking for vulnerabilities to exploit. In addition, attackers likely would have deployed common network scanning tools to create a map to help them decide the next best steps for the lateral movement.

Privilege Escalation: As attackers moved laterally within the Target environment, the objective would be to find privileges that worked with the POS system. As they exploited these known vulnerabilities on the Microsoft and other systems they had identified in their reconnaissance, intrusion, and lateral movement phases, that data was leveraged to elevate themselves to be able to perform the last step.

Exfiltration: The malware was distributed to the POS machines in such a fashion as to suggest it was an automated update, indicating that the attackers had attained privileged access to the central system that updates those machines. Because the malware was custom written, virus scanners did not have their signature to detect it. As the payment cards were swiped, their data was stored in a system configuration file that was shared over well-known ports. This data collection from all the different POS machines was then sent to a compromised server internal to Target's network. The data was then retrieved via a number of electronic "drop" locations worldwide. The Target team in India notified the Minneapolis team of the attack, but they took no action on the warning.

The breach itself took place from November 27 to December 15, 2014. Obviously, we do not know how long the research phase took for the attackers. What the timeline does show is how methodical and clever attackers can be when attempting to ambush a victim. In this case, leveraging the available public information not only got attackers access to the vendor portal, but also gave them candidates from the vendors so they could select one with lower access standards. This breach cost Target hundreds of millions of dollars in direct damage, lost revenue, and reputational costs. Many C-level and lower-level employees lost their jobs, including the CIO and CEO, while the board of directors was threatened with removal as well.

Inside Look: Home Depot Breach

Occurring in 2014, the attacker in the Home Depot breach used a third-party's logon credentials to get into that vendor's environment. Once inside the vendor's network, they leveraged a zero-day exploit for Windows that gained them access to Home Depot's corporate environment. Within the Home Depot network, they deployed memory-scraping malware to the company's POS systems, resulting in over 50 million credit and debit cards numbers being stolen along with a similar number of email addresses. Valid customer email addresses are a gold mine for phishing attacks. Several studies were done on how Home Depot could have installed IDS/IPS, end-to-end encryption, network segmentation, and other technical and process improvements to detect the vulnerabilities exploited by the attackers. Very little is ever mentioned about how a more robust cybersecurity due diligence program would be appropriate for vendors.

This third-party vendor had a connection to Home Depot. While we have focused most of the discussion on data security, there are vendors who will need to connect to your network to perform their business function. These types of vendors pose risks like the Home Depot incident demonstrates: Their inadequate security controls were the beachhead the hacker needed. Legitimate cases can be made that if Home Depot had better security patterns in its enterprise, the attack might have been either prevented or caught much earlier (they lingered for months). However, if Home Depot had taken our more Cybersecurity Third-Party Risk approach, the risk of the beachhead being established would have been reduced.

In this updated approach, we want to look at a few items:

- Did Home Depot have language in its contract with this vendor? Did it have:
  - Appropriate cybersecurity language in the contract with the vendor who had a direct connection to the Home Depot network?
  - Provisions in the contract language allowing Home Depot to perform validation or gain assurance of the vendor security controls?
- A few high-level questions should have been more diligently reviewed:
  - The hardware most vendors maintain at a customer's sites for end-to-end connectivity often falls into a no-man's-land of who maintains it. If the third party owns it, make sure they do so securely. Did they verify it on a regular basis that is pre-established with the vendor to set expectations?
  - What was their access management policy and how did they enforce it in production? If they had a policy, how did it not catch this activity? Was logging and monitoring insufficient?
  - What was the vendor's patch management policy and were they aware of the zero-day exploit available in the version of Windows?

Notice many of these questions are incident management–type questions a cybersecurity incident management team (CIMT) would typically ask internally. In this case, it is a third-party risk team asking similar questions of vendors, leveraging language that is written into contracts, and managing their security as an extension of your own.

Author's Note: Applies to Any Size

While much of this book discusses firms large enough to have the size and complexity for cybersecurity teams and TPRM programs, there are ways to implement the recommendations for even one-person firms. The book speaks often of a "risk-based approach." A risk-based approach allows for any firm to customize the program based upon its needs and size. Whether you are a large, multinational, or a small business serving your local area, this Cybersecurity Third-Party Risk program can be made to reduce your organization's risk.

To illustrate this is possible, we can consider an example of a small one-person organization: a sole owner of a business. This type of business typically does not have access to the cybersecurity or risk management expertise natively. A small-business owner can first start by making an inventory of all their vendors who have their customers' data or a connection to their network (i.e., their computers). Once it's known where the company's data is located, then the owner can ask some questions about how their vendors secure the data.

If the business has more than one vendor with customer data, sort them by the highest risk. The highest risk can be based upon their number of records. Without the cybersecurity expertise, the questions and answers can be intimidating; however, there are options. Search the internet for help and answers. Explore around for a local technology business that, as a small-business owner, you can barter support with for the more technical questions.

Another option is ask the vendor for help explaining some of the more complex items.

When performing the due diligence activities as a smaller entity, it is dealt with in a similar fashion: Design it to meet the risk. Vendors with your data, listed in risk order, allows you, a business owner, to engage and ask questions. Whether you perform just remote assessments (e.g., questionnaires sent to the vendor) or on-site assessments (e.g., physical validation at the vendor site) or both can be determined by your risk appetite. If one or more of your vendors has a lot (or all) of your customers' data, at a minimum, ask very detailed questions on the intake (when you're first deciding if they are going to be a vendor). That is the time you have the most leverage. Once the contract is signed, you will lose much of your ability to effect any change.

Pick a cadence for review of their security. Quarterly, yearly, bi-annually? In risk order (i.e., high to low), send them a questionnaire about their security to confirm nothing has changed. Knowing you don't have the staff or expertise to review 100 questions, ask questions that elicit the answers you require. For example, rather than ask a technical question about encryption, ask it like this, "How is my customers' data protected?" You might get back some technical answers: however, as described earlier, there are ways to cut through some of the technical jargon by reaching out when needed.

The principles and actions suggested in the book should be applicable regardless of the size of your firm. Tailoring it to the needs of the company depend on acceptable levels of risk and priorities.

Conclusion

Cybersecurity, like many technology-based careers, is complex and typically takes a good deal of training, studying, and immersion in the field to become proficient. The basic cybersecurity triad of Confidentiality, Integrity and Availability can serve as guideposts for any risk discussion around data protection and third parties. Information security focuses on ensuring that data stays restricted to those authorized to access it, protected so it is not altered, and accessible to those permitted to get to access it. Cybersecurity can cover a wide spectrum of activities in most enterprise networks, and will be the basis for how due diligence and due care activities are to be performed in upcoming chapters.

Cybersecurity frameworks provide organizations with guides to how to lower their risk to security incidents. Frameworks to focus on include NIST-CSF, ISO 27001 and 27002, NIST-853, Federal Information Security Management Act of 2002 (FISMA), New York Department of Financial Services (NYDFS), and any that are applicable to the industry, country, or region where business is conducted. The adoption and adherence to one or more of these structures informs the customer how the vendor approaches this risk reduction. Speaking to them in their "language" by understanding their framework adoption can ease discussions about gap analysis and remediation steps.

The types of cybercrime and cyber threats are always evolving. Advanced Persistent Threats (APTs) and cybercriminal organizations pose the largest threat to others as they tend to have near infinite time, resources, and energy. The types of attacks are equally varied, but the ones that are most often impactful or seen recently have been phishing and ransomware attacks. Social engineering using fake emails to fool an insider to give away their credentials, or to download malware that encrypts all their files, is often that path of least resistance for a hacker.

Understanding how a breach is performed was broken down into the five steps—research, intrusion, lateral movement, privilege escalation, and exfiltration—and we included a walkthrough of how it was accomplished at Target. The five steps (i.e., phases) illustrated how most of the APTs and cybercriminals approach their work and how the steps are important to when and how a breach can be stopped. If the cybersecurity team's detective work can catch a breach in the intrusion or lateral movement stages, there is a good chance of containing the effects with minimal damage and data loss. However, if their detection isn't until the exfiltration phase (which is often when detection occurs as the damage the hackers have done becomes known), then there's zero chance to stop the loss of data and damage. This is why cybersecurity professionals push tools like as IDS/IPS and DLP, among others, to amp up the detection capability.

3

What the COVID-19 Pandemic Did to Cybersecurity and Third-Party Risk

The pandemic, resulting lockdowns, travel restrictions, and behavioral changes are going to leave a lasting imprint on our lives, businesses, and governments. Because of these immediate effects, cybercriminals quickly acted, swinging their focus and efforts to exploit the panic and confusion surrounding COVID-19. As months passed and other news shaped events, these bad actors continued to change their tactics and messages based on that news. Cyber incidents increased as the focus centered more on how to make the most money and create the most damage during COVID-19. As vaccines are being administered and lockdowns could be ending, data is beginning to predict that trends will continue after lockdowns and travel will return to normal. What's considered "normal" will be different, with those modifications equaling more workers being online and connected, which will lead to more surface area (i.e., more connections + more online users = more targets) for attack.

The Pandemic Shutdown

On March 19, 2020, the first lockdown orders began rolling across the United States. Much of North and South America, Europe, and most of Asia was on a similar trajectory or had already locked down. The rush to send employees to work from home had begun, including all the risks associated with an unplanned massive workforce relocation. While some companies had pandemic plans and/or natural disaster plans set in place to deal with a pandemic, the vast majority were not prepared for a pandemic of this size and scale. When the governmental aid started flowing to citizens in need, the inevitable cybercriminals and hackers took advantage of the opportunity. Everyone's locations and routines were uprooted, which led to security risks being overlooked or unknown.

Prior to mid-March 2020, most cybercriminals focused on where the money is: financial institutions. If criminals wanted data, the easiest targets were often healthcare providers, local governments, and schools because they typically had lower information security budgets and resources. However, the COVID-19 pandemic, with its government-supplemented money and huge disruption to normal work-home life, had these bad actors pivoting their tactics and preying on the changes, fears, and misinformation swirling around the pandemic. Many switched to coronavirus-themed phishing campaigns as well, as ways to extract any relief monies from banks, governments, and the intended recipients.

Several manifestations of this increase in activity could be found. First, hundreds of malicious domains began mimicking legitimate COVID information and relief sites. Cybercriminals use these sites to launch spam and phishing campaigns or to spread malware. Such malware is on the rise as cyberattackers use the pandemic to hide malware in coronavirus websites and maps and use spam emails to fool users into downloading malware. Ransomware is being pushed to hospitals, schools, universities, medical institutions, and local governments as they are overwhelmed by the health crisis. The Federal Bureau of Investigation (FBI) Cyber Division reported up to 4,000 complaints a day—a 400 percent increase from pre-COVID days. Interpol reported an "alarming rate of cyberattacks aimed at major corporations, governments, and critical infrastructure." Microsoft reported that COVID-related phishing and social engineering attacks increased to 30,000 per day.

COVID is the biggest cybersecurity event in history. Forty-seven percent of employees have fallen for a phishing scam due to at-home distractions. Seventy-six percent of companies reported that remote work increases the time to contain a breach. Working from home (WFH) has increased the average cost of a data breach by $137,000. Over 200,000 networking attacks occurred in Asia-Pacific (APAC) from January to July in 2020. Scams grew by 400 percent in March of 2020, with Google blocking 18 million daily malware and phishing emails in April of 2020 alone. IBM reported that the United States had the highest cost of breaches at $8.64 million, but the impact with cyber threats was increasing globally. More concerning were the June 2020 statistics published by SC Media that 65 percent of a cross-section of industries reported they had zero-to-minimal compliance with data privacy and security regulations, while a further 27 percent said they were only partially compliant with the same regulations.

Our discussion earlier of compliance not equaling security is relevant here given these statistics. A large portion of the business community admits that data privacy, security regulations, and compliance are either not done well or not done at all. Being compliant is merely a snapshot of the completion of a requirement and does not mean that the information security program and activities are continually securing data and systems. If 27 percent of industries are only partially complying with regulations, and 65 percent are not complying at all, the gap for actual cybersecurity being performed as a practice is well below those numbers.

The pandemic lockdown that sent millions to perform work, school, and other activities from home was a monumental shift that occurred incredibly fast, and was messy in some cases. Poor cybersecurity practices and processes were exposed as the number of breaches and security incidents increased exponentially. While vaccines are being deployed and the anticipation is that life will return to a new normal, questions still linger about which changes (started in 2020) will continue. Such changes will continue to be high risk to cybersecurity and third-party risk on organizations, work, and school life for years to come.

Timeline of the Pandemic Impact on Cybersecurity

Events happened fast in early 2020, and some of the resulting changes are now considered part of our everyday lives. A large percentage of the workforce will continue working from home well into 2021 and beyond. Some companies, in fact, have opted to shift their workforce to being all remote. Let's look at the pandemic timeline to see what transpired, including notable cybercrime events, and to understand how quickly hackers adapted and exploited the events. To distinguish from COVID-related events, cyber events appear in bold. Watch as the pace and number of these cyber events builds:

- December 31, 2019: The first reported case to the World Health Organization (WHO) of an unknown pneumonia case is seen in Wuhan, China.
- January 7, 2020: Researchers in China announce a new (novel) coronavirus.
- **January 10–20, 2020: The first phase of moving employees to work remotely begins, with about 10 percent working from home by late January.**
- January 21, 2020: The first case of COVID-19 is reported in the United States.
- **January 29, 2020: A Japanese-language spam email pretending to be a public health center is the first known instance of cybercriminals using COVID as a means to hack. The MUMMY SPIDER was distributed the Emotet malware, which was originally developed as a trojan for banks. This malware spreads like a computer worm infecting other systems in the network. MUMMY SPIDER is a criminal cyber gang linked to the development of Emotet.**

- January 30, 2020: WHO declares that COVID-19 is a public health emergency of international concern.

- **February 2, 2020: Advanced Persistent Threat (APT) actors begin using COVID-related lures in phishing campaigns.**

- **February 6, 2020: In China, two types of ransomware are distributed using a COVID-19 theme to fool victims into downloading the malware.**

- **February 15, 2020: Cybercriminals send out phishing scam emails pretending to be from WHO.**

- February 28, 2020: The RSA Conference is held despite many sponsors pulling out at the last minute. Many attendees later test positive for the virus.

- February 29, 2020: The first reported death occurs due to COVID-19 in the United States.

- **March 9, 2020: A "Coronavirus Map" application, which is actually malware that includes the AZORult, is released. This malware is a trojan virus designed to scoop up sensitive information.**

- March 11, 2020: WHO declares COVID-19 a global pandemic.

- **March 20, 2020: An email extortion campaign is launched globally threatening to infect receivers unless they pay a bitcoin ransom.**

- **March 20, 2020: The U.S. FBI's Internet Crime Complaint Center issues a public warning on the rise in cyber fraud due to COVID-19. Another variant of the attack in the U.K. offers the recipient free school lunch if they click on the link.**

- **March 24, 2020: U.S. and U.K. residents receive short message service (SMS) text messages informing them** that they must take a "mandatory" COVID-19 preparation test and points victims to a website that downloads malware.

- **March 31, 2020: Thousands of Skype credentials are stolen using a pandemic-themed phishing campaign.**
- **April 1, 2020: Microsoft sends out a warning to hospitals about the rise of ransomware attacks due to weak security surrounding virtual private network (VPN) use in that industry.**
- April 3, 2020: Half of all working Americans are working from home.
- **April 10, 2020: A successful phishing campaign in Spain uses a COVID-19 remedy as bait.**
- **April 16, 2020: Google releases information reporting it has blocked over 18 million COVID-related emails containing malware or phishing attempts in the week prior.**
- **April 19, 2020: In the United Kingdom, a fake email tells recipients they can receive job retention payments by clicking a link, which directs them to a malware download.**
- **April 30, 2020: Dozens of pandemic-themed phishing and ransomware attacks are discovered in late April. Many leveraged the unknown and panic with emails concerning the Family and Medical Leave Act (FMLA), Paycheck Protection funds, and the delivery of parcels to the home.**
- **May 6, 2020: U.S. and U.K. cybersecurity agencies announce that APT state actors are attempting to hack into healthcare and medical research facilities that are fighting the virus or developing vaccines.**

- **July 15, 2020: Twitter accounts for Elon Musk, Bill Gates, Barack Obama, and others are hacked into using a social engineering technique.**
- **August 5, 2020: Interpol joins the chorus of global law enforcement declaring the increase in cybercrime is likely as a vaccine creation approaches.**
- **August 20, 2020: Cybercriminals posing as contact tracers for COVID-19 scam credit card and bank account information from thousands of victims.**
- **October 21, 2020: The Canadian government warns of a new COVID-19 scam incorporating phishing emails supposedly from the government that are intended to steal personal information from the recipients.**
- November 9, 2020: The first effective COVID-19 vaccine is announced.
- **December 3, 2020: IBM warns it has seen evidence that companies and governments are being targeted by unknown attackers, prompting a rare warning by the Department of Homeland Security.**
- **December 8, 2020: FireEye's internal testing team is targeted by a sophisticated APT that is thought to be a state actor.**
- **December 13, 2020: FireEye makes public the details of the SolarWinds attack.**
- December 14, 2020: The first COVID-19 vaccines are administered to the U.S. public.

This list mentions just some of the notable cyber events; to list them all would take numerous pages. Thousands of other cyberattacks and schemes occurred from December 2019 and are still ongoing. The preceding timeline merely illustrates how quickly the cybercriminals and APTs adapted and pivoted to exploit new vulnerabilities and weaknesses caused by the pandemic.

In many cases the cybersecurity industry is still evolving and trying to catch up. However, it's much easier for the cybercriminals to simply alter their targets and tactics. Corporate and government information security personnel, processes, and systems are usually slower to evolve, which presents a unique challenge to post-pandemic trends and changes.

Post-Pandemic Changes and Trends

Will this level of cyber activity continue, or will it return to pre-pandemic levels later in 2021 as more people are vaccinated and herd immunity occurs, enabling life to return to normal? It's likely there will be a new "normal," and that life will not return to the pre-pandemic normal. While cyber activity might not be at the level it was when full-blown lockdowns were in force, many companies, consumers, and employees have altered their behaviors and won't return to the former. Many companies have shifted their workforces to all or a larger portion working remotely than before. Consumers have changed their habits permanently, opting more and more for online shopping than from traditional brick-and-mortars. All these habits, which before were performed in person, are now going to be performed virtually, enabling cyberattacks to continue as the attack surface increases.

As this increased cybercrime and hacking continues into the foreseeable future, combined with the damning statistics of how few companies perform proper due diligence and due care for their data and connectivity to vendors, we will continue to see the breaches and security incidents growing at the current pace. This necessitates the need to adopt a more aggressive and cybersecurity-focused approach to third-party risk.

Once the lockdowns end, our new normal will begin, creating new changes in many areas. The following descriptions are not predictions, but ideas built on the trends seen building toward the end of the pandemic. While these trends are not going to continue to grow at the same pace, the changes from COVID-19 are widely thought to have moved much of life to where it would have been 10 years or more from now, had it not been for the pandemic. For example, prior to the pandemic, only 17 percent of the U.S. workforce was remote. During the pandemic, it was as high as 47 percent. This percentage will increase past the pre-pandemic 17 percent. Changes to how lives are conducted post-pandemic will shift from an in-person lifestyle to less interaction and a more online, connected work and life presence. This increased amount of web and network traffic increases attack surface for the cybercriminals and APTs.

Work-Life Changes When the pandemic hit, millions of workers were sent home. Adobe, Aetna, Amazon, Ancestry.com, Capital One, Coinbase, Facebook, Gartner, Infosys, Mastercard, Microsoft, Nationwide Insurance, Nielsen, PayPal, Raytheon, Salesforce, Shopify, Siemens, Slack, Smartsheet, Square, Twitter, Upwork, and Zillow have all changed to work-from-home permanently, or for at least much of 2020 and into 2021. Working from home will continue as employees realize its benefits and some employers decide that the risks of the once popular open floor plan are not ideal for the future.

Gaining popularity in the 1980s, these large open commercial spaces were believed to foster teamwork and better communication. The layout flexibility gave companies the ability to modify as their company size changed. Lastly, these were very cost-effective solutions for businesses as long tables took up less space and housed more workers, and cubicles cost thousands of dollars each. By 2017, 70 percent of offices had adopted this open design.

However, this open office plan adoption had its downsides—noise levels grew and privacy was nonexistent. Now the problem is the inadequacy of the ventilation systems against disease. For example, on February 25, 2021, in a Korean call center, one of its 216 employees had flu symptoms. The Korean CDC performed a trace contact for the center's workers and found that nearly half the employees had become infected. The contact tracing further indicated that the virus jumped across the office to cause 94 of the 216 workers to become COVID-19 positive.

Companies are most likely to adapt such open spaces not with a major remodel, but by making tweaks. The first goal will be to reduce density, reducing the work area from 10 workers to a table to 5 or less, as increased space between employees is the social-distancing goal. Clients will not be placed into a conference room deep in the office space but nearer to the entrance or in another space away from staff. All-hands meetings will not occur in person but using a combination of remote and in-person attendance. Elevators that once held 15 people will be counted full at 5 people. This reduced occupancy can result in more employees working from home or a reduced occupancy rate that will require companies to not have all employees returning to work.

Long before the pandemic, many high-tech companies, like Yahoo, had embraced working from home, and had pushed for some employees to work remotely. (Prior to the pandemic, 17 percent of the tech workforce was remote, rising to 40 percent during it.) However, in 2013, Yahoo CEO Marissa Mayer banned working from home, going so far as to tell those who wouldn't make the adjustment that they should find other work. There was an impression among many, outside Yahoo as well, that remote working is not conducive to collaboration or good management.

Yet, the trends during COVID paint a different picture as companies and employees deal with the inevitability of working remotely for a long time. Studies indicated that of the workers new to working remotely, roughly 40 percent wanted to return to the office. However, the other 60 percent wanted to stay full-time or part-time working remotely. The workers new to remote work have had a difficult time adjusting to the distractions of home: needy pets barking, children requiring help with schooling, and no designated office space.

Some of these distractions will lessen over time. Children will return to school and daycare. Pets over time become used to the sounds of working from home as well. Designated work space may continue to be a challenge, but with the schools reopening it will be a lesser problem. New remote personnel will overwhelmingly enjoy their increased family time, flexibility, and work-life balance advantages. On the downside, 15 percent of new remote workers reported a greater sense of well-being, and 32 percent reported being frustrated with remote work due to burnout.

This remote work trend also provides another increased attack surface: collaboration tools. The increased use of WebEx, Zoom, Microsoft Teams, and other video conferencing tools gives attackers more targets. In the pandemic's early days, malicious actors were "Zoom-bombing" meetings due to Zoom's lack of meeting access passwords and easy-to-guess meeting links. The results were predictable: Strangers, often with bad intent, "bombed" a meeting and yelled obscenities or spied on the conversations. Expect this area to be a target for cybercriminals going forward.

Working from Home and Cybersecurity

WFH is going to be a larger part of the corporate, education, and government world for a while. And while this practice can lead to higher productivity and a better work-life balance, it can also lead to data leakage as exposed during the pandemic via security weaknesses and a lack of preparation. There are numerous ways a WFH employee can accidentally release sensitive information, which likely would not occur in an office setting.

The biggest technology threat is the VPN (Virtual Private Network). Every connected remote computer to a corporate network is a potential risk. Just because a VPN provides end-to-end encryption does not mean it *is* secure. You must ask your suppliers the following questions:

Do you require an MFA for remote access?

Remote access with a VPN does provide confidentiality of the data in transit, but it does not provide the security of logging in at a desk at corporate headquarters. Nearly every organization now has some level of physical access controls, from a simple key to enter an office or keycards employees use with a PIN code. Either way, the employee has had some level of verification to enter the corporate network. From home, that physical access is controlled by the employee, not by the company. The requirement of multi-factor authentication can provide a second authentication piece to ensure the person requiring access is the user.

How often are reviews performed on remote access?

Remote access comes with more risk than in-office access. Vendors should be performing at least quarterly reviews of remote access logs. It is better and far less risky if they have them plugged directly into their Security

Information Event and Management (SIEM) for immediate alerting so they can review who had access and when for anomalous behavior.

Do you have geofencing rules on remote access, and how is it enforced logically?

Regulations, industry standards, and corporate rules exist on performing work outside an organization's country of normal operations. In the United States, for example, many non-global companies avoid moving data outside their borders to avoid any unnecessary entanglements with General Data Protections Regulations (GDPR). If your supplier has an internal policy or your firm has a policy it enforces on suppliers, you must know how they ensure that a user cannot connect from outside the permitted area.

Does your VPN connection have an 802.1x implementation that would quarantine or not allow connections from systems out of compliance?

Remote connections of users' laptops are just as risky from an endpoint perspective as that same laptop connecting in the corporate office. The 802.1x Network Access Control tool ensures that if a device does not meet the connection standard, it is either quarantined (i.e., has no connection except to the help desk) or not connected and given a number to call for assistance. This capability should be extended to VPN or remote connections to ensure that they do not wander out of compliance remotely and drag malware into the network.

Do you allow administrator rights to users on their laptops?

In any organization, a "normal" end user should not require administrator rights on their laptop. By definition, a corporate-issued device should have all the software the user

(Continued)

(Continued)

needs installed by the software department, not by the user. Enabling a user to have administrator rights allows them to not only install unapproved (and potentially malware loaded) software, but they can also disable important services like antivirus and malware protection. While there can be exceptions, those exceptions should adhere to a review, approval, and rereview process at regular intervals.

Does remote access require connection with a vendor-owned and controlled laptop? (Do you allow personal devices to connect?)

During the original WFH rush, there were a few instances where some companies were forced to allow employees to connect via their personal laptops. As in the case of both the administrator rights problem and the 802.1x compliance check, allowing non-corporate-controlled devices to connect invites malware and cybercriminals. Vendors should always control what type of devices can connect to their network.

Do you allow Virtual Desktop Infrastructure (VDI) connections for users? If so, do you restrict ability to remove or exfiltrate data?

Virtual desktops are a common way to enable users to connect at scale that does not require the company to provide a physical laptop and the total cost of ownership that entails. However, because a user can connect to a VDI from any device anywhere, some controls must be set in place on the ability for data leaks. Closing down the ability to copy/paste any data out of the virtual environment, along with reduced access to copy the screen if possible, is a start. Restricting the ability to download to local machines is another control.

What Security Training and Awareness do you provide employees and is it mandatory?

The weakest link can be the user if not properly trained on what to look for in phishing emails, social engineering, vishing, and how to report suspicious activity or security risks. It is important that they know where to report potential incidents or they could go undetected or unreported. Cybersecurity training should also be followed up with some testing (e.g., phishing campaigns with fake emails) and annual retraining as new risks need to be communicated.

The remote workforce is here to stay, even if it drops from the numbers seen in 2020. Vendors who do not secure their remote connections certainly pose a risk to your data either directly or through lateral movement.

Shopping Changes   Changes in shopping behavior will likely be more significant and permanent than remote work. Trends that began before the pandemic accelerated in 2020 are now viewed as having more staying power according to continued consumer behavior. Touch-free shopping and the dying of malls both are opportunities for cybercriminals.

Touch-free shopping sharply contrasts to pre-pandemic shopping. Previously, you could walk into a big-box or grocery store and sample everything from food to cologne. Checking out meant swiping a debit card and punching in your personal identification (PIN) code. Changes made to shopping are near permanent. Touchless payments, either via a smartphone or with a smart debit card, are being rolled out by card issuers and the retailers themselves. Retailers are expanding this as well. For example, Price Chopper, a smartphone application that allows shoppers to scan and go, is now used by several grocery chains. Walmart is pushing its Scan & Go mobile app, enabling customers to ring up purchases on their smartphones.

Gone are the samples of lipstick at the makeup counter or the meatballs as you roam the aisles at the grocery store. Lowe's Home Improvement stores are installing lockers where online shoppers can retrieve their purchases without even interacting with an employee. Numerous grocery stores are pushing parking-lot delivery services, which end in-store interactions. Curbside pickup has become the new normal for many retail and restaurant customers. GlobalData reports that 68 percent of U.S. shoppers will use curbside pickup and another 60 percent indicated they will collect online purchases from inside stores in the future.

The trend from mall and department store shopping to online shopping was already occurring well before the pandemic; lockdowns and behavior changes were just rushed forward by years due to it. Malls and department stores had already been struggling when they were forced to shutter in March 2020. Brooks Brothers, Lane Bryant, Ann Taylor, Chuck E. Cheese, Century 21 Stores, GNC, Guitar Center, J.C. Penny, J. Crew, Lord & Taylor, Neiman Marcus, Pier 1, Stein Mart, Men's Wearhouse, and Joseph A. Bank, among others, all filed for bankruptcy protection as the lockdowns during the pandemic sped up their decline. Many may not survive through Chapter 11 proceedings and will cease to exist. Some malls may reopen, but eating at a crowded food court or watching a movie at a theater will be impacted for a long period to come. Coresight Research predicts up to 1,000 U.S. malls will close within five years.

Who was the winner during the global pandemic? Online retailers, whose accelerating adoption is global. It's predicted that China's online sales will comprise over 27 percent of retails sales in 2021, with the United Kingdom at 19.9 percent, and the United States at 16.2 percent. eMarketer predicts sales online will increase over 32 percent in 2021, while traditional brick-and-mortar sales will shrink by 3.2 percent. Compare these numbers to 2019, when online commerce grew by 14.6 percent and brick-and mortar grew by 1.5 percent. These trends will dip lower post-pandemic, and it is not expected to see a 30-percent growth year-over-year in online commerce for 2021; however, the trend accelerated greatly due to the pandemic and will not return to pre-COVID levels. This increased amount of online shopping will increase the targets for cybercriminals.

School Instruction Changes   The way students learn has been forever changed from being in class to more remote learning style, also resulting in increased attack surface. The initial response for most primary and secondary schools was to close and perform remote instruction when possible. However, the technology divide became obvious very quickly as areas with low online adoption and limited broadband access prevented or slowed the ability to teach remotely.

Such changes for educational instruction are similar to those found in the workplace. Cramming a bunch of students into shared spaces like before will not be welcome, despite a vaccine being available. While the number of K–12 students who remain remote will not be at the same level post-pandemic, many trends point to some parents choosing private school or homeschooling at numbers greater than pre-pandemic. Additional online students learning from home also increase the target surface area for cybercriminals.

Another likely trend to increase is the push to move broadband access into previously underserved areas. The rush to educate via remote learning demonstrated that several areas simply could not support the effort due to lacking infrastructure (i.e., broadband access, Wi-Fi availability, and a lack of access to internet-connected devices). Increasing internet access is a necessary and worthy goal, but more participants on the web also increase opportunities for cybercriminals.

One possible beneficial change is the increased demand in technical employment in areas such as cybersecurity. The cyber-criminal and security incident uptick is driving this increased demand for these professionals. As current working professionals and students make career choices, this demand will drive up salaries and increase student draw to the field. Unfortunately, the time it takes to become a skilled security professional is not quick, so it's likely this will be a lagging indicator; changes in the tech workforce will unfortunately increase slowly over time. As a result, this lag will give cybercriminals more time to exploit this gap in resources.

Supply Chain Changes The pandemic lockdown disrupted numerous supply chains. Shuttered factories, disrupted shipping routes, and remote work forces meant many companies struggled to fulfill orders. Many had to rethink and redesign their approach, which likely will impact how Cybersecurity Third-Party Risk is managed. Changes in how supply chains are handled and enabled to grow will be slowly implemented.

Regionalization, where certain regions are self-sufficient in terms of deliverable goods, will likely be a notable trend. Rather than relying on global supply chains to deliver goods globally, regions will be self-sufficient in their particular area. Therefore, if there is an impact in an area due to another pandemic event, it will only affect that region. Others could continue opera-tions without issue. *Onshoring*, where production is moved back from being overseas, likely will be another trend. Survey results from The Institute for Supply Management indicated almost 25 percent of companies would be bringing operations or manu-facturing onshore. Changing these during a lockdown and travel bans is very difficult; however, the work to change the span and size of their supply chains has begun.

Cybersecurity's impact on these changes has yet to be seen, given that such changes have either not been completed, or even started, in some cases. Onshoring work and production to its home country can lessen the impact of performing due diligence on offshore vendors. However, splitting up the production for regionalization likely will increase the attack surface as production is farther spread out.

Lifestyle Changes   Lifestyle changes have become more digital than prior to COVID-19 and will remain that way. How we cook and eat, view entertainment, and perform physical activities have all permanently changed in ways that add risk. These changes are not directly connected to a Cybersecurity Third-Party Risk for all organizations, such as working from home or education. However, our increased online activity and changed behaviors create an increased attack surface.

Before the pandemic, telemedicine was barely a blip on the radar and mostly used for patients who had difficulty traveling or who were located far from medical personnel. The lockdown, however, necessitated remote medical appointments for those needing normal checkups and other issues besides the flu. Telemedicine use increased 154 percent in March of 2020, and its increase of use into the fall season from previous years approached 50 percent. This increase in telemedicine is not confined to doctor's visits but also includes an increase in online prescription orders and the monitoring of remote medical devices by a doctor or nurse over the internet. This online activity increase in the medical field increases risk as the healthcare field has had a high incidence of ransomware attacks. Healthcare has been a target of cybercriminals for a while, and this rise in activity will also provide more opportunities for bad actors.

Home-delivered meals, which originate from online activity, have taken off since the pandemic began. Blue Apron, Hello

Fresh, and Plated all started around 2012 in the United States, with their initial customer base being older millennials with disposable income. The pandemic, however, increased their user base as more people who were seeking convenience began cooking at home. This is not a huge growth area, but there has also been a rise in the use of restaurant and grocery store meal kits into this space. This activity all takes place online and shifted from previous dining out. The move to online transactions for meal kits is one more avenue for cybersecurity bad actors to exploit.

Streaming video was already on track to increase in popularity pre-pandemic, and cinemas were seeing declining attendance as binge-watching became the new normal. Many cinemas closed and have yet to reopen. Regal Cinemas filed for bankruptcy, and AMC is facing it but raising capital in the hope to avoid it. Even after the lockdowns have ended and a vaccine is fully implemented, there will be even fewer options to enjoy a theater experience. The big four streaming services (Netflix, YouTube, Hulu, and Amazon) saw huge increases during the pandemic, growing their subscription bases. This increased subscriber base opens up even more online areas for cybercriminals.

Another lockdown casualty were the local health clubs/ gyms. Many either closed for months, went out of business, or continue to struggle. Large fitness chains began offering online streaming fitness classes. The sale of at-home exercise equipment, such as Peloton, iFit, Mirror, and others, grew exponentially. This equipment is not cheap, and many require a monthly subscription. These online transactions for such fitness equipment and services are great targets for cybercriminals. First, the purchase of expensive equipment and continuing subscriptions are likely tempting for hackers seeking victims with deep pockets. Second, the equipment vendors themselves provide a great target, given they have a customer base that is generally affluent and online.

Although these changes may not directly relate to Cybersecurity Third-Party Risk, they do offer an increased attack surface that will alter cybercriminal behavior. This altered behavior will focus on areas where data and money can be stolen. Whether it's working remotely, studying remotely, buying groceries for curbside pickup, or ordering meal kits for delivery, all these activities involve internet traffic that is subject to attack and will lead to more security incidents.

"But we have a firewall. . . ."

Cybersecurity and information systems have evolved a great deal since the 1990s when nearly all data internal to a company was protected by a firewall. Firewalls are still an important security feature in any enterprise. However, they can be misunderstood by some non-security teams to be "the solution" to a breach or security incident. As discussed in an earlier chapter, security is not reliant on one tool, process, or person to be effective. It is defense-in-depth—a combination of a diverse set of tools inside and outside the network to prevent breaches.

For those not working in cybersecurity, a firewall is akin to a moat around the castle with the entrance having a guard. The firewall is both the moat and the guard, preventing unwanted traffic from entering. The guard knows to let certain packages and people through, based upon the rules given from the king and queen. These rules govern who the guard (i.e., firewall) allows to pass into the castle. At the end of this list is a "deny all others" rule. Meaning, if the visitors do not meet the profile listed on the guidelines, then those visitors cannot enter.

(Continued)

(Continued)

However, the rules for the guard (firewall) only apply to visitors, it does not apply to mail (i.e., email). Email arrives via the mail deliver courier and the guard verifies it is the recognized mail delivery person and truck. A firewall cannot review every email for malware, links to infected sites, or attachments that embed ransomware or protect all the potential network vulnerabilities.

Firewalls are important tools and the next generation of firewalls have great features that can look deep into the network traffic. Combined with tools such as IDS/IPS, DLP, and email protections, they all provide the defense-in-depth (several independent layers of security used to ensure if one fails, another will be operational) required in the 21st century.

Regulated Industries

Several industries are highly regulated where Third-Party Risk Management is a requirement. Financial sector requirements have been listed before, but both the Office of Comptroller of the Currency (OCC) and the Federal Insurance Deposit Corporation (FDIC) have required regulated banks to follow their guidance on Third-Party Risk Management. However, that's just a small sliver of the related regulatory and framework oversight. It includes, for example, the Federal Reserve Guidance on Managing Outsourcing Risk, Federal Financial Institutions Examination Council (FFIEC) Supervision of TSP, the Financial Industry Regulatory Authority (FINRA) Notice to Members 11-14, and Gramm-Leach-Bliley Act (GLBA) Reg-SP Privacy of Customer Information, just to name a few more. In the United States, healthcare is regulated by the Health Insurance Portability and Accountability Act (HIPAA) enacted in 1996. This act prescribes both a privacy rule and security rule for protection of health data.

Other sectors have regulations specific to the third-party risk around data privacy. However, as the number of data privacy laws and regulations have been promulgated worldwide in the last 10 years or more, what most companies haven't taken into account is that virtually every business worldwide that manages protected data for customers is subject to regulation. Except for much of Africa, a few countries in South America, and a similar amount in Central Asia, nearly every other country in the world has some form of data protection laws.

The General Data Protection Regulation (GDPR) is a European Union (EU) law. This is considered one of the most robust and punitive data protection laws in the world and while the application is focused primarily on Europe, there is an extra-territorial effect. A company that is not within the EU is subject to GDPR if it processes personal data of subjects who are in the EU. A formal payment transaction doesn't even have to take place but GDPR is in effect when goods or services are offered for sale.

In the United States, several data protection laws and regulations are in place that are sector-specific and medium-specific. The California Consumer Protection Act (CCPA) is the most well-known, and due to the state's size and economy, it has an outsized impact on how data protection is done within the nation. On top of that, California has another two dozen state data protection laws. Other states are also writing their own data privacy laws. The Federal Trade Commission has the authority in the United States over a wide range of businesses on the data protection area. It is highly likely that if you're doing business in the United States, you have a myriad of agencies and enforcement abilities required of your organization if you process or store customer data.

In other international locations, it is far more likely that you will have some form of data protection requirements than not. Argentina has a very robust privacy clause built right into its Federal Constitution. Australia has the Federal Privacy Act of 1988 and the Australian Privacy Principles. There are also several more regulations specific to the territory (New South Wales, Queensland, Tasmania, Victoria, Northern Territory, and the Capital Territory). Canada has over two dozen federal territorial and provincial privacy statutes and is considered a very robust program.

Many businesses and entities in those sectors that are not highly regulated may have thought they could relax. However, as the list of data privacy protection laws and regulations are shown to be applicable to nearly every company that retains customer-protected data, they're subject to regulatory requirements. While the list of required business practices doesn't go into great detail in the finance or biotech industries, the penalties and fines for failing to follow them can be enough to prevent a business from being a "going concern" (an accounting term for a company that has the resources needed to continue operating indefinitely until it provides evidence to the contrary). Every company that has customer PII or PHI, no matter the sector or location, must perform due care and due diligence for securing that data.

An Inside Look: P&N Bank

In mid-January 2020, P&N Bank disclosed that it had been involved in a data breach involving detailed and sensitive financial information for potentially all its 96,000 customers. The data involved included their names, mailing addresses, email addresses, phone numbers, ages, and account numbers and balances. This breach occurred in mid-December 2019 during a server upgrade at the third party hosting P&N Bank's servers.

Upon becoming aware of the attack, we immediately shut down the source of the vulnerability and have since been working closely with WAPOL, other federal authorities, our third-party IT provider involved, regulators, and independent expert advisers to investigate and protect customers from any further risk. The safety and security of our members' information and funds is our highest priority. Data protection continues to be a focus around the world, and financial systems will always present some degree of risk, so it is important to stress that in line with best practice, we have highly sophisticated security measures and controls in place to protect our customers' accounts.

—*Andrew Hadley, CEO of P&N Bank*

Formerly known as the Police & Nurses Credit Society, most of the customers of P&N Bank are first responders. Luckily, no direct loss of customer funds, credit card details, or bank passwords occurred, and the customer relational management (CRM) database did not contain any passport, Social Security, or health data.

One of the first missteps made by P&N was to send a letter out to the affected customers, stating that "non-sensitive" data was exposed. This statement was incorrect because names, addresses, emails, phone numbers, ages, and account numbers and balances are considered non-public when combined. It resulted in many customers becoming even more disappointed in their breach response.

The customer information was leaked by a social media vendor for P&N named Deep Social. Described as a "freemium" influencer ranking, discovering, and AI-driven analytics platform, Deep Social's server was left vulnerable while undergoing an upgrade. In late 2018, Deep Social stopped providing its service and wound down the company, and its license to use the Instagram platform was revoked by Facebook because it had been found to violate Facebook's policies.

This breach demonstrated how vulnerable a company can become due to a third-party hosting service not taking proper due care and due diligence. What P&N Bank should be ensuring is how its hosting provider secures their instance. We will discuss specifics of what to ask in later chapters, but most hosting providers should provide what is often called a Security Configuration or Security Audit printout. In Amazon Web Services (AWS), it's called a Trusted Advisor Report (TAR), which details important items and flags variances from best practices, such as multi-factor authentication (MFA) for privileged accounts, items left unencrypted, or firewalls not configured properly.

SolarWinds Attack Update

The SolarWinds attack involved dozens of companies and government organizations. As a result, the Cybersecurity and Infrastructure Security Agency (CISA), part of the Department of Homeland Security (DHS), issued a rare direct Emergency Directive 21-01:

> *Section 3553(h) of title 44, U.S. Code, authorizes the Secretary of Homeland Security, in response to a known or reasonably suspected information security threat, vulnerability, or incident that represents a substantial threat to the information security of an agency, to "issue an emergency directive to the head of an agency to take any lawful action with respect to the operation of the information system, including such systems used or operated by another entity on behalf of an agency, that collects, processes, stores, transmits, disseminates, or otherwise maintains agency information, for the purpose of protecting the information system from, or mitigating, an information security threat."*
>
> *44 U.S.C. § 3553(h)(1)–(2)*

Section 2205(3) of the Homeland Security Act of 2002, as amended, delegates this authority to the Director of the Cybersecurity and Infrastructure Security Agency.

6 U.S.C. § 655(3)

Federal agencies are required to comply with these directives.

44 U.S.C. § 3554 (a)(1)(B)(v)

These directives do not apply to statutorily-defined "national security systems" nor to systems operated by the Department of Defense or the Intelligence Community.

44 U.S.C. § 3553(d), (e)(2), (e)(3), (h)(1)(B)

The Emergency Directive also mandated that federal agencies take actions to forensically examine hard drives and memory systems with the SolarWinds product Orion versions 2019.4 through 2020.2.1 HF1. It directed them to analyze all new accounts, especially privileged ones; further, there were indicators released for the compromise that could be used against stored network traffic to give forensics investigators the ability to determine when they were subject to the hack. All SolarWinds products, whether hardware or cloud-based, were to be powered down and until CISA produced a known-clean build that agencies could use, the agencies affected would not be able to (re)join the machines to the enterprise domain.

Steps then included instructions to block traffic from any version of SolarWinds Orion software that had been installed, which really reveals the sinister danger of this hack: The product was sending out leaked information to collectors and this leakage went undetected for a long time. FireEye's incursion began in early Spring 2020. While FireEye is the most publicly visible with its announcement and transparency of the attack, it is clear that the U.S. government also leaked data for much of the same duration. How much data crossed networks for almost nine months across all the *known* victims? The sheer number should make any cybersecurity professional weak in the knees, and businesses and governments are bracing for the worst.

The survey results year after year indicate far too few companies perform adequate or any Cybersecurity Third-Party Risk assessments. As the pandemic swept in a new hyperactive cybercrime activity level, many companies with poor cybersecurity practices were breached (via ransomware, phishing attacks, stolen data) at a level not seen prior. Cybersecurity and Third-Party Risk Management (TPRM) organizations both have work to do in terms of collaborating on the third-party risk domain and finding ways to more proactively lower risk.

On its editorial page on December 18, 2020, *The Wall Street Journal* described the SolarWinds supply-chain attack as the equivalent of the Maginot Line in 1940. France and the western allies relied on a set of fixed fortresses around much of France, with the exception of the part that the Germans ended up exploiting through the Ardennes where there were no defenses. This comparison is appropriate as the fixed defenses are the security that CISOs and organizations have placed around their own boundaries, yet the enemy went through an area not defended sufficiently—the supply chain. The changes by COVID-19 to the world have made this a less safe place for organizations from the actions and intent of bad actors.

Conclusion

The cybercriminals and APTs quickly changed their focus and tactics when the COVID-19 pandemic hit. As the timeline shows, it took only a few short days from each change before the introduction of a new phishing or malware attack that preyed upon victims during these rapid and scary events. COVID-19 and the resulting lockdown to reduce the spread of the pandemic rushed many trends in online and other behaviors that will not return to pre-pandemic levels. The pandemic changed behaviors by employers and their employees, students, customers, and suppliers, and continues to provide more opportunities for the cybercriminals.

4

Third-Party Risk Management

Third Party Risk Management (TPRM) is the process of identifying, assessing, and controlling risks presented through the lifecycle of a relationship with third parties. The Office of the Comptroller of the Currency (OCC) defines a third-party relationship as any business arrangement between a company and another entity, by contract or otherwise. Third parties can perform any number of activities and services both internally and externally at a company, from landscaping and cleaning services, to managing intellectual property, processing customer data, outsourcing business functions, and countless other activities. Businesses also use third parties to grow their existing business (i.e., to attract and grow the customer base) or to improve efficiencies internally (i.e., to allow staff to work smarter, not harder).

The average company has nearly 600 vendors who have access to customer personal identifiable information (PII). On average, nearly 90 vendors can access a company's network on a weekly basis. Because they have access to your customer data or your network, performing due diligence on your third parties is crucial. TPRM amasses all the relevant information from the vendor to gather, review, and provide guidance on their risks. It is an end-to-end process, from the intake of the vendor to their offboarding when their service is no longer needed.

Five main areas make up Third Party Risk Management:

- **Reputation risk**: The threat or danger to the company's reputation (i.e., good name, goodwill, or standing) in the public.
- **Operational risk**: The risk of loss resulting from inadequate, lack of, or failed controls, processes, systems, people, or external events.

- **Transaction risk**: The adverse effect that can occur when monetary exchange rate movements are completed on transactions prior to settlement.
- **Compliance risk**: Threats posed to a company due to failure of complying with laws, regulations, codes of conduct, or other organizational standards of practice.
- **Information security risk**: The impact to a firm due to threats and vulnerabilities arising from the operation and use of information systems and the environments in which those systems operate.

The practice surrounding the management of these five risks comprise the TPRM end-to-end process. The first four risks are important to manage, and examples exist of firms failing to manage them resulting in catastrophic consequences. Companies like Accenture and Enron are two great examples. However, these examples are very few and far between in comparison to the information security risk category. A 2018 survey by Price Waterhouse & Coopers (PWC) indicated that 63 percent of all cyberattacks could be traced either directly or indirectly to third parties. Meanwhile, the same survey reveals only 2 percent of information technology (IT) and security professionals consider third-party security a top priority for their budgets and projects.

The first step to gain better control of these risks is to implement a TPRM framework. The size and complexity of this framework should be in accordance with your company's level of risk. A large firm in a highly regulated sector will have a department of resources with well-defined policies and processes to guide the risk oversight from end-to-end, while a smaller entity will not. Organizations exist that can assist with some frameworks, such as the National Institute of Standards and Technology (NIST), the International Organization for Standards (ISO), Health Insurance Portability and Privacy Act (HIPPA), and Payment Card Industry Data Security Standard (PCI-DSS).

The basics for all these frameworks follow:

- **Inventory**: Design a process to keep stock of all vendors for the company.
- **Risks**: Establish a list of all risks (cybersecurity, in our case) that the company can be exposed to from third parties.
- **Risk-based approach**: Create categories and risk levels (e.g., high, medium, low) to focus on critical risks.
- **Due diligence process**: Design a process to review and produce risk profiles for vendors that fit the risk levels you have set.
- **Stakeholders and decision-makers**: Ensure you have identified a decision-making team for governance and decisions.
- **Benchmarks**: Set thresholds and alert levels to measure your adherence to the program.
- **Lines of defense**: In organizations large enough, create at least three lines of defense:
  - **First line of defense**: Business owners (of the service/product of the vendor)
  - **Second line of defense**: Third-party oversight group
  - **Third line of defense**: The internal/external audit teams (for observance to the policy)
- **Contingency plans**: No matter the size of the company, design plans on how to deal with the inevitable: a breach, incident, or disaster.

TPRM can run the gamut of maturity levels at companies. As evidenced by some of the earlier statistics, far too few perform many of these activities. The list of provided main activities performed by TPRM, implemented and focused on cybersecurity, can greatly reduce the risk posed by vendors. Again, a TPRM framework can be implemented no matter the size and/or sector for a company.

Data Security Is Not Data Privacy

Data security and data privacy are closely related, but they are not the same. The difference is an important one to understand how they operate and to implement them properly. A number of data privacy regulations, such as General Data Protection Regulations (GDPR), California Privacy Rights Act (CPRA), and South Carolina Family Privacy Protection Act (SCFPPA) speak to preventing the misuse and collection of PII data. *Data security* includes the creation of and adherence to policies, methods, and means to secure protected data. *Data privacy* includes the proper use, collection, deletion, and storage of protected data.

Data security revolves around the CIA triad—Confidentiality, Integrity, and Availability—where all the people, processes, and practices involved to secure data are not being accessed improperly (Confidentiality); it's ensured that data is not altered without proper authorization (Integrity), and that it is available to the authorized users when needed (Availability). Any data security program will speak to the requirements to collect only required data, protecting it through encryption and securely discarded destruction when no longer required for use and retention.

When collecting or processing personal data, the users/owners of that data have an expectation to use it in ways to which they agreed for its use and processing. The regulations like GDPR, CPRA, and others are enforcement mechanisms to ensure that if an organization does not correctly inform, use, store, process, or resell private information, it is held financially responsible.

For example, when Cambridge Analytics harvested over 80 million Facebook user profiles in 2016, it was a violation of data privacy. When Facebook allowed the use of that data without prior user consent, that was a violation of data privacy due to its improper collection and use. When a hacker breaks into a database and steals private data because it is not encrypted, that is a break in data security.

The difference is important for businesses to understand how to properly address both data security and privacy. It is the organization's regulatory responsibility to keep private data secure, which translates into keeping employees', customers', and any other private data collected secure. Performing data security through a written and executed policy is a mechanism to ensure data privacy. However, data security will not protect against the improper sale or solicitation to sell private data.

Third-Party Risk Management Frameworks

TPRM frameworks, much like cybersecurity frameworks, are necessary to have an organized approach to reduce risk. The frameworks provide the structure for the execution and internal audit of this activity. The tools in this framework give organizations a guide to performing all the due diligence and due care for third-party risk.

The choice of a TPRM framework depends on the company's structure, risk profile and appetite, operations, size, and location(s). The OCC first guided financial institutions to manage this risk by adopting a risk management process in accordance with their level of risk and complexity of their third-party relationships. Whether you are in finance or any other industry, the same guidance holds true.

We covered some of the frameworks in Chapter 2. HIPAA, PCI-DSS, among others, are used respectively by TPRM as frameworks for the healthcare and payment card industries. ISO and NIST both have risk management frameworks that can be used in the evaluation process for a TPRM program. These frameworks are not size-specific and can be used no matter the size of your company if you follow the OCC rule-of-thumb where a "company should adopt a risk management process in accordance with the level of risk and complexity of their third-party relationships."

Note, the terms *supply chain* and *third party* are not entirely the same thing. Supply chain means the whole end-to-end process of how products or services are provided. Third party most often speaks directly to the vendor or supplier relationship and risk. While we may see both of them used, in the TPRM world, supply chain is often used to ensure that end-to-end security is discussed and acted upon.

ISO 27036:2013+

The ISO 27036 is a four-part standard offering guidance on the assessment and handling of security risks around the supply chain and third parties. The focus is on the direct business-to-business relationships, not retail sales. The scope is focused on information systems security, including:

- Information technology outsourcing and cloud services.
- Any professional services that would have physical or logical access to data and systems, such as source code escrow, consultants, research and development, cleaning and security services, system maintenance personnel, and courier services.

- The provisioning and implementation of any hardware, software, and services that move data or telecommunications.

- Custom-made software, products, and services that are not commercially available (as opposed to commercial-off-the-shelf suppliers [COTS]).

- Required utilities for operations (e.g., water, power, sewer).

- Strategy, goals, business needs, and objectives as they relate to information systems and the supply chain security.

- The security risks listed in the standard, including:

  - The organization's reliance on third parties that would make business continuity and recovery complicated.

  - Physical and logical access controls both internally and with vendors.

  - The shared responsibility model for compliance with security policies, standards, regulations, and contractual commitments.

- **ISO 27036-1: 2014 Information Security for Supplier Relationships Requirements (Part 1)**: Presents the parts of the standard on background, key terms, and concepts as they relate to security in supplier relationships. Information risks are listed that are common for vendor relationships involving sensitive data or connectivity. This part of the standard deals primarily with the organization perspective when addressing security concerns at their suppliers.

- **ISO 27036-2:2014**: Details the information security requirements for the requirements, implementation, operation, monitoring, reviewing, maintenance, and improvement of a vendor and customer relationship. The requirements cover all procurement and vendor products and services and apply to organizations of any size, type, and industry.

- **ISO 27036-3:2013**: Part 3 is a guideline for information systems supply chain security that provides guidance to both the vendor and purchaser on how to secure information systems against malware, counterfeit products, and organizational risk. It also outlines how to incorporate the software design lifecycle into the processes.

- **ISO 27036–4:2016**: Part 4 deals with security for cloud services. It provides guidance on how to gain visibility into the security risks around cloud services and how to manage the risks. Details on how to respond to the specific risks for acquiring services from cloud vendors and the security impact of those services are included.

NIST 800-SP

NIST 800-SP (Special Publication) is focused on NIST SP 800-161 supply chain risk management (SCRM) practices for Federal Information Systems and Organizations. Published in April 2015, it is available free of charge at nvlpubs.nist.gov/nistpubs/SpecialPublications/NIST.SP.800-161.pdf. The document covers the risks associated with information and communications technology (ICT) products and services

that may contain potentially malicious functionality, are counterfeit, or are vulnerable due to poor manufacturing and development practices with the ICT supply chain. This publication provides guidance to federal agencies on identifying, assessing, and mitigating ICT supply chain risks at all levels of their organizations. The publication integrates ICT supply chain risk management (SCRM) into federal agency risk management activities by applying a multitiered, SCRM-specific approach, including guidance on assessing supply chain risk and applying mitigation activities.

The document describes how SCRM is at the junction of security, integrity, resilience, and quality (see Figure 4.1). Security is a familiar topic relating to the CIA triad of Confidentiality, Integrity, and Availability as the data that is contained in the supply chain or data that traverses the third-party chain and how the data about the third parties participates in the supply sequence. Integrity is not the same as the CIA triad here, as it is specific not to the data, but to the products or services themselves that are not altered but are genuine. Also it addresses that the product or service will perform to specifications and not have unwanted additional functionality. Resilience is focused on ensuring that the ICT supply chain can function under stress or failure. Quality is dedicated to lowering the vulnerabilities that expose the product or service to exploitation, reduced functionality, or failure.

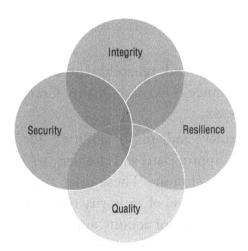

FIGURE 4.1   The Four Pillars of ICT SCRM

Foundational Practices   NIST SP 800-161 builds on a number of other standards that have been published across multiple disciplines. It is critical that foundational practices are utilized to ensure that best practices are used when dealing with third parties. The publication lists 12 examples of these base procedures and practices:

1. Implements a risk management hierarchy and process that aligns with NIST SP 800-39 (managing information security risk) and an organization-wide risk assessment process that meets NIST SP 800-30 Revision 1 (guide for conducting risk assessments).

2. Creates an organization governance that integrates with the supply chain security requirements and includes these in organization policies and standards.

3. Establishes a consistent, documented, and repeatable process for determining impact levels.

4. Uses a risk assessment process on the impact levels being defined that includes criticality, threat, and vulnerability analysis.

5. Builds a quality and reliability program that includes Quality Assurance (QA) and Quality Control (QC) practice and process.

6. Publishes roles and responsibilities for SCRM that requires the appropriate stakeholders to be involved in choices and conclusions. These roles and responsibilities must include the level of authority required to make decisions, accountability for actions, and which roles are in the inform column on activities and decisions.

7. Provides adequate resources to information security and SCRM for implementation of policy and controls.

8. Implements baseline controls as set forth in NIST SP 800-53 Revision 4, Security and Privacy Controls for Federal Information Systems and Organizations.

9. Publishes internal checks and balances for compliance with the security and quality requirements.

10. Establishes a supplier management program that includes both indirect and direct purchase channels.

11. Implements a verified and repeatable contingency plan that deals with the technology supply chain risk issues to make sure the integrity and reliability requirements during events such as natural disasters, economic disruption, and technical outages are maintained.

12. Deploys a robust incident management program to identify, respond, and mitigate security incidents. This program must address and be capable of detecting the cause of a security incident, and include those coming from the supply chain.

These foundational practices are what will drive the tasks and goals for a SCRM. The integration of it into the overall risk management process for organizations is addressed in NIST SP 800-39 Managing Information Security Risk: Organization, Mission and Information Systems View.

Baseline Controls   NIST defines security controls as:

The management, operational, and technical controls (i.e., safeguards or countermeasures) prescribed for an information system to protect the Confidentiality, Integrity, and Availability of the system and its information.
                    [FIPS 200, FIPS 199, CNSSI No. 4009,
                NIST SP 800-37 Rev. 1, NIST SP 800-53 Rev. 4,
                            NIST SP 800-53A Rev. 4]

There are 19 control groups (called "families" in the document) provided by NIST in the 800-161 for SCRM. This specific standard pulled the 19 control groups from NIST SP 800-53 rev 4 that were viewed as applicable to the supply chain, and they specifically state the controls not listed in 800-161 are viewed as not relevant. The following control families listed in the NIST document provide a good deal of detail and reference material to relevant publications; we review them at a high level to ensure the concepts are understood.

The **Access Control** baseline details when the risk that data and systems cross all areas of the supply chain and that this access should be defined and managed to ensure no modification, release, or destruction of sensitive data occurs. An access control policy and guidance for systems integration are clearly specified, along with a separation of duties. Organizations must use the least-privilege principle when it comes to access. Guidance and controls are listed for wireless access, remote access, and access control for mobile devices.

Awareness and Training directs organizations to create a policy for supply chain management and define training needs across the enterprise. Education should target the supply management organization and systems integrators. The policy directs that this training is required for those who touch or impact the supply chain infrastructure, information technology (IT), and Incident Response. It goes beyond the usual cybersecurity awareness and training, but specific risks and roles on Third-Party Risk Management are covered and evaluated.

Audit and Accountability directs organizations to create, protect, and keep systems' audit records to enable monitoring, analysis, investigation, and reporting of any security incidents. It ensures that users are unique and easily identified, all activities on systems are logged, and unauthorized users or devices attempting to connect are identified. Logs must be verifiable and the chain of custody must be clearly maintained.

Security Assessment and Authorization orders that organizations perform periodic security controls' evaluation. The premise is that you cannot improve what you do not measure. The assessment validates if the controls are effective in their application as designed. A mechanism must be in place to take this feedback into production if changes are required due to assessment results. Different assessment options are offered, such as Continuous Monitoring, insider threat assessment, and malicious users assessment.

Configuration Management directly addresses the default configuration on most systems as unacceptable, and that all devices, software, and hardware must be hardened according to policy. This standard security configuration is referred to as a baseline configuration. It also tells organizations about the importance of tracking these systems to know when the last changes were made, who made them, and who authorized them. Further direction states that cybersecurity and information systems are part of any impact analysis for these changes. This family instructs that systems are deployed with least functionality ensuring only those services required are turned on to reduce the attack surface.

Contingency Planning states that parties produce a plan in case of emergencies or disasters. These plans can range from backup systems, disaster recovery, and maintenance activities. Planning and policy for alternate suppliers or vendors of hardware, software, or services are covered. Alternate site storage, processing sites, and telecom services must also be planned out.

Identification and Authentication requires organizations to have a policy and systems that identify and authenticate users and systems processes before allowing access to resources or systems. Guaranteeing that only users properly identified and authenticated have access ensures improper access cannot occur.

Incident Response (IR) plans with suppliers ensure the timely involvement of resources in the event of an incident and are a must for any company. These plans and policies must include detection systems, analysis, containment, and recovery. Communication plans must be detailed in the IR plan for when, how, and with whom to communicate. Incident information must be shared with appropriate authorities (e.g., Federal Bureau of Investigation [FBI], U.S. Computer Emergency Readiness Teams [US CERT], and the National Cybersecurity and Communications Integration Center [NCCIC]). Agreements must reflect that suppliers must notify organizations of any security incidents in a timely manner. Best practice would be to perform a table-top exercise, at a minimum, to run through simulated IR plans. This can show any weakness in runbooks and playbooks designed to deal with Incident Response.

Maintenance of information systems must be periodic and documented. The roles and responsibilities of tools, processes, and personnel should be clear. Controls on who performs maintenance and when it is performed must be documented and logged. Testing and validation are mentioned as requirements for maintenance work on systems.

Media Protection, including items such as backup tapes and paper records, requires organizations to encrypt where feasible and protect them from unauthorized access. Other subjects also include procedure documentation for the transportation, sanitization, and destruction of any media. Any media (e.g., tapes, paper, USB drives) must be documented as destroyed or sanitized once its use is no longer needed or appropriate.

Physical and Environmental Protection of any organization where there is data located specifies typical items such as locking doors, limiting access, and securing areas from unauthorized access. Access must be monitored so that any attempts to gain entry which are not allowed can be traced and investigated.

Physical access controls and the removal of equipment must be documented and any asset must be monitored and tracked.

While **Planning** sounds pretty simple, an organization must create, document, update, and execute a security plan for information systems. This plan includes all security controls currently in place, including any still in development, and a code of conduct for anyone with access to the systems. The organization must ensure that the information security architecture is well understood by its system engineers and system security engineers.

Program Management controls support and gives data and feedback to the organization's supply chain security. It's essential that they have an information security program plan and senior information security offices, such as a Chief Information Security Officer (CISO). Information security procedures must be documented, and the definitions of business processes must be published. Companies must have insider threat and threat awareness programs.

Personnel Security directs that anyone with a position of responsibility, including third parties, can be trusted and meets the security criteria. Vendors that have personnel who do not comply with this policy must suffer some repercussions, including termination for severe infractions. Access agreements for vendors who require it must be documented.

Provenance deals with the origins of any item in your supply chain. All purchases and acquisitions must have their origins documented as they travel through the supply chain. Records of the origins and any changes must be well documented for other staff or auditors to follow. COTS suppliers and external service providers can use the provenance to demonstrate that all items are genuine and not counterfeit.

Risk Assessment of information systems on the organization's operations, assets, and personnel is detailed in this family. The policies and procedures for how risk evaluations are performed with the categorization articulated must be published and validated. The risk assessment should include criticality, threats, vulnerabilities, likelihood, and impacts.

Systems and Services Acquisition dictates how an organization allocates its resources at appropriate levels to protect information systems. They must guarantee that any third party also takes same appropriate action and measures to protect data, services, and any applications that have been outsourced. Systems Development Lifecycle (SDLC) must be implemented to ensure that secure requirements and designs are implemented.

Systems and Communications Protection prescribes controls for securing communications (e.g., emails, network connections, etc.) both internal and external. Typical items that would be deployed include firewalls, Intrusion Detection/Prevention Systems (IDS/IPS), Cloud Access Security Broker (CASB), and other tools to detect and protect data and network traffic.

Systems and Integration Integrity requires companies to recognize, classify, report, and modify information faults in their systems. Once any information flaws are identified and corrected, the organization must protect itself against malicious code being added and monitor security events. If any security incident takes place or is even suspected, it must be reported to the appropriate personnel internally.

Finally, the NIST standard provides for a tiered system, comprised of three tiers. Tier 1 is focused on the development of SCRM strategy, detailing what the risks are with the supply chain and the company's organizational policies around its security. Tier 2 is designed to establish the company's mission and business functions. This tier also covers how to conduct a risk assessment internally and externally, and how to implement the Tier 1 strategies and direction for the organization. Tier 3 takes the other two tiers and directs how to apply them to the specific information systems and IT acquisitions.

NIST 800-161 Revision 1: Upcoming Revision

NIST SP 800-161 was first published in 2015, and since then, there have been a lot of changes in methodology, risks, and technology. In February of 2020, NIST held an open comment time for the updates. The updates were also prompted by revisions of NIST SP 800-37 rev. 2, draft of NIST SP 800-53 rev. 5, and Cybersecurity Framework v1.1. The update addresses any removal, clarification, or adding of information to the updated document.

No date has been given for when Revision 1 will be published and ready. But considering the recent security incidents with the supply chain mentioned in this book, a lot of attention will likely be given to it.

NISTIR 8272 Impact Analysis Tool for Interdependent Cyber Supply-Chain Risks

This tool is designed to provide a means to measure the possible impact of a cybersecurity supply chain event. It does not measure the risk of an event occurring (as an outcome of threat, vulnerability, likelihood, or impact). The focus is on the impact a supply chain incident (security) would have on an organization's specific environments. It provides a wider view into the third-party chain and the importance relative to projects, products, and vendors compared to others in the chain. Understanding the relative importance of these in an organization's supply chain allows it to prioritize its risk reduction and mitigation strategies. The amount of importance can be derived from the amount of access a vendor has to the company's IT network, facilities, and data (in the NIST document these are called *nodes*). The higher the reliance, the higher the relative importance, and thus, risk (see Figure 4.2).

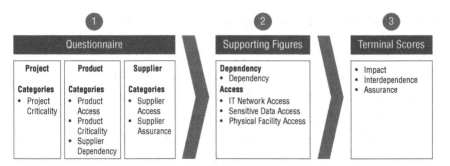

FIGURE 4.2 The Calculation Flow

The website (nvlpubs.nist.gov/nistpubs/ir/2020/NIST.IR .8272.pdf_) provides the software (.csv files, questionnaires, and sample data) for free download. The tool will run on nearly any platform, and the user can create the .csv files as input into the software. It only requires 20 MB of space to run. The questionnaires must be filled out by the correct subject matter experts (SMEs), which go into the .csv file to get the results.

Once any input errors have been dealt with, the results will output a series of scores and visualizations. The intent is to use those scores and visuals to prioritize the high impact and interdependent nodes. As the team reviews them, decisions can then be made about cybersecurity and SCRM. These decisions prioritize relative scores so organizations will know where to focus their risk mitigation. Visualizations are also great for understanding the colors provided for the most important nodes. Impact scores, interdependence scores, and assurance scores will assist in the further identification of significant nodes to the organization. This tool can be very useful for an organization that is unsure of how to prioritize security projects and resources around third-party risk or a TPRM, and for executive leadership seeking to prioritize resource requests from cybersecurity.

Acquisition Security Framework (ASF)

Published by Carnegie Mellon University and operated by the Software Engineering Institute at CERT, the ASF focuses on the security of application development and is ideal given current concerns around the software supply chain and vendors. Designed to give an organization more visibility and control over supply chains for software, it assists in the evaluation of risks and gaps in the current process, development, and the deployment of software systems. It is in prototype mode when an organization is looking for collaborators. Its foundations are well-developed, and it has a high-level workflow diagram that should get any team started on both process in addition to its roles and responsibilities.

The Cybersecurity and Third-Party Risk Program Management

While this author is not one for more paperwork and processes, process does need to be developed in order to run a program successfully. This process can be run ad-hoc for a very short time if there's a newly discovered urgent need to fill a gap, but laying down the structure of how the program is designed and managed should be done early, if not before the systems and resources get to working.

At the top level, there should be a cybersecurity policy that describes the "what and why" of the program. This document sets the standards for how the program is managed, updated, and who is responsible (i.e., CISO, CSO, etc.) for cybersecurity at the company. This document should reference other lateral relevant policies and standards. Other documents are also located at this level, such as access control, personnel security, and physical security. The third-party risk program, standards, and baseline are tied to the cybersecurity policy and program documentation at the top level.

In order to better demonstrate language for policy and program documentation as well as how to execute the program, the following sample company has been created to guide the reader. Note, some assumptions about the company's size and scale have been made and will be referred to in the remainder of the book when required.

Kristina Conglomerate (KC) Enterprises

Let's check out KC Enterprises. It is a medium-sized U.S.-based company with some offshore resources in EU, India, and Philippines. It sells widgets all over the United States and requires its vendors to ship products and manage its inventory, factories, customer service, business processing, human resources, finance, marketing, in addition to all typical corporate functions.

Based in Raleigh, NC, KC has over 5,000 employees, mostly employed in the factories in North Carolina, and the corporate office downtown employs a couple hundred. Much of the non-factory staff are located in the corporate headquarters in Raleigh and in a large office in St. Louis that manages the factory in Missouri (which handles all widget distribution west of the Mississippi). Because KC makes the best widgets, there is a high demand on customer service and support, and thus there are customer support centers outsourced to third parties in Ireland, the Philippines, and India to enable support for customers in any time zone around the world without interruption. In addition, KC has outsourced some business processing to India for financial processing.

KC has expanded in the last 10 years mostly by acquiring other smaller widget manufacturers. However, some strategic purchases of the vendors who make some of the components for widgets have also occurred. Five years ago, a large purchase of an up-and-coming software widget maker was made that was pre-IPO (this is before a company goes public and is traded on a stock exchange). The widget maker is based out of San Jose and located in the heart of Silicon Valley, which is where much innovation for the company started. It can be a challenge for KC's cybersecurity team as it tends to view boundaries as more of a dare or a challenge.

In the last 20 years, KC has been expanding its footprint into digital widgets, which require no manufacturing operations but require IT assets such as data centers to support the backend application developers in creating new demand for the digital widgets, in addition to mobile applications to enable customers to buy digital widgets directly on their phones and send them to friends and family electronically. This has forced KC Enterprises to adopt several different changes and frameworks. Cybersecurity adopted NIST-CSF as the framework, as is typical in many commercial environments. In addition, it matured its technology operations and management.

KC has a CIO and CISO who both report directly to the CEO of the firm. It is a public company and its CEO reports to the board of directors; there is a technology risk committee on the board and the CISO provides reports directly to them at regular intervals or earlier when circumstances require. Remote staff are scattered across the United States, with the support infrastructure growing massively in March 2020 due to the pandemic. The company will likely have fewer people in-office post-COVID, as some decisions to scale back on office (non-production) space is beneficial for the bottom line. (Note, the exact staffing levels and items are less important in this sample company than to provide a consistent yardstick when doing the examples. Whether your firm is smaller and simpler or larger and more complex than KC Enterprises, the sizing and complexity of implementing the items in this book can be adjusted.)

KC has four types of data classification: Public, Internal, Confidential, and Restricted. KC policy dictates that all data internal and above (i.e., not public) must be encrypted. Internal data may be encrypted at the lower level of AES-128, but the top two must be at AES-256 or higher.

KC Enterprises manages its third-party risk and cybersecurity programs as separate teams. TCRM reports into Finance to the CFO, and the cybersecurity program reports to the CISO who reports to the CEO. The CFO and CISO are peers. TPRM and Cybersecurity have their own program and policy statements for their respective areas. Cybersecurity consists of several domains: Architecture, Cloud Security, Governance, Risk and Compliance, Cyber Ops, and Reporting. As is typical, the Cyber Third-Party Risk team sits in GRC (Governance, Risk, and Compliance is a strategy and organization for managing overall governance, enterprise risk management, and compliance with regulations) because it is viewed as a compliance task. The company has several oversight committees and regulators that keep tabs on third-party risk and cybersecurity.

At KC Enterprises, the Cybersecurity Third-Party Risk standards and policies are clear about what the two triggers are for when cybersecurity due diligence is required:

- The vendor will have, process, use, store, or transmit KC Enterprise customer or employee data that is of the top three data classifications.
  Or
- The vendor will have a connection to any KC Enterprise network, whether intermittent or persistent.

As described, KC creates physical and digital widgets—pretend items designed to mimic a thriving business. The regulations for data protection have been adequately described as near universal, no matter what business or operation. The point isn't what KC makes or the services it provides. The risk isn't what your firm or company makes or creates: The risk is in the data you share with vendors or the connectivity you allow them. The use of this company example is to illustrate best practice to lower the risk third parties present to your firm.

KC Enterprises' Cyber Third-Party Risk Program

To run a successful cyber third-party program, documentation of governance, policy, procedures, and oversight must occur to ensure adherence to the program, although the KC Enterprise example we use also demonstrates the foundations of a program. The complexity or simplicity of the policy, processes, and other artifacts are dependent upon a host of differences at your organization.

KC Enterprises' Cybersecurity Policy   The cybersecurity policy document forms the basis for the scope of cybersecurity and the sub-programs that it contains, such as cyber GRC, cyber operations, vulnerability management, and the other functions that run a modern technology-based company and economy.

Scope

Kristina Conglomerate Enterprises and its subsidiaries and affiliates (KC) Cybersecurity Policy (the "Policy") is designed to accomplish the three pillars of Confidentiality, Integrity, and Availability for all KC data and systems owned, operated, and managed by KC (the "Assets"). The policy is intended to provide compliance with applicable regulations, laws, cybersecurity frameworks adopted, and higher-level KC policies and standards. A number of lower-level cybersecurity standards, procedures, and artifacts support and implement the policy.

The KC Cybersecurity Policy is designed to implement and support the Cybersecurity Program (the "Program") as presented to the KC Board of Directors. The Program implements and supports the Policy's goals of the CIA triad to provide security to KC's information assets and systems. The supporting documentation of policies, procedures, and controls are the means to ensure the protection of those assets.

Breaches of the Policy may result in disciplinary actions, up to and including termination of employment and legal action by KC if warranted.

Three (or Four) Lines of Defense for Risk Management

The creation of the program for cybersecurity and third-party risk specifically mentions second and third lines of defense, which stems from the problem with any complex system. All the policies, standards, procedures, and activities require some oversight to ensure that they are completed as documented. Given the number of activities, their interconnectedness, and importance to reducing risk to an organization, having other groups responsible for that oversight provides that assurance (see Figure 4.3).

The **First Line of Defense** is embedded in the daily business operations. Operational management identifies risk and then assesses, mitigates, and controls it. It is there to recognize emerging or existing risks from cybersecurity, business, or technology changes—these are the functions that own and manage risks on a daily basis, oversee the risks, and provide independent assurance.

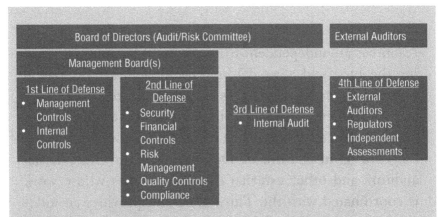

FIGURE 4.3 The Four Lines of Defense Model

The **Second Line of Defense** is comprised of risk management control and compliance functions. Its role is to monitor the First Line of Defense for adherence to policies and procedures. The Second Line of Defense can intervene and provide guidance for corrective action when required to realign the First Line with the policy and procedures. This level is responsible for supporting management policy, and defines the roles and responsibilities and implementation goals. The risk-level frameworks are provided by them along with identifying new and existing risks and issues. The Second Line assists management in process and controls development, along with identifying the organization's risk appetite. This level is responsible for monitoring the adequacy and effectiveness of internal controls, reporting, and compliance activities.

The **Third Line of Defense** contains the internal auditors whose role is to act as independent auditors and advisors to executive leadership and/or the board of directors. The Third Line assesses the effectiveness of both the First and Second Lines and provides guidance when those controls need improvement. It is important that these

(Continued)

(Continued)

resources are independent from the organizations performing the First and Second Line duties to ensure no bias in
findings or recommendations occurs. They must also have
an unobstructed reporting line to all governing bodies
(e.g., the executive and board committees).

The **Fourth Line of Defense** refers to the external
auditors and other external oversight bodies whose work
is coordinated with the Third Line and provides an independent assessment of the previous three lines of defense.
In regulated industries, the primary focus for this line is
compliance with regulatory agencies and their guidance.
These regulatory bodies will also perform a Fourth Line of
Defense in those industries.

These lines of defense, while not required, produce
a more mature program over time as they coordinate and
communicate between each other.

Policy Statement and Objectives

KC Cybersecurity Policy is designed to ensure the appropriate
management review and approval of the Program and to provide
escalation avenues for cybersecurity risk from management to
the board. It confirms the Confidentiality, Integrity, and Availability of its data and assets; creates a baseline for audit, assessment, and regulatory compliance; and provides clear direction to
employees, contractors, and any third party on their due care and
due diligence requirements around the assets.

Cybersecurity Program

The Program provides Confidentiality, Integrity, and Availability of all KC protected data (as defined in the "Classification of

Information Assets" section that follows) from any disclosure, whether accidental or intentional. The Program's implementation is risk-based to align with risk appetite and risk priorities. The Program is based upon the National Institute of Science and Technology Cybersecurity Framework (NIST-CSF) and is reassessed no less than annually to review its effectiveness and updates required due to environmental, financial, or business objectives. The Program advances a defense-in-depth strategy to ensure a layered approach to the protection of the assets.

The Program is periodically assessed by Technology Risk (Second Line), Internal Audit (Third Line), external auditors, regulatory supervisory agencies, and independent evaluations.

KC Cybersecurity has the sole authority to create and modify physical, technical, and logical security standards and procedures to support the Policy. While Cybersecurity will consider business needs and objectives when enforcing these standards and procedures, it retains the sole authority to enforce them to ensure compliance with the Policy. All lower-level standards, policies, procedures, and artifacts support the scope of the Policy and carry the same authority as part of the Program.

Classification of Information Assets

KC Data Classification provides a means for determining the risk of data. The following list describes the four classes of data and their relative risk to the organization:

- **Class 4 Restricted**: This data is the most sensitive data at the company. Losing this data would be equivalent to losing the "crown jewels." It requires the highest level of available protection from misuse or loss. The access criteria must be set to a need-to-know basis and based upon least privilege. The impact of loss or misuse would be serious and adverse to the company and cause severe reputational, financial, and/or strategic damages.

- **Class 3 Sensitive**: These data assets are typically PII, operations, proprietary, and other information that if disclosed or misused would adversely affect the company, shareholders, customers, and partners with regulatory, financial, or reputational damage and penalties. The access criteria can be a bit broader than Class 4 but still should be on a need-to-know basis.

- **Class 2 Internal**: These data assets are often internal and general business communications, documentation, and other items used in day-to-day business operations. The disclosure of this data would have very limited financial, reputational, or operational impact. Access is appropriate for all internal users at KC.

- **Class 1 Public**: Data here is any data that can be found in public forums or online and does not require any protection. There must be no impact to KC or its shareholders if released. Access is open to all internal users and the public.

Incident Response

The KC Cybersecurity Program provides the policy and procedures for detecting, managing, and reporting security incidents in accordance with KC and regulatory obligations and requirements. The scope and details of this plan can be found in the cybersecurity incident management process documentation and artifacts.

Awareness and Training

The KC Cybersecurity Program conducts awareness and training on the protection of the assets to all users. This training occurs no less than annually and ensures a baseline of understanding for the protection of the assets. The awareness and training program is detailed in the cybersecurity awareness and training program documentation.

Third-Party Security and Risk

KC manages the risk of third parties and supply chain security to comply with corporate, legal, and regulatory requirements. The framework adopted is NIST 800-161 for third-party and supply chain risk management along with NIST-CSF for baseline security controls. Third-party security requirements are detailed in the third-party security standard and supporting documentation. All legal agreements with third parties and suppliers that involve protected assets must adhere to the applicable contract addendum requirements.

Cybersecurity Third-Party Risk Program Breakdown   The following breaks down KC Enterprises' Cybersecurity Third-Party Risk Program in depth.

Definition and Scope

KC Enterprises routinely uses third parties to provide services and products that collect, store, process, and transmit confidential customer and business data. KC must adhere to the Cybersecurity Policy and Program requirements, along with all applicable regulatory and legal requirements to secure sensitive data. The Cybersecurity Third Party Risk Program (i.e., the "Program") applies to all lines of business, affiliates, and subsidiaries for the protection of all Assets as defined by the Cybersecurity Program and Policy. The Program's scope is defined, but not limited to, cybersecurity terms in contract language and cybersecurity due diligence efforts for third parties (i.e., Intake, Ongoing, On-site, and Continuous Monitoring).

Objectives

The Program's objectives are designed to support the direction of the board, executive leadership, cybersecurity program, regulatory guidance, and all applicable laws. The board and executive leadership are responsible through the Program for the identification, classification, and controlling of third-party risks. Cybersecurity Third-Party Risk (CTPR) leads the monitoring and assessment of third parties to their adherence to the third-party security standard and procedures. CTPR is the sole authority for these standards and procedures for cybersecurity third-party and supply chain risk management. CTPR provides expertise and knowledge for lines of business and leadership on Cybersecurity Third-Party Risk.

Governance

The Program's governance is performed by second and third line organizations. The primary functions of each workstream are listed below as a means for high-level governance review. Specific actions and functions are detailed in procedure documentation for each of the related workstreams.

Third Party Intake determines criteria for Intake Risk Questions (IRQ) and all intake questions related to cybersecurity. The criteria are reviewed annually for appropriate updates. The reports from these activities are reviewed by quality assurance staff of the department before publication. The activities and process for Third Party Intake are described in the Third Party Intake Procedures document, which guides the staff and management in the completion of IRQ and intake cybersecurity assessments.

Third-Party Ongoing Due Diligence determines criteria for ongoing due diligence and all questions related to cybersecurity. The criteria are reviewed annually for appropriate updates.

The reports from these activities are then reviewed by quality assurance staff of the department before publication. The activities and process for Third-Party Ongoing are described in the Third-Party Ongoing Procedures document, which guides the staff and management for the completion of cybersecurity assessments.

Third-Party On-site Due Diligence determines criteria for on-site due diligence and all questions related to cybersecurity. The criteria are reviewed annually for appropriate updates. The reports from these activities are reviewed by quality assurance staff of the department before publication. The activities and process for Third-Party On-site are described in the Third Party On-site Procedures document, which guides the staff and management for the completion of cybersecurity assessments.

Third-Party Continuous Monitoring (CM) determines the criteria for the CM due diligence and all questions related to cybersecurity. The criteria are reviewed annually for appropriate updates. The reports from these activities are reviewed by quality assurance staff of the department before publication. The activities and process for Third-Party CM procedures are described in the Third Party-CM Procedures document, which guides the staff and management for the completion of cybersecurity assessments.

Third-Party Risk contractual language, contained in Addendums, is determined by Cybersecurity Third-Party Risk. The language is reviewed annually for appropriate updates. Deviations from the contract language are risk-rated and recorded as open risks for a third party in the system of record until the third party physically validates that the gap is closed. The activities and process for Third-Party Risk Contracts are described in the Third Party Risk Contracts Procedures document, which guides the staff and management for the completion of cybersecurity control language in contracts.

Inside Look: Marriott

In September 2018, Marriott was alerted by an internal security tool on suspicious activity around the Starwood guest reservation system in the United States. The internal investigation revealed that the unauthorized access began four years earlier in 2014. The perpetrators were very sophisticated, as the attackers had copied and encrypted data and took action to remove it. By November of 2018, Marriott was able to decrypt the files and determine it originated from the Starwood guest reservation system. The breach affected approximately 500 million guests.

For over two-thirds of the guests, the breached information included names, mailing addresses, phone numbers, hotel stay dates, passport numbers, dates of birth, genders, and communication preferences. An undetermined number included payment card numbers and expiration dates. While payment card information is encrypted and requires two components to decrypt the payment card data, Marriott wasn't sure that both components were taken.

The fact that the attack went for four years without detection, given the size of Marriott, in addition to the breathtaking amount of data stolen, makes this breach one that is a prime case study. A merger agreement with Starwood and Marriott was announced on November 16, 2015. In January 2016, Starwood announced it was the target of a large credit card hack. Following that hack, the company website was attacked using SQL injection. Further reviews by Marriott found a remote access trojan (RAT) and the password-matching tool, MimiKatz. Marriott was fined by GDPR $123 million. The UK's privacy watchdog, Information Commissioner's Office (ICO), fined Marriott another 18.4 million pounds.

In late February 2020, Marriott announced it had discovered that the login credentials of two Marriott employees had been hacked and used to attain guest information. These credentials were disabled, but not before there were 5.2 million guest records pilfered. Internal investigations found that the hacker activity started in mid-January 2020 and was not discovered for over a month. The information stolen consisted of names, addresses, email addresses, phone numbers, loyalty account information, gender info, partial birth dates, and employer details.

Takeaways   Numerous lessons can be learned in this case study. First is employee education for security topics, such as phishing. Educating users how to recognize and reject phishing emails is crucial as these are increasing both in numbers and sophistication. In the Starwood breach, Marriott made the conscious decision to not integrate the security systems. This decision left the Starwood hackers free to roam around the Marriott network without a correlation engine to see the activity. The lack of log analysis on the part of Marriott played a large part in how the attack was allowed to go on for four years.

Conclusion

Third Party Risk Management (TPRM) is the process of identifying, assessing, and controlling risks presented through the lifecycle of a relationship with third parties. There are NIST and ISO frameworks that can be leveraged to design and run a TPRM program. For the purpose of illustration, we've created a fictitious company, called KC Enterprises, to allow for examples of implementation of best practices. This company will be referenced throughout the book as a means to expand on ideas and implementation in a more tangible form to the reader. Depending on the size and risk appetite of your organization, implementation will vary. Building a TPRM program and process are the first steps to lowering the risk that vendors pose to a company, and in the following chapters the cybersecurity focus will further build the program into drastically lowering the cybersecurity risk.

5

Onboarding Due Diligence

A s part of Third-Party Risk Management (TPRM), the first step in engaging the lifecycle of a vendor's due diligence is during intake. As a new vendor is identified by a business, it is required to perform an initial review of the vendor's risk domains. For the cybersecurity domain, this is generally performed via a remote questionnaire or during question and answer (Q&A) sessions. Initially, an intake questionnaire, known as an Intake Risk Questionnaire (IRQ), should be provided to assess the initial risk. This list of questions should be short and determine which risk domains are relevant and require due diligence.

Intake

During this part of the lifecycle of the vendor, a business has all the leverage. Once the contract is signed, good intentions aside, no one will want to renegotiate on stricter cybersecurity terms. Also, items discovered at this point in the process—security gaps, process concerns, lack of required certifications, and due diligence—are all best done *before* contracts are signed. In many cases, even if the vendor can't meet the security or other risk requirements at the time needed to initially, the remediation of those items can be listed within the contract with milestones tied to payments. These milestones require the cybersecurity teams to be actively engaged in the Intake process. See Figure 5.1. which illustrates that we are in the Onboarding phase.

Transparency is the approach needed for the intake; however, the process depends on size and complexity of your company. This book, however, will not spend too much time on the

Cybersecurity Third-Party Risk Vendor Lifecycle

FIGURE 5.1 The Cyber TPR Lifecycle

established TPRM framework process as much as focus on how to inject cybersecurity into the process. How to identify cybersecurity risk earlier in the cycle is the focus for this chapter.

IRQ question lists are not long, but they are designed to aid companies in making decisions about the further required work to vet their vendors. Much of this vetting depends on your company's size and your reach. A local business that ships internationally, a mid-size company of 10,000 people with some good processes, or a large multinational business all have various risk management processes and scales. Common areas of focus are covered next.

Data Privacy

Ensuring data privacy requires asking the vendor high-level questions about how they approach data privacy. Focus on yes or no, Boolean-type questions to ensure clear answers to questions and make quick assessments. For example, "Do you encrypt customer data and at what level?" If your company is a U.S.-based company that doesn't want to have data in the EU and wants to avoid direct contact with GDPR jurisdiction, for example, you would be concerned about data location. If the data is Personal Health Information (PHI), additional questions are possible, such as "Are you Health Information Trust Alliance (HITRUST) certified?" If they are doing credit card processing, then a question about their Payment Card Industry Data Security Standard (PCI-DSS) certification is needed.

Cybersecurity

Cybersecurity requires that you first ask a few simple questions to assess if the vendor can meet criteria to require further due diligence. Cybersecurity due diligence can take some time to complete, as the topic's complexity can lead to more communication to settle any risk concerns. If the vendor doesn't meet the criteria, then they wouldn't require a cyber review and can move to the next step. First, you need to know if they have data that requires protection. This level of protection depends on your data classifications, and the key is deciding the level at which your company requires the data to be protected outside its own network. KC Enterprises, for example, declared that its top three tiers of data classifications, by policy, require protection.

Because the intake process should be quick, getting all the information and performing an honest appraisal of data can be challenging. Who is performing the assessment of the data elements that, by themselves, may be fine but in combination add up to personal identifiable information (PII)? The data privacy regulations that nearly all of us are now subject to, no matter where we live in the world, are often not very easy to understand. This needs to be done by an expert or via some level of investigation by someone with the skills to perform the proper due diligence.

The next dilemma in many typical third-party due diligence efforts revolves around checklists. Due to the number of vendors and people involved in an onboarding process, much of the work can be accomplished using a series of checklists to ensure due diligence is performed, such as ensuring that certain tasks are completed and that milestones are achieved. However, security itself isn't a checklist—it's an ongoing activity. Active security departments may deploy checklists to ensure that certain process upgrade tasks are accomplished, but cybersecurity and information security require something besides checklists. They require conversations between a business and its vendors.

The IRQ contains checklist items to help determine the level of risk for the vendor and a new service/product. However, when certain risk criteria are triggered, it should initiate a conversation with the vendor. While it may not require an actual phone call, it could instigate a process (manually or through your workflow tool of choice) where an email or conference call takes place to attain more detail on a subject. Although some important reasons exist to ask more in-depth questions, quick dives into details with a vendor are helpful during these early stages.

First, you'll want to make sure the vendor can adhere to critical security controls at this early stage, or you must warn your business sponsor (i.e., the leader in the organization who is pushing this new service or product) of the new service/product that it presents unwarranted risk. KC Enterprises requires data to be encrypted because it is restricted and up to one million customer records will be processed by the vendor. A very early discussion occurred between KC and its vendors about how they need their data encrypted and that policy dictates that customer data must not leave the United States. If the vendor, in this example, can't meet these conditions, it requires a much earlier discussion with the business about the risk and possible alternate vendors.

The Q&A process between a vendor and a business can occur via a variety of avenues. If multiple risk domains are involved during intake, then a conference call should take place among the vendor subject-matter experts (SMEs), business sponsor, and relevant SMEs from the internal risk domains. The challenge is getting everyone on a single call, but if that's possible, it will generally lead to better outcomes because all the risk domains can see the entire risk landscape for the vendor at the same time, which can lead to a holistic look at the risk for this broader team. It should be a "gating" activity in most organizations, meaning that all the risk domains (i.e., everyone involved) must approve the vendor for the next step based upon predefined criteria. During this activity, all questions from those at risk can be answered satisfactorily, or the vendor could be denied if any predefined, non-negotiable, standard, or policy items cannot be met.

Amount of Data

If data is going to be shared, ask a follow-up question on the amount expected to be shared and have vendors list the exact data elements. The data types and amounts correlate directly to how much quantitative risk a company is taking on. For example, if the firm values PII records at $200 per record (for direct costs to consumers harmed, not including reputational costs) and the record count is in the millions, that should set off another set of due diligence steps in the next intake round. Similarly, if the data count is very low, and assuming your risk threshold is $1 million in cyberliability insurance, anything under 5,000 records is covered. From a cybersecurity professional perspective and common sense, you would not want to set your risk threshold right at your insurance limit of $1 million. By being conservative and starting at 1,000 records or less, your due diligence can be lessened due to your lower record count and lower risk.

Country Risk and Locations

Another common cybersecurity concern during this intake process that should be covered on the IRQ is location. Are there any offshore concerns that the company might have on items besides data location? Many firms have outsourced development and support, just as KC Enterprises has done. While it's not a deal-breaker, company sponsors should ask in what countries these activities are performed and that the vendor lists these countries up front. If a vendor develops software in a country listed as problematic for computer crimes, then it should be red flagged so your business knows it needs to have a conversation about it before proceeding.

Connectivity

If a vendor and business sponsor check the IRQ checkbox that the service or product requires connectivity, a series of questions must be asked to initially assess that risk:

1. Is the connection leased-line or via the internet?
2. How is access taking place, both physically and logically?
3. Who is the maker of the connectivity hardware?
4. What encryption level are their screening questions?
5. If the third-party's personnel will connect directly to the company, how is that planned to happen?

If a vendor says you must do something not on this list, that's something of concern already. Virtual Desktop Infrastructure (VDI) connections need infrastructure and must be learned early on as well.

Data Transfer

Whether connectivity is static or intermittent, some key questions like the following must be asked to understand if any additional due diligence is required: If data is uploaded/downloaded, what type of secure file transfer protocol (SFTP) do they use?

How does the vendor support an access control mechanism that meets your standards in cases such as an SFTP server upload/download? Again, these are just screening questions, so they should be focused on your security for how your data is moved.

Data Location

It's very common for business sponsors and vendors to have a cloud-based solution. As we've discussed, for this book "cloud" means anything not located in your own company's premises (i.e., from a server closet to your own data centers). This includes Cloud Service Providers (CSPs; e.g., Google, AWS, Azure), co-location providers, or a vendor-owned data center. If the IRQ's checkbox is checked for a cloud-based solution, you should determine early where that data will go. All of these solutions have different security risks. For example, if a vendor is using a CSP, then the physical security of the data center is very low risk. These companies run first-class, top-tier data centers that would put Fort Knox to shame. In fact, you'll never get one of them to allow you a physical walk-through unless you can pull some serious strings.

If the vendor replies they have their own data centers, then it might set off a different security review. Traditionally, data centers are very expensive and can be challenging to maintain at acceptable levels over time as standards evolve and mature. A vendor data center that is 10 years old might be a concern given changes in the standards and tools during that time frame.

Service-Level Agreement or Recovery Time Objective

Service-level agreements (SLAs) and Recovery Time Objectives (RTOs) require the business sponsor and vendor to collaborate productively. The business sponsors should ask what the expected business RTO is (i.e., how long a product/service can be down in hours before it must be restored) and compare their requirements with the vendor's answer to see where they can meet. The goal of follow-up due diligence, depending on any mismatch, is to ensure that these items are discussed and corrected early. In addition, legal implications could be added to SLAs in the contracts if requirements are not met.

Fourth Parties

Questions about what third parties this third-party vendor will use to provide your product/service should also be triggered by IRQ checklists. Are parts of or all of the product developed outside your home country? Information about the access that these fourth parties need to your data, in addition to the third party's answer, will let your company know if Cybersecurity needs to perform any further due diligence.

Software Security

While not enough software security questions are on the IRQs I've seen, given the high risk posed by third-party software, you should ask the following questions to determine what next due-diligence steps would be: Do you have a secure development lifecycle? Do you perform penetration testing against both your enterprise and product?

The intake questions to determine inherent risk is focused on finding alerts that would require further due diligence. The risk-based approach suggested earlier determines the level of risk (i.e., number of records, data type, and criticality to business operations), where the IRQ process is more conversational to ensure there is as much transparency as possible, and that all questions and risks are addressed with more attention. Anything under that threshold would still need to be covered by an IRQ, but it can be more menu-driven than a conversation. Ideally, such a conversation can take place with all vendors. But if resources aren't sufficient, then the risk-based approach to engage with vendors viewed as high risk is appropriate. In cases where the menu-driven format is followed, ensure that examples are used to clarify what data is expected. Use drop-down menus to limit data variance on replies. Another way to handle the complexity of an IRQ is to provide examples of what PII consists of, as many third parties do not sufficiently understand this concept.

KC Enterprises Intake/Inherent Risk Cybersecurity Questionnaire

KC Enterprises sends out an IRQ to its vendors for their input. Again, the IRQ questionnaire is used to give those performing the cybersecurity due diligence a window into what risks this vendor product/service poses for follow-up due diligence. It often requires that some additional meetings are held to gain clarity, depending on the complexity of the service/product and how clear the answers are from the third party.

The following example is KC Enterprises' IRQ. Note that this is a summary of the subjects covered in the questionnaire. You can find the full question set online at www.wiley.com/go/cybersecurityand3prisk.

- **Data Security:** Assess if the vendor will have confidential data, can they encrypt, and can your firm perform security assessments on the vendor?
- **Data Volume:** How much data will determine potential quantitative risk?

- **Data Location:** Is the data going to be at the vendor data center, at a co-location facility, or at a Cloud Service Provider (CSP)?
- **Fourth Parties:** Find out who the vendor uses to provide the service to your organization for any additional risk.
- **Connectivity:** If the vendor requires a connection, this needs to be understood for the risk.

As KC Enterprises' Cybersecurity team reviews each response from the vendor, decisions can be made about whether more or less due diligence is required. As discussed in the section titled "Cybersecurity Third-Party Intake" later, we will take up the work performed from the IRQ for that next due diligence step.

Cybersecurity in Request for Proposals

Request for Proposals (RFPs) are frequently done for larger projects or investments, but far too often the cybersecurity key elements do not get added into them. More importantly, a single list of questions cannot often be used because the RFPs are dependent on the type of service or product the business is seeking to evaluate for selection. However, collaboration between any internal teams, which are managing vendor sourcing or how evaluations are performed, along with the cybersecurity team, can help avoid the pitfalls that usually occur. Such late pitfalls occurring in a vendor's decision produce the appearance that Cybersecurity is once again slowing business down or interfering in operations. Some questions and easy evaluation tools can be incorporated in the RFP's cybersecurity items. While some of them are similar to the IRQ's questions, these are geared to allow Cybersecurity teams to provide feedback to the business at this time.

Next, we'll review a sample of 10 cybersecurity topics sent out on the vendor's questionnaire. This questionnaire starts off as a checklist, but it should not end as such. The expectation is that the vendors all submit their replies to these cybersecurity topics (and likely other topics such as business operations, financials, etc.), which is followed by some type of meeting where the answers are reviewed and clarified. The following 10 RFP topics also include good follow-up questions that can be part of the discussion with the vendors as part of the RFP evaluation.

Data Location

The questionnaire includes data location so that vendors submitting for the RFP can detail where the company's data will be located (CSP, a co-location, a vendor data center), or if it will be on-site at your company's location. These answers are weighed differently because the risk is different for each. For example, if a vendor states your data will be stored at your company's location, the answer is given a higher weight and achieves the best score. Should a vendor answer that they are using a CSP, you should discuss with them how they plan to manage the shared security model with the CSP. Questions must be asked about their alternate sites, no matter what type of data center, to ensure there's a fail-over solution.

Development

This questionnaire section focuses on where a vendor's development is done and if they have a secure development lifecycle. Concerns may surround the development done in some locations, depending on a country's risk. Finding that out in the RFP is an important sorting tool, in addition to whether or not they have a secure development lifecycle. Follow-up discussions can explore what parts of development are done where, and what access developers have to production data, if any; and if developers anonymize data in lower environments (i.e., the test or development environments). On the secure development front, it is ideal to have vendors walk through it at a high level so you can inquire about how they manage open source software.

Identity and Access Management

Identity and access management (IAM) ranges from how the vendor manages identities in their enterprise to how access management is done for the products or services. Do they accept a Single Sign-On (SSO) type that your developers can support? How often do they perform access reviews and what are their password complexity requirements? As vendors answer the initial RFP, there should be more information provided on the implementation of any access controls with the vendor and the company to ensure it is a secure design.

Encryption

While this may seem repetitive of the many other questions coming from cybersecurity, it's because it is very important. Asking a potential vendor questions about encryption at this stage in an RFP will save your company a ton of pain instead of waiting to discuss it before contract signing. Be specific and ask what level of encryption vendors deploy on the products and ask about all three stages of at-rest, in-motion, and in-use. The time spent with the third parties discussing encryption ensures that there are no surprises, and that the vendors can meet your company's encryption standards. Because encryption is vital to data protection, if a potential vendor can't meet your company standard, they should never become a candidate for a contract. If a vendor cannot encrypt your valuable data, you should walk away.

As mentioned, encryption questions should cover the data encryption's state (i.e., in-transit, at-rest, in-use). Too often the questionnaire asks about encryption in a generic form, only to discover later that the vendor thought only "at rest" was of concern. There are, in fact, methods of encryption that are considered out-of-date or deprecated. SHA-1 is fine for some functions, but not others, and 3DES is still acceptable, but updated encryption algorithms have taken their place. It's a must to catch this detail during intake via the questionnaire.

Intrusion Detection/Prevention System

Both IDS/IPS are valuable tools on the RFP that alert a vendor about suspicious activity and prevent it from becoming a breach or security incident. Asking questions about this and the other cybersecurity defenses are a way to understand if a vendor is following the common cybersecurity principle of defense in depth. Vendors should have not just one, but many defensive products deployed to effectively defend a modern network. Once your company is communicating with vendors, ask about the type of IDS or IPS they use (e.g., host- or network-based).

Antivirus and Malware

The RFP should cover whether vendors use antivirus and malware products, what they are, and how often scans are performed. You must ask the following: Do you have a vulnerability management program and how it is managed? What type of antivirus and malware protection do you use and how often are the signatures updated?

Data Segregation

Often not asked about, data segregation is involved in discovering risk. If your data is going to be in the cloud, it's crucial to know if it's segregated from other customer data. Some companies will have customer data comingled and have a customer ID that identifies which data belongs to which customer. If you do not inquire about data segregation, it often will go undiscovered. Ideally, a vendor places your data in its own area, with its own encryption key. As discussions take place around encryption, the data segregation is a common follow-up subject, and it is ideal to find out how vendors will protect your data from other customers.

Data Loss Prevention

While you would think Data Loss Prevention (DLP) would seem obvious, a lot of companies still have not deployed a DLP solution. As indicated in the IDS/IPS topic, the fact that they'd have a DLP indicates they are thinking about the defense in depth. Often, IDS/IPS are deployed as a suite of products that include a DLP product (among others). Great follow-up questions should focus on how they classify data, and if they have a data classification system tied to their DLP to prevent data from email loss. Because data is the primary target, having DLP is a key defense.

Notification

Questions focusing on notification should cover how long it will take a vendor to notify your company of a suspected breach, and it's often a contentious piece of contract negotiations and operational conduct. A suspected or confirmed breach often is a hot topic discussed between a vendor and customer, along with 24- or 48-hour notice. Notification is important, and you must discover early which potential vendor is best positioned to meet your company's expectations. Nail down how they will notify your company if and when they suspect or have confirmed breaches, and how fast they will notify you.

Security Audits

It's best to determine early in the RFP which potential third parties will allow you to perform your due diligence. Whether your company requires on-site, remote, periodic, or annual security assessments is also something to establish now. If a vendor says they will not allow the firm to perform the level of due diligence that is required based upon risk, then the vendor should not be hired. If the opportunity arises, inquire what level of security assessment they will allow and if they charge. Some firms will charge for the time to help your firm perform its due diligence. This information is good to know up front before the bill arrives.

Once the initial questions are answered, the Cybersecurity SME assigned to the RFP should review the answers to determine if there are any immediate flags. Feedback about the responses that miss key security controls need to be given to the business sponsors early. Likewise, if there are respondents that do a great job and provide all the right answers, then you should note them as a great candidate in your feedback. However, don't stop there when reviewing their survey answers.

Whether your company has 2 or 15 RFP candidates, the time spent with the ones that pass the first review is valuable. Often, time spent on a phone call with the vendors' cybersecurity SMEs will produce a holistic picture of how they approach security. Again, security isn't a checklist but an ongoing process. Such discussions can add more context to the RFP feedback from cybersecurity to the business sponsors. The feedback must focus on the security concerns or benefits of the product/service and avoid business value.

One other benefit of cybersecurity involvement in this important intake process is data movement on the next steps. For example, as the due diligence data is collected with the RFP, or as the final vendor is selected, that information can be passed along to the IRQ questions. This will cut down on the time spent by both internal resources and the vendor. RFP questions are very similar to the IRQ, and you can find a sample at www.wiley.com/go/cybersecurityand3prisk.

An RFP cybersecurity questionnaire should not exceed 10–20 questions on an initial screening. As vendors are scored and some are eliminated, hopefully, due to inability to meet some conditions and lower scores, you should engage with the remaining contestants for deeper dives on the subjects.

Cybersecurity Third-Party Intake

After the intake process is completed and the inherent risk of the third party is established, it must be determined if a vendor meets the criteria for further due diligence. Ideally, each of the answers in the preceding IRQ subjects are triggers for the subsequent due diligence, and the process can be very involved and lengthy if the vendor has a lot of sensitive data and other risk factors involved. Much like an IRQ, this next due diligence can be done via a remote questionnaire sent to the vendor, but it often may require a phone call or two to gain clarity.

One concern often laid out at this stage is how many questions to ask and what is considered too much or too little due diligence. There is no set answer to this, but both the RFP and

IRQ questionnaires are designed to include 10 to a couple dozen questions at most. However, once these triggers in the IRQ are met, it's typical for questions to multiply to more than 100 to almost 1000 at larger firms. As with most cases, the best option is the one that works for your firm. Your "goldilocks spot" needs to fit the number of risk concerns that are a result of the IRQ, which is not designed to be a months-long security audit. A suggested path is to list the triggers in your IRQ, then proceed to list the questions that need a follow-up from each of those points. Figure 5.2 shows some important points in each of the three stages from RFP to IRQ to Intake.

FIGURE 5.2   The RFP to IRQ to Intake Process

Data Security Intake Due Diligence

This section's driver is the vendor answering "yes" to the Data Security question: Yes, they will be storing, accessing, or processing customer or employee protected data. This section is broken down into subsections for easier digestion. As we get into each of the subsections, we will assume the role of KC Enterprises' Cybersecurity team to pose sample questions. The sections covered on this form are:

- **Security Policy:** Questions at this level are designed to determine the level of maturity of the vendor's cybersecurity program and policies. The maturity of a security program will often drive how well they secure data and network connections.

- **Security Incident Management:** Security Incident Management, or how a firm deals with threats, speaks to its preparedness for the inevitable: a suspected breach. Because the vendor is going to have sensitive data, it is important to determine their readiness for this activity and questions at this level should reflect it.

- **Application Security:** Also called Secure Development (or Design) Lifecycle (SDLC), application security is applicable if the vendor is providing the software, whether it is in the cloud, on a mobile device, or an internal application. On the internal application, there needs to be some risk-based decisions made because not every application running internally poses enough risk to evaluate. For example, while due diligence on normal office applications (such as Word or Excel) might not meet the threshold, software that moves money or provides critical infrastructure support could. Design your questions, if internal, to assess even more due diligence that might be needed.

- **Access Management:** Access Management domain questions should focus on determining if vendors have sufficient controls to ensure only authorized personnel gain access to appropriate resources. This includes both the enterprise of the vendor and the product.

- **Mobile Security:** Many applications and services are deployed or available over mobile devices. Special questions should focus on these types so that your company can understand a vendor's mobile security risk.

- **Network and Systems Security:** Networks and systems are the core of transport and storage for data. Querying a vendor about how they approach network and systems security can identify any risks to be remediated prior to production going live.

- **Offshore Security:** Some vendor engagement requires an offshore component. Whether it's business process out-sourcing (BPO) or customer support, some security controls are required to ensure data and connectivity security. Questions in this area should help your company understand the risks of a vendor's offshore security.

- **Encryption:** Although encryption crosses the paths of other areas, it does require attention. Here, the concentration is to ensure that a vendor meets the standards set by your company.

Production Data in Lower-Level Environments

There are enough examples of data breaches by third parties and enough ways to get anonymized data (at all price levels) that using production and sensitive data in testing because "it's the only way we can test" is not a valid reason anymore. There, I said it. Let the hate mail begin. Test environments do not have the safeguards given to a production environment, no matter what a cybersecurity team reports. Due to the very nature of it being a test, the value is lower on any risk scale. Policy might even dictate that all environments are treated as equally risky and are protected and monitored the same. However, those people monitoring them might, by that use of nomenclature, devalue them even a smidge, which is all it takes to allow an attacker into the system. Figure 5.3 shows how masking works in lower-level environments.

(Continued)

(Continued)

ID	Last	First	SSN
1001	Smith	Jane	444-22-5555
1002	Smith	Joe	555-11-2222

Production Database

Dev, Test, Analytics Databases

ID	Last	First	SSN
2213	Smith	Jane	XXX-XX-5555
1232	Smith	Joe	XXX-XX-2222

FIGURE 5.3 Masking or De-Identifying Tests in Lower-Level Environments

Far too many risks exist for your customer data already and there are enough ways to solve the testing using complex data to make using production data in testing no longer necessary. Break the cycle and find a way to *close* a risk. A *closed risk* is one that no longer must be managed as a risk acceptance or transfer. The productivity benefit of these types of actions will often go unnoticed, but the work to manage this risk can be focused on finding and managing a risk that is more difficult to mitigate or remediate.

Data Center Security   The Data Center Security section in KC Enterprises' questionnaire has some portions that are applicable based upon the type of cloud deployment involved. Be sure to ask only those questions appropriate to the subject as this is an area where attention can become more focused due to its complexity.

- Vendor-Owned Data Centers:
  - Provide the address of all data centers in scope.
    - Primary data center
    - Secondary data center
    - Others

- Describe the age and any upgrade/maintenance done since established.
- Are data center personnel full-time personnel, contractors, or managed by another third party?
- Are any data center personnel members of an organized union?
  - Yes or No
  - If yes, provide their association details.
  - Have there ever been any worker unrest or strikes?
- Are there restrictions on customer security assessments of the data center?
- How far from corporate headquarters are these data centers?
- Is there an active plan to retire any or all of the data centers?
- Do you have appropriate certifications for the physical security of the premises?

Personnel Security   Some important Human Resources (HR) cybersecurity steps must be taken to ensure that a third party is performing the correct due care and due diligence. Too often, it's an insider threat or a rogue employee that leads to an incident. The Personnel Security section in the questionnaire should cover the following:

- Are all personnel (i.e., full-time, part-time, contractors) required to accept and sign an Acceptable Use Policy or Agreement?
- Are all personnel (i.e., full-time, part-time, contractors) required to accept and sign a Code of Ethics?
- Are all personnel (i.e., full-time, part-time, contractors) required to accept and sign a Non-Disclosure Agreement (NDA)?

- Are all personnel (i.e., full-time, part-time, contractors) required to undergo a background check prior to hire?
  - If yes:
    - What items are checked on background?
    - How often are background checks rerun for any personnel?
    - Does your company policy require forced PTO for personnel who work in Finance or other high-risk areas?
    - Is there a termination policy that clearly describes behaviors that can result in job loss?
    - Are all personnel (i.e., full-time, part-time, contractors) required to undergo annual security awareness and training?

Connectivity Security   As the IRQ is completed and vendors answer that a connection with KC Enterprises is required, you must inquire about the following security controls on network connections:

- Which data centers or offices will the vendor require being connected?
- Is there an existing connection with the vendor?
- What hardware is the vendor supplying for both ends of the connectivity?
- What is the vendor's patch management policy and how does the connection hardware fit into that process?
- Does the vendor agree to share with KC's Cybersecurity team the version of its software running on any hardware used in the connection at least twice a year?
- What level of encryption is used for the connection?
- Are there any out-of-band devices needed for the management or recovery of the hardware?

- Yes or No
- If yes, please describe the hardening done for such devices.

Supplier Management Security This questionnaire section is a great opportunity to discover if your third party is one of those companies that does not sufficiently manage its own third parties. The questions should focus on the following areas of biggest risk:

- Do you have a vendor management program?
- Yes or No
- If yes:
  - Is there a tiering system for vendors based upon risk?
  - How is due diligence performed on the vendor's cybersecurity risk?
  - How often does your company perform on-site security assessments of critical vendors? How many critical vendors does this include?
  - Have any of your third parties reported a security breach in the last three years?
  - Who are the key vendors and products used to perform the service or deliver the product to KC Enterprises?
  - Please provide the vendor's names and what services they provide in the delivery of product.
  - Have there been any disaster recovery tabletop exercises run on an outage at a key vendor for this product?

Next Steps

Risk-based triggers Any due diligence program should take a risk-based approach, meaning focus of the work and attention increases as the risk increases for the vendor. One way to do this is to assign risk based upon cyberliability insurance limits and payouts. KC Enterprises' cyberliability insurance requirement from vendors is $1 million. Any deal where the quantitative analysis places the risk at 90 percent of that insurance level (in case there are times where we have a vendor with more than $1 M), means that the vendor must go through additional analysis. This analysis can be from a complex quantitative analysis model or simple math. KC values PII records of customers at $200 per record. This value is based upon internal calculations done to hire an excess amount of lawyers and an outside PR firm to put out a brave message, to pay for free access to credit viewing and protection to customers affected, and to fire the CISO and look for a new one. (Did I mention hiring more lawyers? They're expensive.)

Low-Risk Vendors At this point, the math necessary is straightforward, but a calculator is still nice to use. The threshold for low-risk vendors is $900,000, with $200 per record, and the trigger for additional scrutiny is 4,500 records. While that might sound very low as thresholds go, keep in mind this is just a threshold to do something: What is the "something to do" above and below the threshold is the important question. Below this threshold, vendors receive a remote questionnaire that asks them the additional due diligence questions in an online form (ideal) or in a locked spreadsheet (keeps the answers from varying too much from them). As the responses come in, staff can review them and look for flags that require follow-up, either via email, direct call, or conference call.

The risk of these low-risk vendors allows KC's due diligence teams to focus on more in-depth reviews of vendors with higher risk. Process the low-risk vendors and keep an eye out for the following flags in the system that set off cybersecurity alarms:

- Are there any red flags on encryption questions (i.e., vendors who do not meet a minimum standard)?

- Are the offshore resource policies meeting KC's standards?

- Does the firm have a defense-in-depth strategy as seen by the responses?

- Would a phone call or follow-up meeting clarify any risk concerns?

Above this low-risk category can be another threshold or two, depending on typical vendor record counts and resource capabilities weighed against the risk of a breach because due diligence missed a key risk. No pressure. The risk-based approach allows for flexibility, but the rule-of-thumb would be to increase the level of hands-on deep dives as the record count gets higher or connectivity gets less secure (e.g., a vendor needs to traverse the network with discovery nodes, which might be a concern given what has been seen in SolarWinds).

Moderate-Risk Vendors Moderate risk at KC Enterprises is considered as any vendor with more than 45,000 records. This value is based upon KC's own cyberliability insurance with the same insurance carrier with which it has business insurance: at $10 million. The same threshold is built-in here, where 90 percent of $200 per record is 45,000 PII records. Anything between 4,501 and 45,000 records gets this additional scrutiny. In this risk level, the following should occur:

- The third party is required to complete the IRQ. Once triggered, then the Intake Questions are expanded to include more questions on data security and the ability to perform more due diligence (i.e., on-site assessments).

- The vendor is required to schedule appropriate subject-matter experts (SMEs) for two one-hour video conference sessions. These two sessions will include time for an initial session of information gathering, in addition to some questions and answers. Undoubtedly, on this first call, not all the answers will be ready as the initial discovery is performed. The second call is available in case the initial call does not produce all the answers.

- Vendors at this risk level must agree to three non-negotiable cybersecurity conditions:
  - **Encryption:** All data must be encrypted at a minimum of AES-256 or equivalent at-rest, in-transit, and in-use.
  - **Right to On-site Security Assessment:** These assessments will be two-day on-site visits by our Cybersecurity team to perform on-site physical validation of security controls.
  - **MFA for Privileged Access:** Any systems that store, process, or transmit KC data must require MFA or a Privileged Access Manager (PAM) to manage escalated accounts.
  - These non-negotiables have only two ways to become negotiable:
- If the vendor agrees to take on additional cyberliability insurance to cover the risk, in addition, the vendor must ensure the insurance is exclusive to KC Enterprises.

  Or

- The business sponsor must present a Risk Acceptance (RA) memo explaining the risk, with recommendations from Cybersecurity Third-Party Risk leadership. The RA must get approval from the company's CISO, the executive owner for the business unit, and the business sponsor.
- The results of a Risk Acceptance must be stored and searchable. An RA doesn't make the risk go away; it must follow that vendor like a "scarlet R" (for Risk!) until it is closed, to discourage it as a practice and so no one loses sight of the risk.

- This RA will be stored in the system of record on the vendor. It will also be logged in the system of record on the vendor as an open "finding"—an identified risk at the vendor—that is not closed until it's confirmed. Meaning, every time the third party has a due diligence engagement, whether remote or on-site assessment, the KC cybersecurity assessors will ask if the finding has been closed.
- An RA quantitative risk estimate will be added to the KC Cybersecurity Risk Register (discussed later), which is a way for the company leadership to view the risk that they have taken on in total.

High-Risk Vendors High-risk vendors at KC Enterprises consist of any vendor with a record count above 45,001 or a vendor with a connection. KC added the connection to this risk category due to a concern of lateral movement. A connection to the network to a cybersecurity professional is like what an open wound is to a doctor. It can be managed with some disinfectant and a band-aid, but the wound is still a threat that can infect the body from the outside. So, if a vendor has only five PII records but has a connection to the KC network, then it is automatically placed in the high-risk category.

At this category level, a vendor is subject to the same scrutiny as the moderate-risk vendors and also to the following additional steps:

- The vendor must agree to the following connectivity audits on any hardware used:
  - The third party must physically validate that the software running on the hardware is at a patch level where there are no critical security patches (i.e., zero-day critical as defined by the hardware vendor).

- Access controls for hardware must meet KC's security standards for third parties.

- These non-negotiables have only two ways to become negotiable:
  - If the vendor agrees to take on additional cyberliability insurance to cover the risk. In addition, the vendor must ensure the insurance is exclusive to KC Enterprises.

    Or

  - In this level, RA becomes more politically expensive for the sponsor. This is intentional by KC's leadership, because they don't want this behavior to happen unless the price of the behavior is outweighed by the whole firm taking this level of risk. The business sponsor must present an RA memo explaining the risk, with recommendation from Cybersecurity Third-Party Risk leadership. This RA must be approved by only the CEO and get reported to the KC Board Risk Committee as well as the Cybersecurity Risk Register.

- Storing the results of a Risk Acceptance so they can be reported. An RA doesn't make the risk go away; it must follow that vendor like a "scarlet R" until it is closed, to discourage it as a practice and so no one loses sight of the risk:
  - This RA will be stored in the system of record on the vendor. It will also be logged in the vendor record as an open "finding"—an identified risk at the vendor—that is not closed until it's confirmed. Meaning, every time the third party has a due diligence engagement, whether remote or on-site assessment, the KC cybersecurity assessors will ask if the finding has been closed.

- An RA quantitative risk estimate will be added to the KC Cybersecurity Risk Register (discussed later), which is a way for the company leadership to view the risk that they have taken on in total.

These vendors and the risk levels help not only with intake due diligence but help KC cybersecurity teams to focus on resources in the Ongoing, On-site, and Continuous Monitoring teams. Because of the high risk and the high oversight, this threshold is a difficult decision for KC to make, which determined that a service model needed to be established for the line of business vendors based upon their risk level.

Ways to Become More Efficient

You can improve the efficiency of these due diligence efforts by leveraging any vendor that has certain certifications or third-party confirmed frameworks implemented. Following are some examples of widely recognized certifications that can be used:

- Health Information Trust Alliance (HITRUST) is an organization that represents and is governed by the healthcare industry. It offers three different levels of certification for its Common Security Framework (CSF): self-assessment, CSF validated, and CSF-certified. A CSF-certified vendor that is going to be handling PHI data can skip much of the due diligence efforts if they can confirm that their certification is still valid.
- Federal Risk and Authorization Management Program (FedRAMP) is a government program that provides a standard approach to cloud security assessments. There are three levels of FedRAMP: low, medium, and high. Depending upon

a company's risk appetite, it could declare that if a vendor is FedRAMP medium-certified, then they can skip much of the cloud due diligence.

- To become certified by the Cloud Security Alliance Security Trust Assurance and Risk (CSA STAR) program requires a rigorous third-party independent assessment of the vendor's cloud security. If they can demonstrate that the certification is still valid, it offers the ability to avoid cloud due diligence.

There are other similar certification programs that could be used to leverage the work the vendor has performed in achieving this level of certification and to lower the amount of due diligence required.

Systems and Organization Controls Reports

Systems and Organization Controls (SOC) reports are common reports requested or required from vendors, as they are mandated by SSAE 16 and SSAE 18. This requirement stems largely from the Sarbanes-Oxley Act (SOX) that made public companies responsible for effective system controls on their financials. Ensuring this control requires that public companies obtain a SOC report to ensure that vendors don't impact their compliance negatively.

A SOC report is performed by a certified public accountant (CPA) from the American Institute of Certified Public Accountants (AICPA) and is a compilation of controls to confirm they are present and audited. There have been a number of versions, such as SAS 70 that was superseded by SSAE 16 in May 2011. In May of 2017, the SSAE 18 mandated a series of upgrades to the quality of SOC reports.

Various types of SOC reports are available: SOC1, SOC2, and SOC3. In addition, there are also different types of each of them: Type 1 or Type II. A SOC1 report is focused on the internal controls on financial reporting. This report is an output from an audit of the accounting and financial controls. Note, these reports are not applicable for a cybersecurity evaluation. A SOC2 report is the one most often used by an information technology vendor. The SOC2 is not an upgrade nor does it provide more details than a SOC1. It is an audit of the controls of the vendor for one or more of the following Trust Service Criteria (TSC):

- Security
- Confidentiality
- Privacy
- Processing Integrity
- Availability

The SOC2 is designed to provide a metric of a vendor's ability to adhere to privacy, confidentiality, availability, and security of its IT services. The different types of SOC2 reports (i.e., Type I and Type II) are vastly different in scope. Type I confirms that the controls exist. However, a Type II affirms that the controls are in place and that they work. It's an important distinction and is why a SOC2 Type II often represents an improved view of how a vendor is performing at protecting your data.

A SOC3 is not an upgrade of a SOC2 report. It is a summary of a SOC2 Type II, so it is not as detailed as either type of SOC2 statements. It is primarily intended to be used too as a seal of approval that can be shared publicly (on the company website or in literature). Because it is not as detailed, it cannot be used for cybersecurity due diligence efforts.

There are four sections to a SOC2 Type II report:

- **Report from the Auditor:** The auditor discusses the audit engagement (i.e., what was audited, duration, and scope). They list anything they have found, good or bad. Most opinions will be one of these four:
  - **Unqualified:** Great result, good-to-go
  - **Qualified:** Good but not great, need some things fixed or remediated
  - **Adverse:** Not good, a failing grade
  - **Disclaimer of Opinion:** Bad, equivalent of not just getting an "F" but getting kicked out of school
- **Management Assertion:** Management responds to some of the audit findings as well as the period, scope, and time of the engagement.
- **Description of System:** An important section because it describes the structure of a company, services offered, in addition to its IT systems and controls.
- **Matrix of Criteria and Testing:** This is usually a listing or matrix of the criteria, controls, and testing, along with results.

When reviewing the SOC2 Type II report, there are several key items to pay attention to ensure that it is relevant:

- **Type I or Type II:** For a SOC2 report to be considered sufficient for cybersecurity due diligence, the auditing and testing must be done at a Type II level where the effectiveness of the controls is evaluated.

- **Coverage:** Does the report cover the services and/or products the company has contracted the vendor for or are there pieces missing?
- **Criteria:** There are five Trust Services Criteria: privacy, security, data integrity, availability, and confidentiality. Does the report cover all five?
- **Sub-contractors:** Is the report inclusive of the vendors' third parties used to provide the service?
- **Exceptions:** If the report has any material exceptions, these need to be reviewed for impact to the risk due diligence.
- **Date:** Check at the date of the examination to see if it is old enough to be considered stale. It should be no older than one year from when the Intake process takes place, and ideally it should be less than nine months, given that the Intake process for a vendor can take a lot of time from start to production implementation.

SOC2 Type II reports are a valid way to have vendors attest to an independent assessment of IT controls. It cannot be a substitute for performing due diligence and risk evaluations. These are point-in-time audits that do not provide ongoing assurance that the vendor is adhering to security controls. The reports are a requirement of public companies to lower their risk of SOX issues or findings. However, they are not ideal for cybersecurity due diligence as described in this text.

Chargebacks

This can be a difficult topic for cybersecurity to discuss with business leadership. However, this model is a largely accepted practice for IT services rendered to lines of business. It is a common way to ensure that business includes the true cost of the ownership of the size of their business. In this case, the requirements for due diligence levels are clearly articulated by KC Third-Party Risk Management and Cybersecurity. The thresholds were established principles and had been working, but management was concerned that the business was taking on a lot more moderate- and high-risk vendors that required more resources.

The lines of business leadership, TPRM, and cybersecurity leadership agreed to a cost model based upon the risk category of the vendor engagement. Pricing was not an actual cost as it passed hands from a department to cybersecurity and TPRM for the resource cost, but the line of business "funded" the cybersecurity resource as part of the project for the duration of the intake review process. Resources can be fully funded and cybersecurity and TPRM can collaborate with each line of business, as part of each fiscal year's planning to establish expected staffing levels based upon funded projects in the upcoming year that would require due diligence. This isn't an exact science, as not all projects may not know if they require a connection or data classification levels or because projects are sometimes added mid-year. Because it's not a science, the three teams work it out in budgeting per the normal prioritization process.

This risk-based approach to how a project is funded, and thus resourced, has some side benefits. First, it provides a "cost" to business on projects with vendors that raised the risk levels at KC Enterprises, so the cost was added into the calculus when weighing options of doing something outsourced or in-house on internal resources and systems. Second, it bridged the gap of friction that is often had between business and cybersecurity overdue diligence efforts. This exercise of establishing vendor risk classifications, based upon quantitative values to having business fund the resources required for the due diligence, was an education for all three teams. Cybersecurity learned business operations and needs, TPRM learned the expected input coming in the upcoming year, while the business learned of the "cost" of cybersecurity due diligence by viewing the activity level required at each level.

Go-Live Production Reviews

Prior to any go-live production, a new vendor service must meet and go through all the due diligence that is required to complete a gate review. At KC, these reviews depend on the vendor risk level. On the low-risk side, vendors are required to have closed any high-level risk findings during the Intake process. All lower-risk cybersecurity items can be risk accepted by the business sponsor and the approval of the Cybersecurity Risk Advisor or their delegate.

Moderate- and high-risk vendors must have an increasing level of go-live preapprovals. On the moderate- and high-risk vendor side, they also must close all high-risk findings prior to go-live; and all moderate-risk findings must have a remediation date of no more than one year from go-live or earlier, depending on agreement with a third party prior to production.

Connectivity Cyber Reviews

Because connections to the corporate network carry a risk, KC requires some additional steps before any line is turned on live. Once the connection is established, changes are hard to make. In addition, if there is a security gap, it could go undetected for a long time, depending on scanning and patch management. The history had shown Cybersecurity teams that these connections can be "forgotten" by the vendors; but because the vendors managed the hardware and were the only ones with access, this meant it could be a challenge once installed to correct bad behaviors of vendors.

Connectivity Cyber Reviews involve Cyber Third-Party Risk reviewing a few key items prior:

- Vendors must confirm hardware and patch level at time of deployment.
- Vendors must confirm that the encryption of the connectivity is per design approval.
- KC Security Architecture must have completed a high-level design of the connectivity with approvals from relevant network connectivity policy. At present time, this is the Enterprise Architecture Council that has all relevant stakeholders across Information Technology and Cybersecurity departments.
- There are no open high risk findings or risk acceptances that directly impact the security of the connection with the vendors.

Once these four processes are confirmed completed, then cybersecurity has performed its approval at the connectivity.

Connectivity Lifecycle   One often overlooked item is connecting the vendor contract with the life of the connectivity. If there is no process to let the network connectivity and security teams know that a contract has been terminated, KC found that equipment often stayed connected. They took corrective steps to connect their workflow tool used for the network service management connected to the vendor management software. The workflow between the two programs meant that if a vendor's contract was being terminated, a flag drove a workflow. If that vendor had a checkmark for "Connection," then it sent a nightly batch file to the workflow in the service management tool. It wasn't magic, but at that point, the appropriate personnel were notified of the need to investigate and coordinate with the vendor management team on when to shut the connection down. Also, the equipment had be returned to the vendor or otherwise inform KC of how to dispose of it.

Final Intake Steps   Once the go-live production steps have been completed, the systems of records must be updated and owners for the data be assigned. Based upon risk, the vendor then goes into the next phase: Ongoing Due Diligence. This phase will decide how often a third party will require periodic assessments and where in the Continuous Monitoring program it fits. It is likely there will be multiple services from single vendors, so there are ways to speed the whole process up as well, by leveraging existing artifacts and due diligence records (that are not too stale) to lower the activity level required for a vendor to repeatedly refill out the same data.

KC Enterprises also establishes a vendor portal that is leveraged for communication. After the service or product is in production use, the cybersecurity team can communicate directly with the vendor contacts. For high-risk and moderate-risk third parties, the cybersecurity Incident Response teams are linked, and the cyber teams have designated points of contact. Through this secure portal, the vendor can be sent surveys or questions to fill in online to lower the risk of data leakage. One future feature request at the firm is to integrate a calendar schedule function that is tied to the firm's risk. The vendor would see, based upon their KC risk profile, that they are expected to have an on-site assessment performed at certain periods. For example, a high-risk vendor might get an on-site assessment every other year, so in an "off" year it would not appear as a vendor requirement on their portal in that calendar year.

Inside Look: Ticketmaster and Fourth Parties

In June 2018, Ticketmaster publicly acknowledged that it found malware in its customer chat function, hosted by third-party Inbenta Technologies. The data that the malicious code was leaking included names, addresses, emails, telephone numbers, payment card data, and Ticketmaster login credentials. The malware ran for nearly a year, from September 2017 until June 2018. Ticketmaster's use of a third-party chat hosting company isn't unique. The cybercriminal gang, Magecart, was behind the attack—a group known for payment skimmers injected into vulnerable website components. Worse was news that as early as February 2018, a number of major banks told Ticketmaster about a large amount of fraud and they failed to take any action. This lack of action caused the U.K. privacy watchdog Information Commissioner's Office (ICO) to fine them over $1.65 million.

This breach is also an excellent way to explain fourth-party risk. In this case, many U.K. venue operators found out what it was like to be affected by a fourth party; one they were unlikely to know about given most operations do not bother to find out their third-party's vendors. Let's say you operated a small music venue in Liverpool. It's likely you didn't do your own ticketing, and had contracted Ticketmaster to perform that service for concerts. Suddenly customers are calling upset about fraudulent charges on their cards after they booked a concert at your place. Good customer service dictates you let them vent but politely remind them they book with Ticketmaster. Your next call made is to the Ticketmaster account representative to find out what is going on. In June 2018, they inform of the breach and how it happened. Likely none of the theater and music operators in the U.K. ever heard of Inbeta Technologies. Yet, they had unhappy customers regardless.

Later chapters will discuss ways to test software from third parties for vulnerabilities and secure development. Another avenue of concern is how Ticketmaster performs its own vendor due diligence on software vendors it uses; what fourth-party questions the venue operators were asking Ticketmaster; and if Ticketmaster uses another third party or parties to provide its own service, and if so, what pieces they are performing.

Conclusion

The process for initial review of a vendor, setting out cybersecurity standards on an RFP, or how vendors are risk classified determines how due diligence depth is adaptable to any size or scale. KC Enterprises is a medium-sized firm with a large U.S. presence, some offshore resources, and regulatory oversight. They decided to take a determined approach on documenting risk levels, identifying their non-negotiables, determining proper oversight of any risk acceptance decisions, and a way to view the accumulated cybersecurity risk of the company to not lose sight of that risk. This "determined" approach meant documenting a policy and process for intake due diligence activities for third parties from IRQ, RFPs, and levels of vendor risk (Low, Medium, High) that are quantitatively based.

CHAPTER

6

Ongoing Due Diligence

Ongoing due diligence is the process, once intake is completed and the vendor relationship is active, for how vendors are continually risk-assessed and the due diligence effort determined. As presented, KC Enterprises continues its high-, moderate-, and low-risk approaches to how ongoing due diligence is performed. The common taxonomy across the due diligence efforts ensures that no "translation" effort is ever needed when discussing the levels. In addition, because the risk levels are based on quantitative numbers, anyone can then understand the dollar amounts (in rough order of magnitude). It's a yardstick used in the cybersecurity organization on vendor risk that traces its way through intake to reporting and analytics.

All vendors who fit the KC criteria (data with the top three classifications or a connection to their network) have continual due diligence in some form. As the vendors complete Intake and are assigned their risk level, the software used to store vendor Cybersecurity Third-Party Risk data provides guidance on the required due diligence. There is some management discretion built into the system. For example, perhaps a low-risk vendor comes to management's attention as a ransomware target on the Dark Web. At that point, due to the that heightened risk of a ransomware event, the vendor could be moved from low-risk to moderate-risk.

Several forms of ongoing security assessments of vendors exist. First is the remote assessment, where a supplier is given a questionnaire either as an online form or a hard copy form to fill out and return for evaluation. These remote evaluations are similar to Intake, in that they have the supplier self-report their security controls. Most often, these activities are done as compliance tasks: Policy or regulatory guidance requires that, at regular intervals, vendors that meet risk criteria must be polled for security and other risk domains.

Taking third-party cybersecurity risk out of a compliance-led activity into a security risk-focused one involves using a risk-based approach. Low-risk vendors, by their definition to an organization, are adequately covered by a remote questionnaire. You should focus on the high-risk items within the low-risk area, which includes encryption, multi-factor authentication (MFA) for privileged accounts, and access control risks. Any changes the vendor admits to in these critical areas are where your follow-up and time should be focused.

Medium- and high-risk suppliers can have increasing levels of activity for due diligence in remote assessments. This increased activity centers around the validation of responses to confirm risk. For example, if a supplier reports closing an open risk that was logged on lack of privileged access controls and does so by deploying a Privileged Access Manager (PAM), then it would be appropriate to request they submit physical proof of deployment. The higher the vendor's risk to the company, the more work spent identifying, monitoring, and reducing risk is time and energy well spent.

The next ongoing due diligence activity is on-site security assessments, which will be discussed at length in the next chapter. On-site evaluations are reserved for vendors that present a high enough risk to warrant the time and energy for this activity. On-site security audits take more time to schedule because the vendor subject matter experts (SMEs) must be available during the time and dates they are scheduled. In addition, travel is involved, either in the same town or across the country or world. Lastly, employees who are best able to carry out these on-site assessments are more experienced, and thus, are the higher compensated staff of a Cyber Third-Party Risk team.

Continuous Monitoring is part of ongoing due diligence and provides near real-time security risk data on vendors who are included in this activity. The team working on continuous monitoring engages suppliers on specific alerts and attacks to lower risk. Continuous monitoring is designed to bridge the gap between the point-in-time assessments that are typical of Cyber Third-Party Risk. Nearly all other due diligence, onboarding and ongoing, are performed on a specific date, which means there are at least another 364 days before they are assessed again. The constant cybercriminal activity does not wait for that length of time, so this ongoing activity helps to close that monitoring gap.

Following are examples of how KC Enterprises handles its ongoing due diligence efforts. KC takes a risk-based approach, which requires less time and energy spent on the vendors who pose less risk. As a vendor's risk increases, KC requires more time and proof to ensure that they have an accurate picture of the supplier's cybersecurity controls.

Low-Risk Vendor Ongoing Due Diligence

Third parties at this level have been evaluated and determined to present a level of risk to the company that deserves their lowest level of resource commitment. Because some risk with these vendors has been transferred to cyberliability insurance, KC can lower the level required for oversight. The team adds these to the Continuous Monitoring Low-Risk vendor category and then the vendor is scheduled in the vendor portal for the next security assessment. Low-risk vendors receive an annual security questionnaire that confirms some items and asks about any potential changes to the relationship. It queries the following:

- If there are any open risk findings, has the vendor been able to remediate them since last update?
- Have there been any material changes to the vendor list that support the delivery of products or services to KC (i.e., fourth parties)?
- Have vendors complete this short cybersecurity survey:
  - Data Classification:
    - Can you confirm that the data classification of (Internal/Confidential/Restricted) is still correct?
  - Data Privacy:
    - Please describe the amount of data records kept on a month-to-month basis.
  - Data Location:
    - Has the location of KC's data changed (e.g., from vendor data center to a Cloud Service Provider)?
  - Encryption:
    - Can you confirm that the encryption of data at-rest, in-transit, and in-use remains at AES-256 or higher?
  - Access Management:
    - Can you confirm that privileged accounts are required to have multi-factor authentication or are managed by a Privileged Access Manager (PAM)?
  - If a condition of your contract was to complete an annual certification (SOC2 Type II report, for example), please attach it to the survey.

Notice that there aren't a lot of questions. Also of note is that the annual engagement is used to confirm some key features.

Data classification and the amount of data are the first two questions. KC's Cybersecurity team wants to confirm if the data classification has traveled up or down the scale. If it was originally internal, but has since moved into restricted, this changes the risk. More importantly, the second question asks about the record count. Very often, business relationships evolve with a vendor, and with no ill-intent (hopefully), the type and amount of data changes over the course of a year or more. This question determines if a vendor can remain in the low-risk category.

Once vendors have confirmed the size and risk of the data in the first two questions, the attention goes to where KC's data is located. As noted earlier, a data center is an expensive operational item, and as time goes on, a vendor may decide to downsize or eliminate it altogether. Moving the data to a Cloud Service Provider (e.g., AWS, Google, Azure) will offload the expense, but sometimes a third party can forget their legal obligations to provide notice. We discuss cybersecurity legal language in a bit, but this notice type should be contractual. If vendors fail to notify KC or the data relocation is just in the planning stages, then this question can ensure that the risk is confirmed.

Encryption is the next question as it's an opportunity to confirm that the protections agreed to with the vendor are still in place. Key management is also important as it's crucial to preventing unauthorized access to confidential information. Managing these keys with proper care and rotating the keys at set periods ensures that the data stays secret because the keys are protected and managed. The specificity on in-use, in-transit, and at-rest encryption is to ensure none of these states have changed either. Access Management and Privileged Access Management are vital in protecting the "keys" to the kingdom. Because these accounts have higher privileges, it's best to ensure that the vendor has kept their security on them to the level expected and agreed upon.

The data size and classification, encryption, and access management questions are all connected back to how KC determined its risk level for their vendors and their non-negotiables. The approach's consistency ensures that cybersecurity staff know how to approach all vendors dependent upon their risk levels. These questions are all asked via the vendor portal, and KC's internal supplier manager is responsible for ensuring they complete them on time.

Failure to complete the questions on time sends an alert to Third-Party Risk Management (TPRM) and Cybersecurity Third-Party Risk staff for next steps. The intent is to work with the vendor to resolve and finish the task. However, if something has changed—for example, the vendor now has over 10,000 sensitive customer records—then a reevaluation of their risk must take place. This reevaluation requires an abbreviated process to determine that it is now in the moderate risk category (as discussed in Chapter 5). Due to the increased vendor risk, the risk due diligence requires Cybersecurity to have a couple of discussion sessions to review their security controls, and to ensure that their non-negotiables (i.e., encryption, right-to-security assessment, and MFA for privileged accounts) meet the moderate risk standards. For example, if there was a Risk Acceptance (RA) for one of those controls, it was likely assigned and agreed upon at the low-risk conditions. The business sponsor is required to either have the vendor remediate the gap, increase their insurance level, or have the RA redone at the leadership level required.

If third parties successfully complete the questionnaire on time without any changes that trigger further action, then the cybersecurity analyst who validates it will schedule another review for the next calendar year. The analyst has some rescheduling flexibility, but the review date must not be more than 365 days from the previous security assessment.

Moderate-Risk Vendor Ongoing Due Diligence

Moderate-risk vendors are also required to fill out the annual survey, but it includes more questions, physical validation is required for some questions, and the category is subject to a less frequent on-site security assessment (than high risk). The low-risk category questionnaire consists of a few questions, and the ongoing monitoring focuses on finding any material changes to the vendor risk. At this increased risk level, the increased effort is again risk-based and must determine with physical validation that the vendor is adhering to security controls as agreed. The queries cover the following:

- If there are any open-risk findings, has the vendor been able to remediate them since the last update?
- Have there been any material changes to the vendor list who support the delivery of products or services to KC (i.e., fourth parties)?
- Vendors must complete a short cybersecurity survey:
  - Data Classification:
    - Can the vendor provide physical confirmation that the data classification of (Internal/Confidential/Restricted) is still correct? Please upload a sample of the data into the secure portal.
  - Data Privacy:
    - Can the vendor demonstrate the amount of data records that are kept on a month-to-month basis? Upload evidence to the secure portal.
  - Data Location:
    - Has KC's data location changed (e.g., from vendor data center to a Cloud Service Provider)?

- Encryption:
  - Can the vendor confirm that the encryption of data at-rest, in-transit, and in-use remains at AES-256 or higher? Please provide the evidence as a screenshot on the secure portal.
- Access Management:
  - Can the vendor confirm that privileged accounts are required to have MFA or are managed by a PAM? Please upload evidence to the secure portal.
- Ensure there is Security Awareness and Training for things like phishing, clean desk policies, and other security best-practices by employees performed at least annually.
- Ensure the vendor has an Acceptable Use Policy that details what is permitted and consequences for failure to follow.
- If a condition of your contract was to complete an annual certification (SOC2 Type II report, for example), please attach to the survey.
- Has there been a vulnerability scan performed on the service or product provided to KC in the last year? If so, please provide evidence via the secure portal.

They use physical validation to verify the level of assurance required for the risk. Having a cybersecurity employee verify evidence is a bigger time investment, and it's likely some vendors will push back on sharing this data as it can be considered sensitive. The KC Cybersecurity and Supplier Management team needs to negotiate the level of evidence sufficient to meet their needs while not breaking the vendor's own data protection policy.

As the process is managed by the supplier manager for this yearly security review, the cybersecurity analyst is reviewing the artifacts provided. Once the evidence is deemed sufficient, it's attached to a vendor's file in the system of record for evidence. Again, the analyst and supplier manager will schedule another security check in less than 365 days.

In the low-risk category, we described how the process would work if it was discovered that material changes occurred to the risk, bumping it up into the moderate-risk level. The same process holds true if a moderate-risk vendor annual security review necessitates it to move into the high-risk category.

Finally, the last potential avenue for this annual review process is when a vendor refuses to comply with the assessment. Regardless of whether a vendor is considered low, moderate, or high risk, if they fail to complete the survey or a security due diligence activity, there are risk-based consequences. In the low-risk category, the vendor is flagged being as "non-compliant," and their contract cannot be renewed nor can services be expanded with them until it is corrected. Moderate-risk third parties that refuse to complete the required due diligence activities can also be restricted on contract renewal or expanded services; this issue also can get escalated to senior management, including the CISO, Legal department, and executive business sponsor, to determine if the vendor relationship presents sufficient risk to sever it.

A high-risk vendor that refuses to perform due diligence can be escalated to senior management quickly, and for good reason. For example, the process at KC has additional triggers: If a third party refuses to complete the required due diligence and also has any high RAs or high-risk open findings, then the escalation is immediate to the CISO, Legal department, and executive sponsor. The timelines are left to management because these events are not frequent, and each varies. However, the intent of the process is to quickly determine if the risk of failure to comply with the due diligence and any open risks should equal suspension of activity plus any legal remedies.

High-Risk Vendor Ongoing Due Diligence

KC spends most of its resource time and energy on ongoing due diligence. As expected, their surveys occur once a year, but much of their energy is spent on on-site security evaluations at this risk level. The online survey is identical to the moderate-level questions in the Intake assessment, but a few more questions are required, as shown here:

- If there are any open risk findings, has the vendor been able to remediate them since the last update?
- Have there been any material changes to the vendor list that support the delivery of a product or service to KC (i.e., fourth parties)?
- Has the vendor completed this short cybersecurity survey?
  - Data Classification:
    - Can the vendor provide physical confirmation that the data classification of (Internal/Confidential/Restricted) is still correct? Please upload a sample of the data into the secure portal.
  - Data Privacy:
    - Can the vendor demonstrate the amount of data records that are kept on a month-to-month basis? Please upload evidence to the secure portal.
  - Data Location:
    - Has KC's data location changed (e.g., from vendor data center to a Cloud Service Provider)?
      - If the location of the data is a CSP, please submit a security configuration report via the secure portal for the area where KC's data is stored and/or processed.
      - If the location of the data is a co-location facility, please provide an appropriate SOC2 Type II for

the facility's physical security and an attestation that the areas managed by the vendor meet their own physical security standards.

- If the location of the data is a vendor-owned/controlled data center, please provide an appropriate certification or attestation to the physical security at the data centers.

- Encryption:
  - Can the vendor confirm that the encryption of data at-rest, in-transit, and in-use remains at AES-256 or higher? Please provide the evidence as a screenshot on the secure portal.

- Access Management:
  - Can the vendor confirm that privileged accounts are required to have MFA or are managed by a PAM? Please upload evidence to the secure portal.

- Has there been a vulnerability scan performed on the service or product provided to KC in the last year? If so, please provide evidence via the secure portal.

There aren't a lot of questions here, as the on-site assessment will go into more depth. Much of this questionnaire is aimed at attaining evidence for the analyst who will go to the vendor's site. The analyst who manages this process will attach all the artifacts to the third-party's record, so the person who performs the on-site assessment can use them for their process.

"Too Big to Care"

Some companies and organizations are big enough or secure enough in their position to not care about what a customer wants or requires. We call them "Too Big to Care" because they know their position is secure enough that their attitude is almost a "take it or leave it" one when negotiating with a potential customer. Such organizations can be government entities that a company uses to report transactions or a large multinational software company with a lock on its product market. When engaging with customers, they often dictate the terms of their contracts, due diligence efforts, and choices for security. They know customers have little choice in who provides them with their services or products, and they act like it. However, there are ways to work with this type of vendor to reduce risk to your organization, even if they will not cooperate. While the better option would be to find another vendor, there are cases where this may not be possible, so it's good to have a plan and process ready for those who are "Too Big to Care."

The onboarding processes for such vendors can be challenging because they are so large and likely have a prescribed way of engagement with new customers. The IRQ and Intake questions may not be answered fully, or they may provide your company with a standard response set that does not match exactly with the questions asked. IRQ and Intake are not the same questions. An IRQ should be short to determine appropriate risk domains that require due diligence. The Intake question is (in the case of this book) the actual due diligence questions that the cybersecurity risk domain will ask if the IRQ indicates it is required. The process for dealing with such vendors is to work with the business sponsor to fill out as much of the questionnaires as possible with the information provided. Simply note the missing pieces and send just those questions over to the product's sales leader. Salespeople are still motivated by a commission no matter if the company is considered "Too Big." Explain that the process at your firm cannot be completed, nor the sale finalized, until those final questions are answered. If that does not work, again note the missing information and risk rank it. If there are any that are non-negotiables, an escalation to the business sponsor is warranted.

The contracts for these vendors are often done on their "paper," meaning their contracts and terms are provided to your company by them. This situation does present a challenge as the terms are often very favorable to the vendor. It likely does not contain the cybersecurity terms that should be discussed in your contract. The vendor can also take your contract language and edit it to the point where it's unrecognizable as your company's contract terms and conditions. Either situation poses a problem for onboarding these "Too Big to Care" vendors. If the contract terms are unacceptable or present a high enough risk to your company, there is little recourse if the vendor is the only game in town for their product or service. In those instances, if the contract terms present too high a risk (based upon your company's risk appetite), then one option is to look at cyberliability insurance to cover the risk, transferring the risk to the insurance carrier. That's the best risk-based approach in that situation.

The due diligence efforts involved in the ongoing section of the lifecycle do not get any easier with these vendors. The contract terms for performing on-site assessment is a common pushback from these suppliers due to the number of customers they support, combined with their attitude of not really needing to accommodate customer requests. One option is to negotiate a virtual on-site assessment: Use video conferencing and collaboration tools to perform the security due diligence without physically being at the company. This can be more appealing to a vendor because they don't have to dedicate a conference room or personnel to escort customer visitors to the assessment, and it can be accomplished over a few days to accommodate varied schedules.

Lastly, here are two more options: If the industry your company operates in is a highly regulated one (e.g., Finance, Energy, Government, Biotech), there are often regulatory requirements to have a TPRM program perform cybersecurity due diligence. The regulatory directives to perform these actions are the price that the vendor must pay to sell to companies in those sectors. If that does not work, then an exception process in the TPRM policy can be incorporated to deal with the vendor. Provide a section in the policy titled "Special Contracts and Supplier Relationships" that details steps to get a vendor to agree to as much as possible of the TPRM due diligence process. Whatever cannot be negotiated is then accomplished as an exception process for risk acceptance. These instances must be RA approvals done by senior staff reporting to the Board or other oversight roles, and should be well-documented to ensure it does not happen too often.

A Note on Phishing

Phishing is a counterfeit email that attempts to steal sensitive information, and is considered a social engineering technique used for deception. The email claims to be from a trusted party and asks a user to click on a link, which covertly injects malware or provides the user's logon credentials to the attacker. The word *phishing* is a homophone (i.e., a word that sounds the same as another, in this case *fishing*) combined with the beginning of the word *phreaking*. Phreaking is the slang term given to the activities of experimenting and exploiting weaknesses in the telecommunications equipment and systems.

Phishing is on the rise. These attacks comprise 32 percent of all data breaches according to a Verizon 2019 Data Breach Investigations Report. The rise in recent years has been on *spear phishing*. Spear phishing targets users with elevated privileges, such as executives or senior administrators/owners of data. *Whaling* is also another similar term that applies directly to a phishing attack aimed at senior executives and high-profile targets. The techniques used in phishing can be broken down into four categories.

Link alteration is the most common form of this social engineering attack. An untrained user looking at a uniform resource locator (URL) such as www.myinsurance.sample.com might assume they are going to "myinsurance," but they are in fact going to "sample.com," which is a website the attacker created. The phishing emails that hide the actual URL with displayed text that fools the user with what appears to be a correct destination are clever. However, the code underneath points to the attacker's website. One way to detect link alteration is to hover over the link to view the actual website's destination in the status bar. Still, there are more advanced techniques that allow a hacker to override this in the status bar, and mobile applications do not have a status bar.

Filter evasion, which is the ability to get around email anti-phishing scanners, is generally done by using images rather than text. These images make it more difficult for the software to detect the phishing attempt and allow it through to the end user. Newer email filters have leveraged optical character recognition (OCR) abilities to counter this new trend. Websites that are scanned for phishing attacks use a multimedia object, such as Adobe Flash, to hide the text inside the object to avoid detection.

Website forgery uses JavaScript to hijack the address bar and point the victim to the target website. Cross-site scripting is leveraged in these attacks where the hacker exploits flaws in a legitimate trusted website to direct the user to the hacker's own site for the attack. The user signs in to the site thinking they are logging in to their bank, broker, or service, but in fact the site is collecting their data for exploitation later. Website forgery is very hard to detect and often the user is not aware that they have been tricked.

Covert redirect is similar to link alteration, but the difference is that a real website is used with a malicious login popup that disguises the attack. For example, a victim receives a phishing email with a link that appears to be for Twitter. The user clicks the link and a popup box requests the victim to authorize the application. Once authorized, the application then sends a token to the attacker and the victim's data is exposed. If not authorized, the attacker can try to redirect the user to a malicious website to further compromise their data.

Phishing emails are one of the biggest security risks for most organizations, and thus need to be part of a company's ongoing due diligence. While 90 percent of phishing emails are caught by email scanning software, the sophisticated nature of the ones that make it through are enough to expose a company to malware. It only takes one user to expose an enterprise to the ransomware or other phishing attacks. On average, 1.5 million phishing websites are created each month. The average spear phishing attack results in the loss of $1.6 million, and 95 percent of all attacks on enterprises are caused by successful spear phishing campaigns. The statistics are terrible, and while there is software that filters for phishing emails, the best defense is training and education of the user community.

Be sure your vendors are queried about their User Awareness and Training for phishing. This training must be done at least annually and require the users to be tested or validated. The testing should be performed during training but also as part of an anti-phishing campaign. These campaigns involve using software tools to send out fake phishing emails to test the user community for retraining opportunities. It would be better to see the supplier also have a spear phishing awareness campaign that tests executives and other likely candidates. These victims should have special emails crafted and sent to see if they are fooled. Request to see how your company's vendor deals with employees who "fail" these campaigns. Are they required to take additional training? If they continually fail, what are the corrective steps taken to ensure this user does not endanger the enterprise?

Intake and Ongoing Cybersecurity Personnel

The analysts at this level of due diligence can be in the junior or early levels of cybersecurity expertise. KC Enterprises requires their analysts at this level have 2–4 years of cybersecurity experience that demonstrates an ability to find information security risk. Knowledge of topics around encryption, access management, and data privacy are key areas during the interviews. While not necessarily an entry-level position, it can be if the candidate is paired with a more seasoned analyst for a defined time period. Such staff is required to take a certification course commensurate with their skill level within the first year of employment if they are without any certifications at time of hire.

This staff job grade varies at KC from entry-level Cybersecurity Analyst to Senior Cybersecurity Analyst. These roles are ideal for growth into the other due diligence roles in the Cybersecurity Third-Party Risk team or into another more capable role in another information security domain. Often, these assessors will train to become an on-site role, which requires more experience. Certifications should be a goal for these individuals if they do not already possess one in cybersecurity.

Ransomware: A History and Future

Ransomware is malware that encrypts your data and demands a payment (i.e., ransom) to release the data back to you, the victim. This type of attack is on the rise exponentially, with a 350-percent increase in the last several years and 68 percent of them delivered via phishing attacks. It is predicted that a ransomware attack will occur every 11 seconds in 2021. Fifty percent of IT professionals do not believe their company is ready to defend against a ransomware attack. In 2021, this malware is expected to cost $20 billion globally.

The biggest ransomware attack in history was the Wanna-Cry attack, and it is illustrative of some of their root causes, how to reduce their occurrence, and what to engage with vendors on for due diligence around their controls to prevent them from occurring. In May 2017, WannaCry targeted older Microsoft Windows operating systems. It encrypted the data and demanded ransom payments in bitcoin currency. Microsoft released patches to close the vulnerability, but there were more than enough systems left unpatched for the exploit. Many of the systems exploited were end-of-life versions of Windows, such as Windows XP and Windows Server 2003. These systems lacked necessary manufacturer support, and had not had any security patches available since 2014 and 2015, respectively. Windows 7 also had a large attack surface as it was widely used, and many users did not patch it on a regular basis. In fact, much of the data reports that up to 98 percent of the infected computers were Windows 7.

The day after the attack, Microsoft released additional patches for several end-of-life products: Windows XP, Windows 8, and Windows Server 2003. The patches were created in February when a tip was received about the vulnerability in January 2017. Given that these systems were still running and had been lacking any security patches for so long, it meant that many of these systems continued working unpatched for days after the attack. They were already not being managed for patching and continued to be unmanaged in the days that followed, making the spread of WannaCry more extensive.

What followed was a series of cat-and-mouse games by the attackers and defenders. A security researcher found the kill-switch domain hardcoded inside the malware. This kill switch worked as such: If it could not contact the malicious domain used to spread the malware, it would proceed with the encryption of the data. If it could connect, the software would stop the attack. Microsoft created a sinkhole (i.e., a fake address for the website) that stopped the further spread, but it did not fix the already infected systems. Several other back-and-forth volleys occurred between attackers and defenders with new WannaCry variants to get around the sinkholes, and eventually there was a version that avoided the kill-switch domain altogether.

The lessons learned from this type of ransomware attack go directly to how due diligence efforts for vendor risk should focus on some key controls. Because one of the main delivery vehicles for ransomware is phishing emails, the education, training, and testing of anti-phishing campaigns as described previously are a key control. Additional areas can request more information from vendors that can help reduce the risk of ransomware.

Asset Management

Far too many organizations were running end-of-life, end-of-service software. Whether they knew this was the case and ignored the risks or were unaware due to a lack of an asset management process, the results were the same: They were vulnerable to the attack. There are questions on intake and ongoing processes that require vendors to declare their asset management process. These question focus on the process and how they prioritize. However, questions should also focus around end-of-life and end-of-support software and hardware. They can be asked in a general way, such as "Does your organization currently support any hardware or software that is end-of-life and/or end-of-support?" For software or hardware that is of a specific concern, such as an operating system or major component (e.g., web server software, networking hardware) of systems, asking pointed questions about them is advised. Furthermore, you should ask the supplier how they scan and monitor for these types of vulnerable systems that are unable to be patched.

Vulnerability and Patch Management

How an organization updates software and hardware is inquired about along the way during many due diligence activities. As demonstrated in a situation like WannaCry there are still millions of unpatched systems that are vulnerable to this day. They will likely stay like that for a long time, and for that reason it is not enough to take a vendor at their word when they say they perform patch management. Dig deeper into the process. Ask how they prioritize and what their strategy is for patch and vulnerability management. Many organizations deal with hundreds of thousands (or millions) of vulnerability alerts a month, and there are not enough resources or cycles to test and deploy all of them. What is the strategy for which ones are done and those that are postponed?

802.1x or Network Access Control (NAC)

This access control protocol is now essential in mid to large enterprises. NAC acts like a security guard to network access. These products take time to deploy, as the enforcement of the rules for entry into a network can stop normal business operations. They are typically deployed first in a discovery mode, where the administrator software reports all the types of hardware and software connecting to the network. The team can then focus on the types that will have issues connecting due to lack of support for the NAC standard (e.g., network printers, many IoT devices, older VoIP phones, and legacy equipment). Hardware and software that does not support NAC is added to a MAC Authentication Bypass (MAB) list and are managed separately but securely.

Ask your vendor if they have deployed NAC globally in their network or in segments. Are they in discovery or enforcement mode? If in discovery mode, what is the rough number of devices that are not supporting NAC and descriptions of them? If in enforcement, how did they deal with the non-NAC supported devices? Was it MAB or did they disable NAC on the network port? Disabling NAC on the network port is one way to get around the problem, but it means that the port is then unprotected. Should a user plug an infected computer into that port, the whole point of NAC would crumble at that enterprise.

Ransomware is expected to continue to increase in 2021 and beyond. Advanced Persistent Threats (APTs) and cybercriminals have recognized how much money this can make them and are currently untraceable due to ransom being paid in cryptocurrency. Questions about ransomware as well as how to lower its risk of being successful should be the main focus of your vendors in this area.

Inside Look: GE Breach

Between February 3rd and 14th, 2020, GE's 200,000+ employees had their personal information (i.e., passports, birth certificates, marriage certificates, death certificates, direct deposit forms, drivers' licenses, tax withholding forms, medial child support orders, etc.) exposed by Canon, a third party to GE. Canon allowed the leak via unauthorized access to an employee email account. As described by GE, their systems were never directly impacted; however, the effect was the same as if they had been: GE employee-protected information was leaked, and while Canon was responsible, GE took the reputational hit.

The attack and stealing of this data type is a gold mine for cybercriminals. The information attained can be sold on what's referred to as the Dark Web, which consists of essentially online forums and areas where illegally obtained data is for sale.

The phishing attack at Canon was not sophisticated; it was a simple email that was looking for an email login password. This is where questions to your vendor about whether they perform and require employees to undergo Security Awareness and Training is important. Another key question is whether they require MFA as it was not enforced for the breached account used to exfiltrate the GE data.

Another item of note here is that this was not GE's customer data, but the data of its employees that was stolen. Often, the focus is on customer data, but employee data is indeed just as valuable. In fact, former employees sued GE over the data loss, alleging the company failed to adequately safeguard their data. As a result, Canon had to provide coverage for GE employees impacted by the breach with two years of identity protection and credit monitoring.

Conclusion

The frequency of ongoing assessments for all risk categories at KC is annual. The primary reason that *all* risk categories are surveyed is to ensure no material changes to risk are left unidentified. As the levels of risk increase, the scope increases and the questions require physical validation. At the highest risk level, going to the vendor is required to ensure validation. Incorporating a risk-based approach where activity increases as risk increases focuses an organization's resources and time where it is needed most. How a company chooses the thresholds for when an on-site versus a remote assessment is required is driven by their risk appetite. At KC Enterprises, it was chosen using a simple quantitative analysis. They knew how much cyberliability insurance they carried, and at the point their insurance would not cover the losses was when the risk increased enough to warrant more due diligence activity. There are ways to transfer this risk for some higher risk vendors, by requiring they take out additional cyberliability insurance of their own. Be wary of that though: Usually that coverage is not confined to your specific company but for all customers damaged in the breach.

Remote assessments are an important part of ongoing evaluations. They should increase in activity and requirements as the risk to the company increases. However, on-site security assessments are the gold standard for verification when performed properly, and we will delve into that in the next chapter. Regardless of whether the assessment is remote or on-site, when the risk warrants it, you must step away from the checklist approach and have conversations about the security process and controls with your vendor. Conversations entail eye contact and body language that builds both trust and transparency. As mentioned, the time and energy to perform on-site assessments is reserved for vendors with more risk. Because they are often also vendors that are more critical to operations, it makes sense to treat them like partners in some ways. This partnership should extend to security controls and due diligence. Having conversations at the due diligence of intake, during an on-site assessment, and continuous monitoring processes continue to build that partnership.

7

On-site Due Diligence

The act of going to a vendor site and performing due diligence is an investment in time, resources, and money, and is best left for vendors that a company has determined require this level of commitment. KC Enterprises reserves on-site assessments for high-risk vendors and moderate-risk ones that meet a certain risk category. Vendors with data in a Cloud Service Provider (CSP), such as Google, Azure, or AWS, also will get on-site assessment due to the risks surrounding the Shared Responsibility model.

The system of record notes both the risk level and last on-site due diligence visit when required. KC averages 50 vendors in the high-risk category year after year and another 10 in moderate risk who fit the criteria for a trip to the vendor directly. As business operates normally, some third parties are dropped for others or their relationship changes and they drop to a lower risk category.

This due diligence effort intentionally stays away from checklists. The visit to the vendor, where you are physically at their location and having eye contact with them, is an opportunity that a checklist sent via a portal cannot provide. The purpose and training of the senior analysts who perform this verification visit are taught primarily through on-the-job training with leadership emphasis on vendors as partners. (More about job training for this KC role will be discussed later on.)

On-site Security Assessment

There are five phases to the On-site assessment: scheduling, investigation, assessment, reporting, and remediation (if required). Let's begin our discussion with the scheduling phase.

Scheduling Phase

Like it sounds, this phase is where a vendor and the analyst from the Cybersecurity team work together to schedule agreed-upon dates for the visit. The dates and duration of the visit depend on some variables. If the vendor has their own data center or a co-location facility, then some time must be set aside for a physical tour. CSP deployments do not require a physical tour because it's widely known that they (e.g., Google, AWS, Azure) do not give physical tours (unless you have some really good contacts in senior places at them). The visit for KC cybersecurity assessments take a day and a half: One day for the time at the company site, and a half day to tour the data center.

The decision on where to visit the company is mostly left up to the vendor. An overwhelming majority of visits are conducted at the company headquarters. The vendor sets aside a conference room and books the subject-matter experts (SMEs). The visit to the data center or co-location depends on how far from the company location the first-day visit takes place. Again, history at KC indicates these are generally within driving distance of the initial location. If another flight is required, this is also scheduled.

A number of subject domains are part of the On-site Assessment. They require a wide array of SMEs from the vendor, and it's best to allow them to determine the schedule of when they are available to appear. No advance questionnaire is given to the third party, as they dictate the hours and time slots when the SMEs are ready to answer the assessor's questions.

Once the visit is agreed upon and scheduled, the vendor portal reflects the expected dates and times. Process dictates that the staff performing the on-site assessment should send an email no later than two weeks prior providing the full names of those coming from KC and to ensure no changes are needed. The life-cycle of the On-site is illustrated in Figure 7.1.

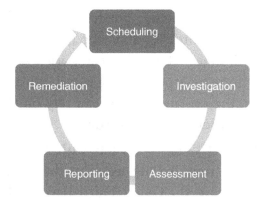

FIGURE 7.1   The On-site Assessment Lifecycle

Investigation Phase

The Investigation Phase is where the analyst performs a series of work in preparation to go on-site. The time spent with the vendor is not to be wasted "learning," or worse, discovering that a potential risk already in any system of record is unknown and should be explored. At KC, the process is defined in a few stages to ensure that all the artifacts are collected and the process is completed. Here are the process stages:

- **Internal Due Diligence:** Because this vendor has already undergone the Intake process, there should be, at minimum, a record of the data collected. Reviewing those records and keeping an eye out for any open findings or Risk Acceptances that are currently still open occurs in this stage.

- **Latest Annual Survey:** Before the on-site assessment can be scheduled, the annual survey must be completed per process at KC. The vendor's responses are required to be analyzed for any triggers for investigation prior to the visit. These items should be documented and reviewed as much as possible prior to ensure that time is spent not hashing out work that could have been completed prior.

- **Continuous Monitoring:** The team that performs this due diligence will monitor vendors who have on-site visits more attentively because their risk categories match all other teams. As this team is performing continuous monitoring on the vendor, the on-site assessor can rely on them for great intel on any potential items to cover.
- **Threat Intel:** KC has contracts with several cyber intelligence firms, traditionally used by the cyber operations teams. In this case, the Cyber Third-Party Risk teams leverage the same data for the vendor intelligence gathering.
- **Systems of Record:** The on-site assessment is performed on an enterprise level for the third party. Oftentimes, a vendor will supply more than one good or service. What services the vendor performs and details about the arrangement (e.g., data types, data amounts, current open issues, open Risk Acceptances [RAs], etc.) are key details to understand to prepare appropriate and contextually relevant questions.

This data is all collected into a standard share drive that ensures that artifacts can be found, and if needed, audited. If there are any items that should be discussed and potentially settled prior to the actual visit, then the analyst has the discretion to perform any due diligence required.

Lastly, the analyst sends an email to the vendor point of contact at least two business weeks prior to the scheduled visit. The email confirms the impending dates, the legal names of those scheduled to visit, and any other information needed or required for the visit. Two weeks is chosen mainly due to any possible need to change flights and hotel reservations without penalty to the company. However, any vendor pushback at this point is generally viewed as having "cold feet" and is met with equal pushback from KC's cybersecurity leadership.

If a vendor communicates at this late stage that it isn't going to complete the on-site audit, at KC Enterprises there is an automatic escalation to the manager for the on-site team. They then engage with the supplier manager about getting the vendor back to their original commitment. If this escalation fails, then a quick email is sent from KC legal (language already agreed to and ready for "insert vendor name") stating something to the effect that "you committed to this, we spent money and time to do this, complete as expected or we'll send you a bill." This always ends the discussion.

Assessment Phase

The Assessment Phase is also known as the Execution Phase. A KC cybersecurity expert shows up at the vendor site at the agreed-upon time. They are expected to look the part by wearing a KC Enterprises polo or button-down shirt or what's considered to be appropriate for the vendor's dress code. All KC personnel are issued name tags with the KC logo, stemming from the drive to have a connection with all customers and the public. The same is expected of the assessors greeting the vendor contacts.

What might not be seen through this personal and direct contact is that their assessment begins as they soon as they drive into the parking lot: Are there appropriate physical barriers that one would expect for the location, such as concrete or solid bollards to protect soft entrances? Is there a large body of water in front of the buildings to act as a physical barrier? How many exits are viewable? Where are the outdoor cameras and do they cover all entrances and exits? Are there gates and fences of adequate height to deter jumpers? Did the security guard or receptionist insist on seeing a government-issued, valid identification card upon entry? Was there an effort to match our identification with our faces? Is the camera coverage in the lobby sufficient? Do they have visitor Wi-Fi and how easy is it get into?

The analyst is trained to be polite, but as they are escorted to any conference room, they are trained to look around and further their assessment: Are desks clean of information and are any workstations unlocked? Are there any maintenance doors propped open "because it's easier for the painters to come in and out," or is a fire door clearly open without the alarm going off? Many employees miss these items at their own workplaces due to "it was always like this" or "no one else said anything" type excuses. This is a flag that security itself is paramount for physical security personnel.

For example, the key role of a receptionist at most front offices is as physical security and is part of an analyst's assessment: As their station is approached, is the receptionist paying attention and ready to greet you? Did they ask to see identification and perform a face comparison? Unfortunately, many folks in this role do not realize how critical to physical security they are. Many social engineering attacks focus on this vulnerable role. Declaring a package delivery or an urgent familial issue are common ways hackers can manipulate an untrained receptionist to allow unauthorized entry.

Once the introductions are completed and the agenda is stated, KC's security assessors are trained to assure the vendor of the purpose of the security assessment via this statement:

> KC Enterprises views its vendors as partners, and this is not designed to be viewed as a "gotcha" game or to embarrass anyone within their company. This assessment is part of our due diligence program with our partners to ensure that our security delivers on our expectations of the customers and our employees.

These *exact* words are part of the training for this team. As they engage with vendors, it is expected that they convey it via their own words. What is also expected is that its spirit is carried through, however they define it to the third party.

Depending on how the vendor has scheduled the SMEs, the domains will be covered in that order. The survey for these assessments is not shared with the third party, largely because this is a conversation. As we review the KC On-site Survey, it focuses on domain levels to start with and relies on the highly experienced and trained KC staff to dive into the details as the discussions evolve. The way it is often described to a vendor upon introductions is in a mock conversation:

KC ANALYST: *"Do you have an access management policy?"*

The point is to start at the top domain level; in this example, it's Access Management. There are some security standards that KC has for access management, but it does not dictate how policy is written at the third parties.

VENDOR SME: *"Yes, let me bring it up on the projector."*

One of the advantages of the on-site assessment is that controlled access documents like policies or artifacts that they would otherwise be reluctant to share can be displayed. This approach allows for a full view of the security posture for the third party, not just individual controls.

KC ANALYST: *"Show me the version control section."*

Looking at the version control serves a couple purposes. Most policy or standard documents require an update period and approvals. Typically, they are required to be reviewed and updated once a year. If the analyst notices there is a gap of more than a year, it can be a sign that the vendors are not paying attention to policy. Not paying attention to policy is a good indicator that they are likely not following policy.

KC ANALYST: *"I notice that it has not been updated per the control statement at least annually. Is there a plan to review and update soon?"*

VENDOR SME: *"Not sure, I will need to check with the document owner and get back to you."*

The analyst notes this and the policy being out-of-date for review in the survey. This might spark another conversation.

KC ANALYST: *"Great, thanks. Please turn to the section on password complexity requirements."*

Now the analyst drills down into specific controls' validation by looking at how they are specified in the vendor's policy or process documents. As the document is flipped electronically on the projector to the password complexity section, the analyst notes the requirements.

KC ANALYST: *"I see that the password complexity rules are at least eight characters, with one uppercase, one lowercase, and a special character. Please show me this in production, either a screenshot of your group policy for the domain, or any other way that would demonstrate that it is enforced."*

VENDOR SME: *"Sure, here is a screenshot, dated yesterday, of our domain group policy showing the complexity rules."*

KC ANALYST: *"Is this the only domain internally used for access management?"*

VENDOR SME: *"No, we've got our cloud deployment in Azure that has a separate domain controller and a one-way trust from internal corporate DC to Azure DC."*

KC ANALYST:	*"We will do more cloud security later in that domain, but do you have available the same type of screenshot for the domain policy in Azure?"*
VENDOR SME:	*"No, that's owned by the cloud security team, when they come in to do the cloud security section they can show you that."*

Again, a note is made to follow up about confirming the group policy in the cloud instance, and the analyst then goes on to other sections in the access management like privileged account management and many others. Each of the domains are conducted in the same fashion: The analyst looks at the top-level policy or standard, then finds the specific security controls for the vendor physically validate then.

On-site Questionnaire

The on-site questionnaire is an important document and due to its size, you can find and download it at `www.wiley.com/go/cybersecurityand3prisk`. Following are summaries of the main sections.

Data Confirmation This section confirms with your vendor the services they provide, the amount and type of data, and if a connection is active, ensures that the data on it is correct. If there are discrepancies, it directs the analyst to talk to the supplier manager to ensure their records are accurate or to reveal if there was a miscommunication that needs clarifying.

The Security Program This is a cybersecurity-focused on-site assessment. For the vendor to be successful at their own cybersecurity, they must have a documented Security Policy and program. The vendor must show a Security Policy document that articulates how information security is run at the vendor. It should provide answers about the following:

Access Control   The questions in this section focus on a couple of key areas within the domain. First, the review is on the top-level policy for access control. In addition, there must be a policy for network access.

Asset Management   If a vendor does not know what assets it has, then it cannot control them. The KC analyst will ask for and get physical validation on a number of key security controls in this domain. Vendors must show the analyst a Configuration Management Database (CMDB) or some repository where asset records are stored and analyzed.

Encryption   The analyst takes a keen eye to the encryption policy to ensure that it matches the level of encryption expected.

Application Security   If the vendor creates software or applications for KC, then this section must be completed. Look at the vendor's secure development policy (if they have one) and find specific security controls in it.

Supplier Management   As has been described in some breach examples, one of the best ways to avoid a fourth-party breach is to ensure that your third parties have a robust vendor risk management program themselves. Review their TPRM policy and test them on how they perform due diligence, how often it occurs, and how deep they go. View some sample documents of their vendor due diligence. Focus on the fourth parties already known to be critical to the service that the vendor delivers to KC Enterprises.

Network and Operations Security   This section can be one of the longer ones to complete and evidence can be challenging. The analyst reviews the high-level policies for network security, logging and monitoring, backups and recovery, vulnerability management, and electronic communications (email). For network security, they must find evidence of network controls, segmentation, and Intrusion Detection/Prevention Systems (IDS/IPS) in use. The logging and monitoring should be managed by Security Information and Event Management (SIEM), and the vendor should be able to show its use.

Human Resources Security   Insider threats are overlooked by many companies. We want to trust our team, but whether it's intentional or accidental, many breaches or security incidents are caused by end users. How a company screens and then educates its employees can answer if they are doing it the right way to lower the risk.

Incident Management   When a breach or security incident occurs, and they do happen far too often, this section can help confirm that the third party has the correct policy and procedures in place.

Evidence presented by the vendor can be sensitive, so merely focus on attaining proof that they are following their process; seeing evidence of an actual security incident may be something their Legal team frowns upon. Rather than create a conflict, KC analysts are taught to look for ways to physically validate without placing the vendor in a situation that violates their own policies.

Data Protection and Compliance   Compliance by vendors can be an important judge of how they are performing information security. Ask if an independent review of the vendor's cybersecurity is done periodically and ask to see the report. Oftentimes, the full report is restricted, so looking at the cover page and enough details to see dates and who performed the review is sufficient.

Disaster Recovery and Business Continuity This is an enterprise security assessment, so while the analyst determines if the vendor has a Disaster Recovery (DR) and Business Continuity (BC) plan for the service(s) offered to KC, there is a need to validate the enterprise, too, by asking questions appropriate to this domain.

Physical and Environmental Security Physical security is often overlooked. As the analyst approached the building and gained access, they were already evaluating some of the physical barriers. Another step is to walk around the building with a vendor escort. Check break rooms and mail rooms for unsecured assets like laptops or hard drives. Find the secure containers for shredding and confirm they are locked. Look for doors propped open or access points that do not make sense for security to be maintained. View the employees' desks or cubes for clean desk policy and unlocked unattended desktops.

The next sections depend on how data is deployed: Is it in a vendor data center, a co-location, or a Cloud Service Provider (CSP)? The sections that do not apply are not graded.

Data Center and Co-location Facilities If the vendor has their own data center or co-location facility, then the following questions and physical security review must be conducted:

- What are the physical controls for entry into the data center?
- Examine perimeter security: How high is the fence around the data center?

- Is there a clear view all around the building or are some views obstructed?
- Where are the cameras located outside the facility and is the building not descriptive of being a data center? (It should not be clear this is where a company stores data.)
- Are there bollards protecting critical entrances?
- Did the security guards check identification properly?

Inside the data center requires more attention to detail by the KC analyst, who must review and note the following:

- Is the data center partitioned and is there sufficient camera coverage to see down every aisle and corner?
- How much reserve fuel does the physical plant have (e.g., heating, ventilation, and air-conditioning [HVAC]; backup power; Uninterruptible Power Supply [UPS provides emergency power]; generators)?
- Does the facility have at least two fuel suppliers in case of a shortage?
- What type of fire suppression system is used and how often is it tested?

Speaking of testing, the vendor must demonstrate through logs that they test the physical plant systems like backup power, generators, and batteries. The analyst must validate if doors are propped open and if the loading dock is segmented from the main data center floor. They also check around the data center's floor for cabinets left unlocked, non-vendor personnel walking unescorted, or if the area is untidy and not maintained properly.

CSP Security We cover more information about how KC secures cloud data deployments later, but for an on-site assessment, the physical review is not conducted. CSPs will not allow tours of their facilities; however, the big three (Google, AWS, and Azure) run top-notch physical security. The focus for the KC analyst in this on-site assessment is the logical security in the cloud.

Access controls into the cloud are a top priority. Is MFA turned on for administrators and can they demonstrate it? Access management should be able to show how accounts are provisioned and deprovisioned, and it should be noted if the developers and administrators have special access into the system.

Data security is critical, so there must be several physical validation steps taken. First, vendors must be able to show that encryption is enforced and at what level. The vendor must demonstrate that the lower levels (i.e., testing and development) do not contain production or sensitive data. They must also be able to note where the encryption keys are stored and how access to them is managed.

If the application the vendor is deploying is internet-facing, an analyst will ask if they run a Web Application Firewall (WAF), who manages it, and where the logs are monitored. Because a cloud deployment is another instance of the vendor's network, analysts look at and validate all the normal security controls in their cloud: IDS/IPS, DLP, a SIEM, and firewalls.

Upon completion of all the survey's domains, the analyst wraps up with a discussion of any outstanding items the vendor needs to produce. Owners are assigned and dates are set for providing any of this follow-up information. The analyst can discuss with the vendor any preliminary findings or gaps. This is part of the partnership with the third party and not a surprise game to set them up for failure. This information provides them with some preparation of what gaps they will be called on to remediate.

Reporting Phase

The next phase, the Reporting Phase, occurs post-visit and is where the analyst takes the data from the on-site assessment and uses it to develop a report on their findings. All the preliminary data collected at the visit is sorted and the gaps are identified according to domain. This report draft is then sent to the vendor to confirm the gaps or to give them an opportunity to correct them. Sometimes, a vendor may not have the physical evidence ready at a visit or simply misunderstood what was being validated. This check with them gives them an opportunity to provide evidence that it is not a gap. They must provide physical proof; it isn't acceptable to just say it is done. It is most often done by uploading the evidence into the vendor's secure portal at KC.

Once the two teams have agreed to the findings, the report is finalized. On the occasion where a third party refuses to agree to the report's contents or drags out the process beyond policy (at KC, responses from vendors are expected within two business weeks), then the original gap or finding stays as reported until they prove otherwise. Gaps are given risk ratings based upon the analyst's analysis of the risk. There is a quality control process that reviews the reports prior to publication, which pushes back in instances where the risk ranking of the finding seems misdiagnosed. This quality control role reviews all reports.

When the QC work is completed and the vendor has agreed to the findings, they must also agree to the remediation steps and timelines.

Remediation Phase

Finding the risks and security gaps is a key activity, but more important is closing the gaps in the Remediation Phase. At KC, the Cybersecurity Third-Party Risk team works with the vendor to establish a timeline for the closure of the risks. There is a standard internally to guide them on schedules. Low-risk items should be remediated within 120 days. Moderate-risk gaps are targeted for closure in 90 days, and high-risk gaps in 30 days or less. However, discretion is left to the analysts.

For example, say one of the findings was that the vendor did not have a PAM deployed. Let's say the analyst rated this as a moderate risk due to the compensating controls of MFA required for privileged accounts. Deploying a PAM solution in 90 days or less would be a challenge for most companies. As it would take time to tune these systems from deployment to full use. Partnering with the vendor to determine a reasonable set of milestones to completion is encouraged. If the vendor says it will take them a year to fully deploy PAM, have them commit to some interim milestones to ensure that they stay on target during that period. If they start to slip on milestones, a conversation can be had with them about priorities and schedules.

Any findings get logged into the system of record with warnings and triggers tied to the vendor in the secure portal. As dates approach for their remediation to be completed, the vendor as well as the cybersecurity staff receive notices. The analyst who is in charge of working with the vendor to close the finding works with them to get the evidence loaded into the secure portal. Again, this is a physical validation of the successful completion of risk closure. If the vendor completed the PAM deployment, then some screenshots showing it in use (possibly blurring any confidential information) would be expected as evidence.

The Remediation Phase is the most important from the due diligence perspective of closing risks. The teams find these security control gaps during the on-site assessment and work with the vendor to agree on the risk rating and timeline to fix it.

In cases of high-risk gaps, interim milestones may be deployed to compensate controls while the final product, service, or process is deployed to close the risk for good.

Virtual On-site Assessments

Restrictions on travel during the pandemic lockdown made it impossible to conduct physical validation at vendor locations. Either the travel was too risky, companies had restrictions on business travel, or vendors had similar restrictions on their ability to accept visitors. These limitations should not stop the practice of physical validation of security controls. Just as businesses, governments, and organizations adapted with collaboration and video-conferencing, so can these due diligence activities adapt.

Recognizing that some of the physical security assessment cannot be done, such as a physical tour of a vendor data center or of their building for clean desk policy, there is the ability to check the logical and other physical controls. A virtual assessment can take some negotiations to establish. Many vendors will share documents and artifacts at the regular in-person on-site assessment because they can control the environment and be confident that there is a low probability of data leakage of sensitive internal documents. Video conference and collaboration tools raise the risk of data leakage because screenshots can be taken and disseminated. One way around this is to have the vendor host the video conferencing and collaboration tools. Obviously, having a Non-Disclosure Agreement (NDA) in place is crucial, and additional language can be added for these virtual events to occur with more assurance to both parties.

There are some benefits to offer to a vendor who wants to perform a virtual assessment. These events can be broken up into a couple of sessions, lasting only two to four hours each. A physical on-site assessment cannot be broken up into smaller chunks, but allowing the vendor to schedule SMEs over a couple days in a virtual assessment can allow for more flexibility, and also avoid the time and energy it takes to host guest personnel from the customer. For virtual assessments done during pandemic lockdown restrictions, it is often the case that the physical tour of facilities still must occur but is scheduled for a future date once travel restrictions are over.

Post-COVID-19 lockdowns and travel restrictions, these virtual assessments still have a place going forward. As a risk-based approach to more in-depth security controls validating the higher the risk, using the virtual on-site assessment model can provide more assurance for vendors who are not high enough risk to perform a physical on-site assessment, but who have a requirement for physical validation of their security controls.

In these cases, the program must clearly articulate the risk criteria for when a physical versus a virtual on-site assessment is called for. The ideal candidates for a virtual assessment could be those who use a CSP such as AWS, Google, or Azure. Because a physical tour of these data centers is not going to happen, a vendor with no open high-risk findings or issues related to physical security is a good candidate. A supplier with their own data center should not have a virtual assessment unless there's a plan to take a physical tour of their data center at some later time as part of the due diligence work. As indicated, vendor data centers can often be problematic on physical security controls.

Another vendor type that is best left for a physical on-site assessment is one that processes any physical records or has access to production data that is in a top data classification tier (i.e., PII, PHI, Legal). A supplier that processes paper documents should have a physical security controls validation for clean desk policy adherence, doorway and entryway security, guest and employee physical security checks, and how document destruction is handled. These controls require a visual inspection to ensure that the vendor is fulfilling the requirements.

In the case where a vendor is processing highly sensitive production data (not on paper, but on the computer), the physical checks are best accomplished in a physical visit to the vendor's location. Often, these can be offshore locations where extra security is required for the service provider. For instance, where production data is processed, employees at this offshore location should not be allowed to have any recording device in this area, such as a smart phone, tablet, or a camera. There must be a physical separation from work being done in a lower environment (i.e., test and development) and the production-level data that includes PII or higher. This type of physical check can be performed via viewing camera recordings when getting to the offshore location proves a challenge; however, these offshore on-site visits should require looking at how the security checks bags for recording devices, how the physical separation is done between test and production areas, and how secure the area is from a physical breach (e.g., a door propped open or without an alarm on it). These checks cannot be seen from security tapes, so require an assessor to examine them firsthand.

On-site Cybersecurity Personnel

On-site cybersecurity personnel are seasoned cybersecurity professionals. Positions for these roles are advertised as requiring operational experience in at least one, preferably two, of the following areas: cloud, cloud security, IT operations, networking, cybersecurity, or similar. Cybersecurity certifications are required for these roles and the required years of experience are listed as five years minimum, but typically hired candidates have 10 years or more. The focus on operational experience is aimed at the analyst noticing what does not seem correct. Having run operations in one or more IT fields gives them the ability to know how they should run.

One additional skill for these individuals is communications. This team is not only very knowledgeable, but they must be able to communicate effectively at many levels. Internally, they often talk to senior leadership about risks at vendors and need to be able to do it in a way that explains the risk to someone not likely to be a cybersecurity expert. Also, the conversations with the vendor's SMEs at the visit are more than just a checklist. As described previously, the on-site security assessment is a conversation designed to build trust and transparency. During interviews for this role, managers always look for clues as to how the candidate effectively discusses difficult and technical subjects.

One last item that management ensures for each candidate before any interview takes place is travel expectations. A physical visit to a vendor's site naturally involves getting in a car or on a plane and staying a night or two. KC Enterprises expects these employees to travel up to 40 percent of their time, and not everyone with this level of technical competence is a road warrior. Taking the time to explain the job's travel commitment is used as a screening question and is an important part of any interview as well.

Due to these requirements for the role, KC places these individuals in a job grade that is the highest level for Individual Contributors (ICs). The roles listed as a Lead Cybersecurity Analyst and peers in this job grade have a Principal Engineer or Architect or Manager title. This level of job grade compensates them for their experience as well as all the travel.

Also because of these requirements, this staff tends to stay in these positions for no more than two or three years. That level of travel, unless tied to a commission bonus as is typical for sales/travel roles, wears on personnel. KC has looked for ways to retain them by finding manager roles when available, principal engineer or architect roles in other domains, or another senior role in the team that takes travel off the plate for a period of time.

On-site Due Diligence and the Intake Process

On-site assessments are built and best conducted for vendors with an existing relationship. However, there can be examples based upon risk where performing one on a third party in the Intake process must occur. KC Enterprises requires this level of due diligence when it is a high-risk vendor with over 1 million customer or restricted records in a CSP or co-location facility. In this case, the TPRM and cyber teams have determined that the most concerning risks are the controls for the cloud deployment.

As discussed previously, a full on-site assessment can take time to schedule and complete due to all its moving parts. In Intake, while speed is not the goal, due diligence as a full on-site assessment will likely impact the ability to close a deal on time. In these cases, the team does a focused physical validation of the cloud controls virtually. At least two, but up to four, one-hour sessions are scheduled with a video conferencing tool to work with cyber and cloud SMEs at the vendor.

These virtual sessions focus on cloud security controls similar to an on-site assessment, but are done over the web conference. Like a virtual on-site assessment, the SMEs for the vendor's cloud security will be made available to answer questions related to their Shared Responsibility Model and how the vendor enforces the controls. It is reasonable to expect a few sessions to take place as some answers elicit more questions, and vendors aren't always ready to answer every question at the first conference.

These assessments should be done by staff with experience and/or certifications in evaluating cloud security. The process must be documented in Intake or even in the IRQ. Vendors who meet the criteria should be identified early to avoid any delays in the process for the cloud security physical validation. The procedure can be adopted from the questions and domain area focused on cloud and logical security. The cloud security SMEs are part of the Intake due diligence effort because all the other relevant third-party risk domain due diligence still must take place. This effort is solely focused on the cloud security controls.

Because these are virtual assessments, analysts cannot perform any in-person physical assessments. For a CSP or co-location provider, this can be an acceptable trade-off. However, if it is a vendor-owned and managed facility, then a virtual assessment will not find any of the physical security gaps that can sometimes be present at one. The team can deal with these in one of three ways: Accept that the risk might exist until a physical on-site assessment can be scheduled, accept an independent assessment of the physical security of the data center for purposes of Intake, or refuse to do virtual assessments altogether.

Vendors Are Partners

Third parties are key to business success. It would be difficult, if not impossible, to name a successful company that did all the work, from nose to tail, without the support of at least one vendor, if not hundreds. As such, the view of KC Cybersecurity and Third-Party Risk is that vendors are partners. They are not something to be driven away or shamed for not meeting standards. This is a partnership to drive revenue for both companies, and working together to strengthen the security is the goal.

Whether it is the Intake, Ongoing, On-site, Continuous Monitoring, or any other interaction with the third party, teams are trained to not view this as an adversarial relationship. Identify cybersecurity risks, explain the risk to the vendor, get an agreement on remediation, and work together to validate when done.

This further develops trust with the third parties that engage with this team and helps with transparency.

Consortiums and Due Diligence

This level of due diligence, along with the remote questionnaires demanded by customers, is reaching a level of concern among some in the industry. One of the ways this is being approached is by some larger business service consumers forming groups to perform these assessments (from intake to on-site assessment) and to provide the data as a service to their owners and subscribers. There is real merit in this, and KC has investigated the use of these services.

Like much of its decisions, the risk-based approach has dictated that, on occasion, KC secures the data from one or more of the consortiums. The primary use for KC Enterprises for consortium data is when in intake, a vendor is flagged requiring an on-site assessment due to heightened risk. If resources are not available internally, then purchasing the consortium's data from their visit is, per policy, an acceptable alternative. KC has decided that the data to use for risk assessment is sufficient to outweigh moving resources from existing or higher priority risk commitments. Vendors who are determined to be low-risk and have a remote assessment completed with a consortium (of which KC is a member), the risk-based policy allows the cybersecurity team to use the consortium report to perform the risk assessment. This allows the focus of resources on high-risk vendors while not ignoring the low-risk ones.

One of the decisions clarified from the onset by KC leadership was that the consortiums were another tool in their TPRM. Even as they saw the benefit in their own customer vendor assessments they were getting (yes, turnabout is fair play), it was not a one-size-fits-all solution. In fact, the Financial Stability Board recently had commented that similar to KC's view, these groups could lead to problems with risks specific to members of the groups. Perhaps as the industry around third-party risk matures long term and there is a more transparent way to transfer risk information, consortiums will work. But for now, the approach at KC has been to use them as part of an information stream.

These consortiums are information or data streams to third-party risk. Consortiums are not there to perform the activity of what that vendor poses for risk to your company. KC and other firms take this data—the responses by the vendors participating in the consortium—and review it for how it views the risk. Another firm getting the same report on the same vendor will likely have a different risk assessment process and outcome. This is data and will not tell any company consuming it how to declare the risk.

Experience has also taught leadership that these consortiums tend to be prone to two conditions: group think (i.e., lots of the same industry and fields) and bloat. KC has gone to great lengths to ensure that all due diligence is based upon the risk the vendor poses to them. This is expressed in how much due diligence each vendor receives and can be clearly seen in how few questions low-risk vendors are asked compared to high-risk ones. However, consortiums treat all vendors the same because they cannot know how each consumer of the data views the risk of the vendor. Not only do the extra questions add to vendor frustration, but it is extra data that internal KC teams have to sift through. This is where it can get tricky legally at KC: If the data is available to them and it is not risk assessed, what happens when something goes wrong that is related to that unevaluated data?

Conclusion

On-site assessments are the gold validation standard of vendor security controls. Just like an internal or external auditor who physically validates transactions or compliance with internal policy, the on-site assessment evaluation provides a level of assurance not available in other ongoing due diligence efforts. The COVID-19 lockdowns did alter the ability to perform them at the vendor locations, but tools are available that can enable up to 90 percent or more of an on-site assessment to be done virtually. Post-pandemic, the use of these virtual assessments can aid in lowering the cost to the vendor and customer, while still performing at a level near what the physical visit to a supplier can provide.

8

Continuous Monitoring

We have described some common due diligence efforts: Intake, Ongoing, and On-site assessments, which are point-in-time due diligence activities. In normal circumstances at KC Enterprises, a high-risk vendor has a physical on-site assessment only once a year, which leaves the rest of the 364 days for something to go wrong. It is not that KC expects a vendor to undo any security controls once an evaluation is completed; the concern is that a lot can happen in those days between the point-in-time appraisals. The development of a Continuous Monitoring (CM) program was a logical next step for finding ways to engage with vendors when risks were observed between normal visits.

What Is Continuous Monitoring?

KC's Cybersecurity team developed this program around the concept that they would be like a team of cyber threat analysts. Their roles contrast with the roles of the other analysts from other parts of the Cyber Third-Party Risk team. Cyber threat analysts are trained to look for cyber risks internally at most companies, and are trained to look externally at vendors for the same risks. This may require an additional set of tools because KC cannot run scans or vulnerability tests against vendors directly. Let's look at the tools used as we discuss how the team performs its actions.

Vendor Security-Rating Tools

Vendor security-rating tools are a relatively new capability, and have not been on the market for a long time. Some of their earliest software makers started as late as 2011. These security-rating tools provide scores and details on how a vendor's attack surface relates to their overall cybersecurity posture. Most are provided as a Software-as-a-Service (SaaS), wherein a web front-end vendor can be added to view their scores. How these systems produce the data varies, but many use sinkholes (silent vacuum cleaners on the internet that sweep up the data coming from the vendor's network) to find information on key security controls like patching cadence, open server ports, botnet detections, spam propagation, and so on.

These tools are useful for one data point for KC's Continuous Monitoring staff. All the vendors that meet the criteria for due diligence (data of the top three data classifications or a connection to the KC network) are loaded into their vendor security-rating software. Within the tool, vendors are sorted according to their risk levels (i.e., high, moderate, and low), and are given an overall score or grade. However, that overall number is not useful for this due diligence effort. Instead, KC has designed a number of triggers and thresholds in the tool to indicate further action is needed.

Open-Server Ports   Open-server ports are TCP and UDP ports that are set to accept packets (network traffic). (TCP is a connection-oriented protocol and UDP is a connection-less protocol. TCP establishes a connection between a sender and receiver before data can be sent. UDP does not establish a connection before sending data.) When these are set to accept traffic it is easy for an attacker to scan and find them open. The vendor server-rating tools describe in detail which ports are left open on the vendor's externally facing servers. Sometimes, these ports are open for valid reasons. A mail server, for example, should have the common mail protocol ports open. However, it should not have an open FTP port. Sometimes, a vendor fails to close all of its unused ports on servers, which can be exploited by hackers. The vendor server-rating tool tells the team if there are any unexpected ports left open that need to be closed or disabled.

Patching Cadence   Patching cadence is how often an organization reviews its systems, applications, and networks for necessary updates that will fix security vulnerabilities. The vendor security-rating tools communicate to KC analysts which vendor external-facing systems require remediation; those systems are the ones most often used by an attacker to perform breaches. If these systems are not patched properly, then an unpatched security flaw may become a point of attack. If the patching cadence rises to a critical level, an alert is raised for that vendor, signifying that attention is needed.

SPAM Propagation   SPAM, or the sending of unsolicited email, is a problem for all organizations. The worst SPAM producers are often hijacked unsecured systems that send out thousands or millions of emails to its victims. If the vendor security-rating tools software detects this type of email spewing from a vendor, it can indicate that a system has been compromised. The likelihood that something else is unsecure is increased due to this alert, as it suggests the vendor is unaware of the SPAM being sent and/or a bot infection.

Botnet Infections   A botnet is a network of hijacked computers used to carry out cybercriminal activities. Hackers use botnets to grow, automate, and speed up their attack capabilities. Malware is used to make a computer a bot, which then carries out data theft, malware deployment, and access disruption. Alerts of botnet infections, much like SPAM propagation, indicate that systems within the vendor's network have been compromised.

File Sharing File sharing is the act of distributing or sharing access to digital media. Torrent is a good file-sharing example. When a vendor security-rating tool indicates file sharing is occurring, it indicate a vendor's internal systems are possibly not well controlled. File-sharing services are sometimes referred to as peer-to-peer (P2P) applications, which share music, movies, and other copyrighted material (e.g., Napster). Nearly every firm blocks these types of activities as they generally violate acceptable use policies. Usually, no justification can be provided for having a file-sharing service running at a business. The following risks make file sharing high-risk for any organization.

Installation of Malware

The installation of malware is highly possible when utilizing these applications. When using a P2P application, downloading software or entertainment files opens a user and their enterprise to malware. Nothing guarantees that the downloading files are free of malicious code, and often hackers use these platforms specifically to distribute malware.

Exposure of Sensitive Information

Exposing sensitive information can be easily done with these P2P products. This software often requires a user to open ports and share directories in order to work. Because there's no way to know who else is accessing those shared files and folders or how many have accessed them, your personal data can be relatively easy for an attacker to expose when you're using a file-sharing application.

Denial of Service

While not common, denial of service can clog the network with unnecessary uploads and downloads from the file share. Because the programs provide no business value or need, they unnecessarily congest normal required business traffic and can impact a business's productivity and availability.

Legal Trouble

Legal trouble is also a likely outcome stemming from the use of P2P software. Because much of these applications are used for distributing copyrighted entertainment, pirated software, and pornography, there's a high likelihood that the copyright holder may pursue legal recourse. In addition, pornography distribution is another legal and human resources (HR) issue that can be avoided by stopping the use of the file-sharing software.

Much Easier Attacks

When P2P software is being used by a potential victim, hacker attacks are much easier. As said previously, most attacks require the user to open ports and loosen their restrictions on sharing. Some advanced P2P programs even have the ability to alter firewalls and penetrate them without a user's knowledge.

Exposed Credentials   Exposed credentials are only mentioned here because it's important to note how problematic such alerts can be. As discussed previously, the number of records exposed or compromised credentials are in the billions. There is likely not a person on the Earth who doesn't have an old password and user ID floating around for sale in the internet. So, what should we do with these alerts? Focus on any that can be identified as administrator or privileged accounts. Because it's difficult to remediate, it is a trigger or alert that is very useful to be monitored as a risk.

The alerts and thresholds can vary from each software maker for the vendor security-rating tools. What other companies choose depends on which tool they have selected and how it is used. At KC Enterprises, the team leveraged the tool's application programming interface (API) to tie it to the vendor management system of record so that confirmed alerts go into the vendor's record.

The vendor security-rating tools are just one tool in the Continuous Monitoring toolbox, and they have some challenges. First, most of them drive their intelligence from public records. The most important public record they use is the known IP ranges of the companies monitored. These IP addresses are publicly available in several locations searchable on the internet. However, they are not always accurate. Companies grow and shrink, selling or buying new IP ranges along the way, and they do not always go back and update the public records of these changes. As the alerts come in and a threshold is triggered to engage with the vendor, there is a need to confirm that they own the IP range that contains the alert.

Internal Due Diligence   At KC Enterprises, every vendor that falls into the cybersecurity criteria for the Cyber Third-Party Risk team has had some internal due diligence done. Whether it's only an intake assessment or has been expanded into ongoing and/or on-site assessments, data exists in the system of record on the security of the vendor. If there is a trigger or alert from the vendor security-rating tool, the CM threat analyst reviews several items:

- **What is the vendor's risk level and information?** If a vendor is in the high-risk category, this gives them priority over a low- or moderate-risk vendor for further investigation. Look into the system of record for how much data they process or hold. The high-risk category has a range of data they can have; find out specifically the number of records for a closer quantitative analysis.

- **Are there any open findings or Risk Acceptances (RAs)?** Have any of the due diligence efforts produced the finding of a security gap that has yet to be remediated? Does the third party have an RA that could be related to the alert?
- **What kind of connectivity data does the vendor have?** If the vendor has a connection, are there any risks or findings on that connectivity that combined with the alert raise concerns?

These second steps of internal due diligence data gathering enables the threat analyst to connect any dots between the alert and known risks or security gaps for the vendor. Thresholds are set for when further action is required and when the risk is low enough that no action is needed. As an example, say a vendor is in the low-risk category and an alert is received about exposed credentials on an FTP server. Reviews of due diligence show no open findings or RAs. The threshold here is not met per the process at KC. The exposed credentials are not confirmed to be administrator level, due diligence efforts have not produced any gaps, and it is a low-risk vendor.

Cyber Intelligence Forums   The last step in the CM process before engaging with the vendor is to perform some research on the specified threat. KC has found that going to a third party with specific data on the type of threat and the risk it poses aids communications with the vendor's cybersecurity teams. Approaching the vendor with "your vendor security rating is terrible" is non-specific and does not produce a lot of information for them to remediate it.

The KC's cybersecurity operations team has existing contracts with a number of cybersecurity intelligence forums and companies. These service offerings provide data about how widespread the threat might be, how long has it been around, what risks it poses, and the known threat actors who use it.

As the team gathers detailed information about the threat, this information is combined with information from the previous two steps to provide a fuller picture of the risk to the analyst and eventually to the vendor.

Continuous Monitoring Vendor Engagement Once all three steps have been completed (i.e., the alert from the vendor security software meets the threshold, the due diligence points to potential risks with open findings, and threat intelligence determines that the alerts or threat all rise to the level that the vendor needs to be informed of the risk), different phases of the CM engagement begin. Note, there are four phases in this process: discovery, investigation, reporting, and closure (see Figure 8.1). The best way to demonstrate them here is to perform a mock engagement for KC Enterprises.

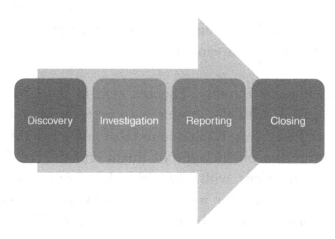

FIGURE 8.1 The Continuous Monitoring Process

The Discovery Phase

In KC's discovery phase, data is collected to discover if the threat (a detected botnet) meets the threshold to engage. However, it has not yet been confirmed as a risk to the vendor because KC has not received confirmation from the vendor; they own that IP range. The analyst puts together an artifact to be shared with the third party through the supplier manager at KC. The vendor is in the high-risk category and has, on average, 100,000 records of protected data (personal identifiable information [PII]). There is an open finding that they allow end users to have administrator control on their corporate laptops. As the team investigates the botnet, they discover that this botnet comes in the form of a browser add-on for Windows machines. Further, this browser add-on is capable of key logging.

The analyst gathers all the data together into a document sent to the vendor through the supplier manager. In this case, this document describes an alert from KC's vendor security software, which detected a botnet coming from an IP address that is tied to the vendor. Upon investigation, the CM team again notes that the botnet has a potential to key log, and it is a browser add-on. Looking at the timeline of the botnet alerts, the team discovers it began in mid-March 2020 when numerous workers were sent to work from home (WFH). The third party is asked if they can confirm that the IP address noted for the botnet infection is tied to their owned range.

From KC's perspective, it appears that because the vendor does not prohibit end users from installing software, and the time the botnet began was when their workforce was sent to WFH, it's likely one or more users have installed this malware.

The Investigation Phase

Once KC's vendor receives the information about the alerts and research collected on the threat, KC's CM team follows up with them based upon the risk. In this instance, because the botnet is a known key-logger and they have a lot of data located at this third party, the CM team follows up daily until an answer is produced or the alert stops. Often, the alerted supplier uses the data to fix the issue without replying, and the CM team simply notes that the alert has stopped subsequent to the vendor's notification. In this example, the alerted vendor replies that they are investigating the data and do own the IP range noted on the alert. Within a day, the vendor returns a response on the secure vendor portal to the supplier manager that they found the infected laptops, quarantined them, and had the end users send them in to be analyzed and subsequently wiped.

The Reporting and Closure Phases

The Reporting Phase is where the threat analyst records the outcome. In cases where a vendor does not acknowledge the alert but it stopped after the vendor was notified, it is reasonable to assume cause and effect. The CM team then updates the vendor's file noting that the risk has been reduced due to the botnet no longer being seen. If the third party confirms that they do not own the IP range, it's noted in the vendor's record that it was a false positive, the reason why is given. In this example, the vendor acknowledged the security issue, took steps to remediate it, and resolved the case.

One more item the CM team must follow up on with on this vendor is the issue of end users having administrative rights on their laptops. Allowing users to install any software is an unnecessary risk that clearly presented itself as an issue with this third party. A discussion on their progress to closing this gap is warranted and is an appropriate part of the engagement.

KC Enterprises decides that point-in-time assessments are valuable, and develops a robust risk-based program for the intake, ongoing, and on-site security evaluations. However, as a cybersecurity incident arose in the early days of the pandemic, it became clear that something needed to be done to monitor and reduce risk between these important activities. CM was found to be so successful that the management team decided to grow the capability with high-risk vendors into a process called Enhanced Continuous Monitoring.

Inside Look: Health Share of Oregon's Breach

The State of Oregon's largest Medicaid organization was victim of a large data breach (over 650,000 PII records) when their third party, GridWorks, had a laptop stolen that contained the data. (GridWorks provided medication transportation to Health Share of Oregon.) The stolen data included names, addresses, phone numbers, Social Security numbers, and birth dates— nearly 650,000 instances of enough data to open millions of fake credit cards and other uses for stolen personal details. To make matters worse, the data was located on a laptop stolen during a break-in and the hard drive was unencrypted.

A key takeaway is always ask third parties if they encrypt the hard drives and memory for mobile devices and laptops. What could have been a small expense to GridWorks snowballed into a major data breach not for the third party, but for the Medicaid company. The loss of nearly three quarters of a million personal data records on a laptop could've been an easily avoidable mistake if the Health Share of Oregon had the proper Continuous Monitoring in place.

Enhanced Continuous Monitoring

Normally, KC Enterprises has around 50 high-risk vendors. In addition, TPRM keeps a list of vendors identified as systemically critical (or known as critical). These critical third parties are defined as such because if one of them were to go offline, KC Enterprises' main operations would cease either instantly or quickly enough that a replacement service or product could not be found in time. This list of systemically critical vendors averages half of the high-risk vendor list of 25 critical vendors. This critical list is a subset of high-risk vendors and all critical vendors that are also high risk, which is considered to be normal and anticipated because they are the large relationships that move the firm day to day and year after year.

The critical vendor list was discussed several times in KC's recent risk committee meetings at the Board level. They posed a question to the Cyber Third-Party Risk leadership if they should perform more due diligence on this list to lower the risk of a breach even further. Reviewing the other due diligence efforts, they found little to do on the intake, ongoing, or on-site assessments except to ask more questions. However, the problem is that these programs are well-developed and still focused on a point in time. With the pandemic, the landscape had changed and a huge increase in cybercrime and activity meant they needed to focus more on the Continuous Monitoring side.

So the team created was called Enhanced Continuous Monitoring, which focused on four key areas of risk (Software Vulnerabilities, 4th Party Risk, Data Location, and Connections) based upon the history of third-party breaches and typical weak security points.

Software Vulnerabilities/Patching Cadence

As seen in some of the breach case studies in the book, the KC team noticed many were caused by vendors not updating software per their own patching and vulnerability management policies. There is a need to understand what software and versions they are operating in order to provide service to the company. While there was an element of KC's Cybersecurity team taking on a vulnerability management program for the vendors, the risk was elevated enough to make it worth the investment. Any vendors that are systemically critical to your company must provide a list of the software used in providing the service to it.

Fourth-Party Risk

Fourth-party risk is real, and KC had observed instances of its competitors and other companies being breached by them. However, there was a problem with the scope of managing fourth parties. At KC Enterprises, there are hundreds of vendors, each with potentially hundreds of their own vendors (i.e., fourth parties to KC) and too much data, and the approach is not risk-based. KC decided the systemically critical risk category was small enough and important enough to also invest in learning what fourth parties these vendors use to provide the service or products to KC.

Third parties listed as systemically critical to operations are required to list all the vendors (i.e., KC's fourth parties) that are needed to provide service to KC. This list is validated at several points in the due diligence cycle. During the Intake process, this list is gathered and validated at the on-site assessment as well as during any Continuous Monitoring engagement. In addition, the Master Services Agreement (MSA) contractual obligations for these vendors requires them to update KC when any material change is made to a fourth party.

Data Location

When it comes to data, it's all about its location, where it travels, and how is it protected. Throughout the due diligence process at KC, the question of data location is asked, and these critical vendors are required to more extensive monitoring around this risk item. For vendors located at CSPs, there is an attempt to leverage the available monitoring APIs provided by them to have them alert KC's third-party risk staff. At a minimum, the vendor must supply a security configuration report on a quarterly basis through its secure portal. If the data is located in a vendor data center or co-location facility, then the vendor is required to have the on-site team perform a data center physical and logical security evaluation annually.

Connectivity Security

Not all critical vendors have network connections to KC, but those that do will have quarterly checks of their software running on the connectivity hardware. In addition, the vendor must turn over the logs for both ends of the connections during each quarterly software version check. This transparency is viewed as critical to ensure that these vendor connections are not being compromised.

The KC Enterprises Board approved and funded the request as some additional resources are required for this additional due diligence. The cybersecurity team hired another four cyber threat analysts to focus on these critical vendors full time. Working with the supplier managers for these 25 critical vendors, they developed and delivered an online questionnaire on the vendor portal.

By having a relationship with your vendor and holding conversations at each due diligence step, your company is able to grow that trust and partnership. A checklist does not build trust, nor does it provide any growth in a business relationship. It is something that must be done, that's all. KC's TPRM leadership, supplier managers, and Cyber Third-Party Risk team creates a slide deck and pitches it to each of these critical vendors. Part of the deck plays to the vendor's ego and how important they are to KC Enterprises' success and how both companies benefit. The other part of the pitch explains how strong the partnership is and also extends into the Cybersecurity and Third-Party Risk space. Lastly, the environment that both companies were now in, each vendor and customer, was a dangerous one from a cybersecurity perspective. It required KC and critical vendors to partner on how they could help each other.

In some cases, KC's vendors wanted a bit more money to cover the additional oversight, and if the request was within a range that did not overstate the risk, it was approved. Given that it was just over two dozen vendors, it only took a few weeks to accomplish. The real work started when the data was collected a month later.

Production Deployment

During the CM production deployment, KC's CM team collects all the data from the critical vendors and places it into a database. The typical vendor management software system of record, unfortunately, did not have the capabilities to store and report on the data in ways that the team had planned. So, they opted to deploy front-end business intelligence software to present the data. This detailed data is now tied to the vendor security software tool, the vendor risk management software, and other data sources as triggers.

Software patching and vulnerability data requires the CM team to find triggers and thresholds for the software reported by the critical vendors. In most cases, the software is common across them (i.e., Microsoft Server, Unix Server, Oracle databases, Apache Web Servers), so they tie significant and zero-day alerts from these software makers directly into the business intelligence engine to match any of the maker and version information. Other less common software was harder to automate, but these were found to be few in number. As the significant or zero-day alerts are announced by the makers, notifications go to a distribution list to take action and investigate.

Fourth-party risk data can be tackled by counting the number of total fourth parties submitted by critical vendors. Recall the question was about what fourth parties the third-party uses to provide services or products to KC. This is expected to be a few dozen for each at most, and with 25 vendors, it ended up being 250. The decision was made to add licenses to the vendor security tool so that these fourth parties could be monitored along with the rest of the vendor pool. The licenses are held in a separate folder in the software and are monitored in the CM program like any other vendor.

Data location trigger data is tied to the cloud solution that the vendor chooses. As described previously, some vendors who used CSPs were courted to collaborate and use APIs for monitoring the security health of the instance. These triggers will be explained in Chapter 10, "Cloud Security," but they enabled both the vendor and KC to alert on specific criteria, such as MFA for root access no longer being required or encryption of the instance being disabled.

In addition, the CM team notes that the data's location is in the cloud (e.g., if it is in AWS, it's noted if it is US-EAST or US-WEST), which allows the team to do two things: First, the team can alert when one or more of the zones or data centers experiences high latency or is offline. Second, the team can look at the *concentration risk*. Concentration risk, in this case, is how many of KC's critical vendors are concentrated (i.e., located) in the same data center(s). If the concentration risk is too high, the team can work with the respective third parties to find ways to dissipate the concentration.

Connectivity security alerts and triggers are tied to significant and zero-day notices from equipment manufacturers of the connectivity hardware. Because KC's CM survey of critical vendors collected the hardware and software versions, this provides an ability to get urgent notices of security patches specific to these hardware and software versions. Also, the team can set up "patch management" triggers in the database so that once the software running on the hardware is of sufficient age, it warrants a patch according to policy.

As the KC Cybersecurity team and TPRM leadership looked to mature their program, they found a need to lower the risk that systemically critical vendors presented to their operations and security. Always looking to take a risk-based approach, they identified four critical risk areas for these third parties to provide more transparency and collaboration on. It took some convincing of certain vendors, but the partnership that the team developed over the preceding years of due diligence finally paid off. It merely had required an investment by the senior leadership and the operational managers to develop the program. However, the additional capabilities on a small but important vendor community allowed the team to lower the risk.

Continuous Monitoring Cybersecurity Personnel

The staffing requirements for this team are very different from the other teams. Here, skilled personnel are focused on hunting. They look at screens and searches to locate potential risks and then, like a good hunter, stalk the prey until it is killed. In this metaphor, the risk is reduced, or the personnel confirms the risk does exist. The teams that typically make up Governance, Risk, and Compliance are fighting off regulators, or audits, and ensuring the rest of the company is following cybersecurity policy and standards. At KC, these work streams are important, but the purpose of the CM team is to find problems, not prevent them.

Typical candidates for this CM team role are cyber threat analysts, networking security experts, or cloud security experts. Years of experience will vary depending on needs of the team, but at least 2–3 years is preferred so the staff can hit the ground running. KC Enterprises has found the most successful CM cyber threat analysts were threat analysts in their previous jobs, as they are trained to seek out and find clues to security breaches or incidents. Managers are looking to hire analysts who have the tenacity to find evidence and are constantly curious.

Third-Party Breaches and the Incident Process

It's never a question of "if" there will be a breach by a third party, but when. Just as you would want to ensure that vendors have a plan to handle security incidents, so, too, must the Cyber Third-Party Risk team have a plan of how to be alerted, and to investigate and close any incident involving a supplier. At KC Enterprises, this activity is handled by the CM team who are trained and focused on continuous engagement, as opposed to the other due diligence teams who are more point-in-time focused. The Third-Party Incident Management (TPIM) process is documented, followed, and validated to ensure that the team does not make a mistake on this important activity.

Third-Party Incident Management

The first step in a TPIM process is to create a playbook detailing the end-to-end process. In most organizations, the cybersecurity team handles internal incident management, and they are owners of the end-to-end process for Incident Management. At KC, the Cyber Third-Party Risk team engages with the Incident Management team to build a separate process for when an incident involves a third party. While the Incident Management team still owns the Incident process, the Cyber Third-Party Risk team manages the process as they investigate and resolve vendor-related incidents.

An incident alert can come into the organization in multiple ways. Regardless of how they do, the process is broken down into four parts: discovery, investigation, reporting, and closing. Similar to the four phases of CM vendor engagement, these four parts of TPIM enable the team to ensure that each part is successfully completed before they move onto the next one. The communication and artifacts involved in each part of the process are all stored in the system of record, while a workflow tool is used to provide smooth hand-offs from the third-party risk team to the Incident Management teams within cybersecurity. A reporting requirement is built into any incident management process, along with escalation points when certain conditions are met.

The Discovery Phase   The Discovery Phase involves how the incident is brought to the company's attention. The Cyber Incident Management Team (CIMT) has a number of threat intelligence and other sources it combs regularly for signs of a potential vendor compromise. Listings of exposed credentials or data for sale on the Dark Web are often the first indicators of an incident. When such things are discovered, the CIMT team performs a cursory search in the vendor management system of record to see if there is a match. If the supplier is listed, then they notify the CM team to go to the Investigation phase.

Another avenue for suspected incidents is the CM team itself. The vendor security tool has the ability to report when a breach has been publicly announced and alerts the team. Just as the CIMT team reviews threat intelligence forums and the Dark Web, the CM team has access to the same tool sets and also looks for keywords that match the vendor list they manage.

The last avenue is notification from the vendors themselves, which always arrives in the form of a letter from their legal representation. The breach's discovery through this official chan-nel doesn't require a lot of Discovery phase work, except to note the source of origin. It can also shorten the Investigation phase as they might have determined the root cause and damage already.

The Investigation Phase   The Investigation phase is designed to confirm the security incident and scope of damage. If the vendor has not self-reported the breach, then the CM team assigns an analyst to the investigation who opens a ticket in the workflow tool for tracking and reporting. All these investigations are the highest priority for the analyst as time is crucial in these events. The analyst has a prescribed list of actions to take and artifacts to use to ensure consistency and accuracy.

First, they contact the supplier relationship manager listed in the system. They are required to receive a response from this manager within four hours of their initial notification. Initial notice can be sent via email, but if they do not respond within two hours, the directive is to call them via their listed cell phone number. If there is no response after four hours, they are expected to escalate their notification to the vendor manager's manager until an acknowledgment is provided. The email describes the information received thus far internally, including potential breach source, and the email requests the vendor's direct contact information to include phone numbers.

While this communication occurs, the analyst queries the systems of record for the vendor's risk data. They pull any existing due diligence reports (i.e., Intake, Ongoing assessments) and view any open findings or RAs for relevancy to the potential incident. If the number of records on a vendor is high or their risk sensitivity level is high, it indicates to the analyst that attention must be given to this issue immediately.

Once the vendor's contact information is acquired, the analyst begins a similar process for response and escalation (if necessary) with the vendor contact. First, they email, then follow up with phone calls as appropriate to obtain responses. Initial contact requires a response within 24 hours. The escalation paths and times are clearly noted in the vendor's documentation: If there is no response within the required time, then the analyst's request is escalated from the vendor's manager to senior contacts at the supplier as required.

The vendor receives a PDF questionnaire containing the following questions to which they are expected to respond.

Vendor Incident Management Questions:

- Does your organization acknowledge the security incident or breach?
- Did you engage your Incident Management process?
- Was there any impact to KC Enterprises' data?
  - If yes, what is the data type and how much was potentially or confirmed as exposed?

- Was there any operational impact to the services provided to KC Enterprises?
- Has the incident's root cause been determined?
- If the root cause has been determined, what corrective actions are being planned or taken? If planned, when will they take effect?

These questions are succinctly designed to obtain the necessary information and not delay the vendor's response. Additional questions can follow in the coming days and weeks, but more urgency is placed on determining if the incident is sufficient enough to require the Reporting phase to be initiated. When a small number of records are exposed (less than 50), it's up to the discretion of executives or regulators if it should be reported. Typically, these are instances when one of KC's processing companies (accidentally) switches recipients on an email or postal letter for billing on a few customers. While not ideal, these incidents are handled with a direct communication with the handful of customers affected.

The Investigation phase is concluded when the team has complete confirmation of a security incident taking place. If a security breach is confirmed by the vendor, then the final step is to ensure that all the information requested is completed on the questionnaire.

The Reporting Phase The Reporting phase involves the required updates being sent to executive leadership and any regulatory supervisory agencies. This phase also includes the legal partners. Reporting to executives, regulatory bodies, and potentially affected customers is best left to the Legal team to ensure that actions do not open the company up to any further risks or issues.

Executive leadership is made aware if the breach or incident confirms a loss of data that regulators and customers must be notified about. Regulatory notification is handled by the Legal team as well, with all communications channeled through them.

Reporting continues until the incident is considered complete from notifications to regulators and executives. The length of the Reporting phase depends on the number of records and amount of damage. For a large event, reporting can last until all the customers are notified and any actions promised to compensate and/or provide additional monitoring services have been delivered.

The Closing Phase   The Closing phase involves updating any system of record with the final information about the incident. In addition, due diligence efforts may be required as a result of the breach. Calls about an on-site assessment should be scheduled as soon as possible for the physical validation of security controls that required remediation due to the incident.

There are potential contractual implications for any vendor who is breached at KC Enterprises. First, all vendor contracts that meet the criteria of having protected data or a connection have language that enables severing of the contract in the event of a breach; severing the contract is not required but gives KC the option to do so if they choose. At the Closing phase, the Cyber Third-Party Risk team, CIMT, business leadership for the areas affected by the breach, and appropriate senior leadership have a process to complete that decides if the contract is terminated or continues. If the decision is to terminate the contract, Legal takes over those steps to offboard them. If the decision is to continue the relationship, then additional due diligence is added for a prescribed time to lower the risk of another incident.

A vendor who has been breached or had a serious security incident is 30-percent more likely to experience another breach or incident within the next year. As a result, KC Enterprises designates any supplier who has been breached or had a serious security incident as "high risk" to ensure they receive the appropriate due diligence for at least two years past the event. These vendors also go into an annual review process dictated by TPRM to review their progress to remediation and overall security control adherence.

Inside Look: Uber's Delayed Data Breach Reporting

In 2016, a cyberattack on Uber netted hackers the personal details of 57 million customers and its 600,000 drivers. This information included full names, email addresses, and phone numbers. It occurred because the company developers published code with their usernames and passwords on the software repository site GitHub. The credentials were privileged accounts and allowed the attackers to access their AWS servers where the data resided.

What made the situation worse was that Uber hid it for over a year before disclosing the incident. The breach occurred in October of 2016, but it was not revealed until November of 2017. Uber paid the hackers a $100,000 ransom to keep them quiet about the breach and to delete the data they had taken. Uber failed to disclose the breach, which violated federal and state disclosure laws.

The act of not disclosing the breach is the most egregious and Uber paid dearly for the mistake. It was fined $1.7 million by the British and Dutch privacy authorities. According to ICO Director of Investigations Steve Eckersley,

> This was not only a serious failure of data security on Uber's part, but a complete disregard for the customers and drivers

whose personal information was stolen. At the time, no steps were taken to inform anyone affected by the breach, or to offer help and support. That left them vulnerable.

Uber should consider itself very lucky that the breach occurred in 2016 before GDPR came into effect, or the fines could have been in the tens or hundreds of millions. GDPR dictates fines of up to 4 percent of global annual revenues or 20 million euros, whichever is more.

Inside Look: Nuance Breach

In December of 2017, Nuance, a Massachusetts-based company that provides speech-recognition software, was hacked by an unauthorized third party that accessed and exposed 45,000 PHI records. Worse, this was following a breach caused by malware NotPetya in June of the same year. The SEC filing for 2017 indicated that the NotPetya attack caused $92 million in damage, and they lost about $68 million in revenues due to service disruptions and refund credits related to the malware. Another $24 million was spent on remediation and restoration efforts. Nearly $200 million in one year is enough to ruin most companies.

The perpetrator was thought to be a former employee who broke into Nuance's systems and exposed the data. It included names, birth dates, medical records, and other sensitive data. The malicious former employee is a fine example of insider threats. Because employees have the knowledge and time, if mischievous, they have the ability to exfiltrate data potentially undetected. Logging and monitoring, access reviews, and ensuring least-privilege are all controls that should be checked to reduce this risk.

Conclusion

Continuous Monitoring is an important ongoing due diligence activity designed to bridge the gap between scheduled point-in-time activities. While it can present some challenges in how to engage a vendor with this process, there is software that can provide alerts, and existing due diligence and cyber intelligence forums that can be leveraged to perform this Continuous Monitoring.

Enhanced Continuous Monitoring builds on the success of CM to target specific high-risk vendors that management targets as needing additional oversight. This process enables CM teams to focus on an expanded set of vulnerabilities within a smaller set of critical third parties, as identified by business and cybersecurity. Insight into fourth parties, software vulnerabilities, data location, and connectivity details helps the CM team laser focus on those key risk control areas that are most concerning. This level of engagement with a vendor requires a partnership, but if they are a critical third party, then that should be a goal itself: a partnership to lower risk mutually.

Third-party breaches are going to occur. A defined process, whether it is owned by a CIMT team or third-party risk team directly, is important to ensure delays in notification and resolution are avoided. Many states and governments require specific notification periods, such as within 48 or 72 hours of the company becoming aware. Failure to report the incident can result in heavy fines. More importantly from a cybersecurity perspective, the sooner the work is done, the more quickly damage can be assessed, customers notified, and steps taken to address the breach.

9

Offboarding

Over a sustained period, nearly every third party will eventually stop being a vendor—requirements change that the third-party cannot perform, the vendor goes out of business, or any of the other countless reasons why a customer-vendor relationship ends. When this happens, it's important to follow the proper steps for offboarding in order to protect your company's assets. The offboarding process is often missed by organizations for a variety of reasons. Systems of record or supplier managers may not notify a company of an impending cancellation of a vendor relationship, or the process might not be defined because many companies are focused more on the Intake and Ongoing steps of the due diligence. However, the steps to offboarding a vendor are equally important to ensure both due diligence of the security controls and due care of any data, assets, and connectivity risks.

Vendor offboarding is a process, from administrative, financial, and other systems of record, during which the vendor's relationship is officially ended with a company. However, their removal from the systems of record is not the goal. The vendor's records should remain inactive/closed in any system for a retention period to comply with any regulatory requirements. The ability to lower risk by following the offboarding process includes cutting off access, destruction of data, and the return of any company-owned assets. There are additional steps for the Legal and Financial teams, but offboarding here focuses on the cybersecurity elements for closure.

Access to Systems, Data, and Facilities

At KC Enterprises, the TPRM process requires vendor managers to notify all appropriate parties about a contract termination no later than 90 days prior to the planned end date. Furthermore, the TPRM team has a workflow tool form that the vendor's supplier manager must fill out to begin this process. This completed form is then forwarded to all the appropriate stakeholders, depending on what the system of record says the vendor needs to complete prior to offboarding (i.e., assess to data, assets, connectivity). Each of these potentially require collaboration with other groups within the company.

Data security is the first concern for most of this process. When a vendor has your company's protected customer or employee data, it is very important to establish that the data will not remain with them once the contract is terminated. The exception to this, however, is for any legal, regulatory, or contractual obligations for retention beyond the life of the contract. These instances are usually the exception, though, and can be handled on a case-by-case basis; the overwhelming majority require the data be returned and/or destroyed.

Data destruction methods vary according to the type of medium used to store the data. Whether it is stored in a database, on a laptop, or in a server-based location, there should be a certificate of destruction (COD) produced by the vendor during offboarding. A COD is a document that includes all the relevant details about the data and describes how it was destroyed. However, not all CODs are created equally, as some are printed and others are digital certificates. Your company should always require a digital certificate because they provide greater assurance than paper.

Printed certificates of destruction carry no legal or financial protections because there is no measurable way to validate that they are accurate. Many data destruction companies provide these certificates as part of their ongoing services when they shred or destroy digital data. However, there's no industry certification for their paper CODs, so nothing legally supports that the data was, in fact, destroyed. In trusting the paper COD certificate when there is no guarantee, your company is running the risk of data leakage later. A paper COD provides zero legal or financial protection for the original data owner.

Digital certificates of destruction, however, are what is required to ensure the destruction of data was actually completed. Digital certificates can only be created when the data destruction software a vendor is using completes the software-wiping process. This data-wiping software automatically tracks and records the destruction process from beginning to end. When the process is complete, the software issues the digital COD. A digital certificate should include, at a minimum, the following:

- ID number
- Customer name
- Type and model of equipment
- Serial number
- RAM
- Hard drive size
- Hard drive model and serial numbers
- Methodology used for disk sanitization
- Number of passes performed
- Number of bad sectors found

Digital CODs are auditable and can be used in a court of law to defend against the accusation that the data was not properly destroyed. When the offboarding process begins, there should be an initial discussion with the vendor and business about the timing of the data destruction. Some lag may need to be included after the contract is terminated and services stopped before the data is wiped. This activity needs to be planned early to allow time for the vendor to locate and schedule their data destruction vendor. However, depending on the circumstances, the actual gathering of the CODs and recording them internally can happen well after the contract is terminated. This lag may require an interim contract to deal with the relationship until the data (or connectivity) is wiped from the vendor.

Connectivity termination is also high on the list of risks that must be closed when a vendor and customer are terminating their relationship. At KC, the process requires that notification is sent both to the Cyber Third-Party Risk team, network operations, and the data center physical security team. These teams are then required to coordinate the connectivity changes. Similar to the data destruction, planning for these terminations needs to start early but may lag a bit beyond the contract termination if there is a business need.

Most connections to companies terminate in a data center or data room, depending on the size of the company and where the need is for the connectivity. KC Enterprises decided a few years back that allowing vendors to gain access to the company data centers for installs, maintenance, and the removal of hardware for connectivity was a risk and resource drain. In addition, they wanted to obtain a faster and bigger pipe to the internet for them and their customers, so they contracted with a co-location facility to perform the demarcation for all connections to KC networks as well as outbound/inbound communications for corporate and the internet. When a vendor needs to remove equipment, they schedule with the co-location facility and the physical security manager for KC's cage at the co-location data center. Also, the vendor and KC Enterprises must ensure any connectivity to

KC's cloud environment and any out-of-band connections are also terminated.

Whether it is in a co-location or your data center or room, the planning for terminating the connectivity starts with a conversation between the business leads and vendor where they discuss what type of connectivity the vendor is using (e.g., leased line, virtual private network [VPN], upload/download via Secure File Transfer Protocol [SFTP], etc.). Each type of connection requires different actions to ensure it is no longer available. A leased line requires coordination with the carrier to terminate it, and while that is usually faster than installation, it can take a few weeks or more depending on their availability.

A VPN tear-down varies based on how it is managed. If the VPN is device-to-device (one-to-one), it can be handled in much the same way as a leased line (by coordinating with the carrier). If the connectivity on the VPN is for individual users to connect using some form of MFA (like a remote access token or app on their phones), the VPN administration must be turned off. Removing the hardware should follow the disabling of all the accounts attached to it. Ensure that the accounts have been disabled (not deleted) in case any forensic work needs to be done in the future (should there be an incident).

Connectivity that is intermittent, such as an SFTP or a shared drive, requires that some important checks are performed to ensure that nothing is left open. A secure FTP connection has accounts that need to be disabled and the FTP location restricted. The recommendation is to leave the location restricted but not deleted for a period after it can be confirmed there's no need for it. After a period of, say, 30–90 days, the location can be deleted, but not the user account(s). User accounts should only be disabled. Online storage, such as a drop-box–type share, requires a couple of steps to completely disable it. First, determine who manages the environment (e.g., the vendor or customer). If a third party manages the location for access management, there must be a physical confirmation of your organization's accounts being disabled and all content destroyed with a digital certificate of destruction.

Physical Access

Many vendors require physical access to a company's data storage locations, including data centers, offices, network closet space, and factories. The physical access revocation involves revoking keys, entry codes, and key cards, and making updates to any physical guard that manages entry. In locations with automated entry systems using pin codes or key cards, the team who controls these systems must be notified of the day and time when the access should be terminated.

Physical keys are rare these days as means to manage entry by a supplier, but if they are used, their revocation requires an extra step for assurance to the customer. Keys can be easily copied, even ones with a marking that says, "Do Not Copy," which is a recommendation, not a physical impediment to copying the key. Because of this, it is recommended to avoid keys as a rule. If their use is unavoidable, then during a termination of contract, it is advisable to have a legal document signed by the appropriate officer of that vendor, stating that they have made no copies. Furthermore, if possible, changing the locks to those keys is also recommended.

Security guards and entry points must also be informed of these changes in a vendor's status as well. While a key card or pin can be deactivated and likely prevent access to the building, updating the personnel who manage entry also prevents a social engineering attack. People like to be helpful, and a malicious actor could take advantage by using the familiarity they have with a security guard to bypass this control. Sending this physical security team a regular update of suppliers who are no longer permitted access is a sound policy to prevent any further attempts at entry.

Return of Equipment

Vendors often have use of customer's equipment to perform their service, which goes back to a sound asset management policy and process at your company to track and identify these assets. The inventory of these assets should include any data, information, and intellectual property to allow for high-risk assets to be located and returned. Smaller items, such as MFA tokens or similar hardware that may not be worth the expense and time to return, can be destroyed via mutual agreement. Again, any of these destroyed items must be accompanied with digital CODs.

Contract Deliverables and Ongoing Security

The time from onboarding to offboarding can be extensive. During that time, it's not uncommon for relationships to change and the scope of engagement to shift. What might have started out as a small interchange of data has ballooned into millions of protected records being sent to a vendor. In cooperation with the vendor's Legal department, review their contract terms for their cybersecurity obligations. Data retention and destruction, termination provisions, and other areas should be reviewed before *any* discussion with the supplier takes place about contract termination. Make any conditions or items requiring completion part of the discussion and checklist for offboarding.

In addition, a discussion with the vendor about the ongoing security that needs to be done post-contract must also occur. Often, there are requirements for them to continue the confidentiality and privacy of any data that remains. Get a commitment from the supplier that they will persist in adhering to the contract provisions on these security controls, even after the relationship has ended.

Update the Vendor Profile

When the relationship ends, the vendor data in any system of record must be updated to reflect that status. Do not delete the record, but update it. Although the contract is over, there must be a way to look up that connection for any future work needed. For example, there could be an alert a year from the contract termination that the vendor has had a breach. Keeping that record of data deletion (via proof through a digital COD in the vendor's record) indicates to the team there's no risk that your customer data was leaked.

It is also possible that a former vendor might become a vendor again in the future. Keeping all their due diligence records, information on security gaps that remained open, how they dispositioned the termination, and other data can inform how to approach them in any potential onboarding process in the future.

Log Retention

When a relationship ends with a vendor, it is important to not end everything. Any logs and monitoring data need to be retained for a period of time that meets policy. Retention should be no less than 90 days, but that time period could depend upon regulatory or legal requirements. In addition, any user accounts should not be deleted, but disabled to allow for re-enablement if required. Although the contractual relationship has ended, there may be reasons for this data to linger. This data includes logs for everything involving the vendor, such as logical logs, physical access logs, and equipment use logs.

For example, the logs and monitoring data might be needed later for an investigation. The investigation could be the result of a suspected breach that occurred during the period that the logs cover. Retaining those logs could provide crucial evidence for any forensic investigations. Secondly, if there ends up being any litigation, then those logs could be key evidence. Keep the logs for a period of time that the cyber incident management team (CIMT) and Legal teams agree is sufficient.

Deleting user accounts is generally not standard practice due to the ways that they are unique. When a user account is created for user "grasner" in a Windows domain, it is given a unique identifier, called a Security Identifier (SID). This SID, generated when the account is created, is a long string of characters. It is not "grasner" that is exclusive, it is the SID. When a user account is deleted, that SID is gone forever. An administrator can create another "grasner" account, but the SID will be different. When an account is deleted, that SID is used to gain access to all the resources the account had when active. Should there be a need to re-enable the account for any reason (e.g., forensics, forgot something in a folder that only they can retrieve, etc.), then deleting the account makes that retrieval impossible.

There should be a policy of disabling accounts using a Windows group policy labeled for disabled accounts. These accounts will stay in that group for the period of time prescribed (again, as determined with the help of stakeholders such as CIMT, Legal, and Windows Domain Administrators). Once the account's threshold for deletion is reached, it is considered "safe" to expunge it.

Inside Look: Morgan Stanley Decommissioning Process Misses

The process for terminating a contract or getting rid of equipment as mentioned previously is important but often overlooked.

In 2016, Morgan Stanley disposed of some old hardware from their data centers. In doing so, they forgot to properly sanitize the data from these systems, which contained Social Security numbers, passport information, and account data. As a result, several class-action lawsuits were filed against Morgan Stanley by customers in federal court.

The court filings claimed the data left on the hardware was sufficient to allow any attacker to use it for creating false identities and committing fraud. While Morgan Stanley maintained that there was no evidence of data leaking from the mismanaged equipment, they clearly failed to live up to their own internal processes and the expectations of their customers on data security and privacy. The lawsuits are seeking over $5 million in damages.

In October 2020, the Office of the Comptroller of the Currency (OCC) fined the bank $60 million for failure to properly dispose of equipment that contained data from its wealth management customers in two of its U.S. data centers. They noted that Morgan Stanley "failed to exercise proper oversight" in decommissioning the hardware, failed to assess or address the risks, had lack of risk assessment and due diligence for third parties, and made an insufficient effort to maintain an inventory of customer data stored on the hardware. Also disappointing was that Morgan Stanley had similar vendor control breakdowns in 2019 for the decommissioning of other hardware, but the OCC let it slide as they had seen sufficient evidence that the bank had taken corrective action.

The need to protect data extends beyond the Intake and Ongoing assessments. When a vendor is let go or hardware or software decommissioned that contains sensitive data, there must be a documented process for staff to ensure that the data is properly sanitized.

Inside Look: Data Sanitization

Data sanitization involves the process of irreversibly destroying data stored on a memory device (e.g., hard drives, flash drives, mobile devices, CDs, tapes, DVDs, etc.), and is an important stage in the data's lifecycle. Using insufficient data removal methods is the most common mistake made by data owners or custodians. Formatting, overwriting, or other tools that do not provide an auditable trail are inadequate, as they are not secure and leave the company open to legal and financial penalties.

Avoid keeping a large inventory of out-of-use equipment for long periods, as it invites the kind of trouble Morgan Stanley found itself in. When a device is placed into storage for disposal, it must be kept under lock to avoid it being used before it can be properly sanitized. A clear chain of custody for this equipment should be maintained, along with a designated owner or role for the sanitization. Records of the digital certificates of destruction must be maintained as long as is required for legal and regulatory obligations.

The NIST SP 800-88 is an ideal framework for ensuring this task is done correctly. This NIST publication is titled "Guidelines for Media Sanitization." The publication defines sanitization as "the general process of removing data from storage media, such that there is reasonable assurance that the data may not be easily retrieved and reconstructed." They list four categories of sanitization: disposal, clearing, purging, and destruction. They are described as follows:

- **Disposal:** The sanitation level is the tossing out of media with no sanitization performed, and is not a recommended option for hardware with protected data.
- **Clearing:** This level of sanitization protects the confidentiality of data from a keyboard attack. It cannot be done with

a deletion of the information, which must be overwritten to ensure that it is not retrievable by keystroke recovery or file recovery utilities.

- **Purging:** This sanitization process protects the data's confidentiality from a laboratory attack, or when an attacker would use resources and knowledge, along with advanced recovery systems, to recover the data. Ways to counter this type of advanced attack on disposed equipment is a firmware Secure Erase command or *degaussing* the media. Degaussing involves using a high-powered magnet to destroy the data on the hard drive or memory device.

- **Destruction:** This is the best and most secure method of sanitization. Physical destruction of the memory hardware with disintegration, incineration, pulverizing, shredding, or melting are all acceptable destruction methods.

The policy at KC Enterprises for which method to use depends on the next intended use for the memory. If the memory with protected data is not going to be used by the company any longer, then it must use the destruction process. If the memory is going to be reused within the company, then clearing or purging are deemed sufficient.

KC provides its internal users and operators with the following list of media types and how to properly clear, purge, and destroy for each.

Floppy disks:
- Clear is accomplished by being overwritten using internally approved software.
- Purge is done via degaussing using an NSA-approved degausser.

- Destruction must take place by incineration or shredding methods.

ATA hard drives:
- Clear is accomplished with internally approved software to overwrite the disk.
- Purge can be accomplished with secure erase, degaussing, or disassemble and degaussing.
- Destruction options are incinerate, shred, pulverize, or disintegrate.

SCSI drives:
- Clear options are to overwrite the data.
- Purge is done by secure erase, degaussing, or disassemble and degaussing.
- Destruction options are incinerate, shred, pulverize, or disintegrate.

Magnetic tapes:
- Clear should be done by overwriting on a system similar to the one that originally recorded the data.
- Purge is best done by an NSA-approved degausser.
- Destruction involves either incineration or shredding.

Optical disks (CD/DVDs):
- There is no Clear or Purge method that is acceptable.
- Destruction is the only acceptable method of sanitization and should be performed by using an optical disk grinder device, incineration, or large shredding machines.

Flash media (USB thumb drives, memory cards, and solid-state drives):
- Overwrite is a possible Clear method for USB and memory cards. For a solid-state drive (SSD), the overwrite method must be validated using multiple overwrites.
- There is no accepted method of Purge for USB and memory sticks, but SSDs can use the secure erase functionality.
- Note that degaussing is not an approved method of destruction for flash media. However, all can be destroyed using incinerate, shred, pulverize, or disintegrate.

Documents (paper):
- Incinerate: Material must be burned in an incinerator that is hot enough to burn all material, and it must be separated to ensure that all documents are incinerated.
- Shredding: Requires 1mm × 5mm cross-cut shred size (or smaller) to ensure it cannot be reassembled.

Verification of the sanitization and disposal of the hardware with sensitive data is an important step at KC Enterprises. There are contracts with some vendors that require an employee be present to validate this destruction. All disposal contractors for the company must be certified by the National Association of Information Destruction (NAID). The vendor must have a valid NAID certification at the time of the destruction.

Records of the sanitization are required. The information in the record must include what hardware was sanitized, when the activity occurred, the amount processed, the methodology used for sanitization, whether there was any verification performed, and the final disposition of the media.

Not all media for data storage can be cleared, purged, or destroyed the same way to ensure sanitization. Providing clear instructions for vendors on the expectations for each type will ensure data leakage from disposed equipment is as low a risk as possible.

The roles and responsibilities for data cleansing involve several stakeholders. The responsible and accountable party is the data owner who must ensure that the data is no longer available for use after sanitization. Consultation takes place with Cybersecurity and/or the Privacy staff on methodology and verification upon completion. Informational roles are often the Legal teams, so that any legal obligations on data destruction are confirmed as fulfilled.

Conclusion

Offboarding a vendor is often a missed process in many companies. Whether this is due to the focus being on the important due diligence efforts for intake and ongoing or due to insufficient systems to alert and take action when a vendor is being terminated, the results are missed risks that can lead to a breach. Always ensure that data is destroyed through a digital COD. A paper COD is not sufficient for either legal recourse or as support that the data is really "gone."

The termination of the contract also entails ensuring access is terminated. Physical and logical access are usually managed by different teams and require confirmation of their closing. Depending on the type of mechanism used for physical access, the activities need to be tracked and completed. The deletion of logs and user accounts should not be done until a prescribed period of time has elapsed; until it is reached, disabling the accounts and storage of logs is best in case of future needs.

Have a process and methodology defined for how data is to be cleared, purged, or destroyed, as different types of media require different methods for ensuring that the process is done correctly. This direction must also match with clear roles and responsibilities for holding data owners accountable and responsible to ensure that data is not left for others to leak when decommissioning equipment.

10

Securing the Cloud

The definition of the *cloud*, for this book, is anything outside the network that's controlled by the company. Using our example, KC Enterprises reviews the cybersecurity risk for their cloud anytime data classification meets the criteria, and the data is not going to be located in a KC data center. Referencing back to the earlier analogy, when your computer (containing your hard drive with sensitive data) is at your own home, it's sufficiently secure in your locked-up home. However, if you need to store it at your neighbor's house, your security risk changes. While you don't think he's going to do something bad, you want to be sure that he stores your computer (with the sensitive data) somewhere out of the normal traffic area in the home, preferably in a locked area of the house.

Why Is the Cloud So Risky?

We view cloud risk the same way we view risk for data that is located outside our company's data centers or networks. KC's security due diligence process demonstrates this risk view, via its developed programs and processes that perform specific security control reviews to lower the risk with cloud deployments.

A vendor's cloud security can be optimized by using frameworks and patterns. Not only does this provide clarity to the vendor on what is expected on the cloud, but it also provides a way for their cloud security reviews to be more transparent. Understanding the Shared Responsibility Model (unlike in internal data centers, where everything is your responsibility, in a cloud deployment, some of the responsibilities are yours, some are the cloud provider's) is key to understanding the security risks posed by each of the different deployment models.

Introduction to NIST Service Models

There are three service models described by the National Institute of Standards and Technology (NIST): Software-as-a-Service (SaaS), Platform-as-a-Service (PaaS), and Infrastructure-as-a-Service (IaaS). SaaS is a complete application that is managed and hosted by the vendor that a user accesses with a browser, mobile application, or an application connecting to the SaaS application. From a customer's perspective, in a SaaS deployment, the product is managed by the Cloud Service Provider (CSP) or vendor. Platform-as-a-Service (PaaS) is an application that abstracts and delivers an application, development environment, storage, processing, or an application programming interface (API) to provide the features of a SaaS, but the customer does not manage the servers, networks, or other infrastructure. A PaaS is different than an IaaS, which provides computing, network, or storage that the customer manages for quick deployment but does not include resources such as the operating system (OS) or applications. A SaaS deployment places much less responsibility on the vendor (i.e., cloud customer) than an IaaS, where the cloud provider has minimal security responsibility.

The Cloud Controls Matrix, by the Cloud Security Alliance (cloudsecurityalliance.org), provides a great framework for not only how to secure your assets in the cloud, but it can be useful as a vendor assessment tool that deploys solutions in the cloud. This matrix can provide the level of controls required according to the deployment type (e.g., SaaS, PaaS, or IaaS).

Author's Note

As a practice, cybersecurity makes no real value judgment on whether the cloud is riskier than an in-house deployment of an application or service. Deploying to the cloud has significant advantages for many businesses, and there are plenty of instances where an application is developed, deployed, and managed internally that is not secure. The issue from a cybersecurity perspective on the cloud is not to place a value of "risky" automatically on a cloud product or service. However, in the context of engaging a third party for a cloud-based service, many companies view this as riskier than engaging an internally deployed product. The fact that management views cloud products as having more risk is linked directly to the company's risk appetite, and it feeds how a Cyber Third-Party Risk team would risk-rate its vendors.

Vendor Cloud Security Reviews

KC continues to look for ways to improve the due diligence and security of the cloud deployments that their vendors use. One well-explored idea came from the Security Architecture world: patterns. A security architecture pattern is a defined, reusable solution. These patterns are used by internal cybersecurity teams to provide conditions and requirements to those deploying into production operations. Experts use their experience with best practices and document them into easy-to-understand formats or patterns. For example, KC uses SAML 2.0 for federated identity management. A security pattern has been developed for how it is implemented securely and repeatedly as new vendor software is added to the enterprise.

Due to the number of vendors and types of implementations, KC decided to review and propose a number of ways a pattern or its equivalent could be leveraged for vendors deploying to cloud. Security Configuration reports are produced by the provider's CSPs, as are existing published cloud security patterns, baselines, and benchmarks. Lastly, the industry has a number of certifications that can be leveraged as a pattern or model that can be used to provide guidance on required controls. We discuss each of those instances next, and some of the ways they can be reused as security standards for a vendor's cloud.

Note, KC's Cyber Third-Party Risk team was tasked with developing a repeatable, easy-to-use guide using several of the most well-known Cloud Service Providers to ensure that their vendors knew the requirements and could easily implement them.

The Shared Responsibility Model

In order to understand and assess the risk with cloud deployments, it is necessary to understand the Shared Responsibility Model. In a traditional data center, all the responsibility for security falls to the company. However, when a company's services or products are located in a CSP, the responsibilities start to become the duty of the Cloud Service Provider.

Defining cloud computing is the first step in understanding the Shared Responsibility model. NIST defines it as follows:

> Cloud computing is a model for enabling ubiquitous, convenient, on-demand network access to a shared pool of configurable computing resources (e.g., networks, servers, storage, applications, and services) that can be rapidly

provisioned and released with minimal management effort or service provider interaction.

The ISO definition is similar to NIST's definition: Cloud computing is a "Paradigm for enabling network access to a scalable and elastic pool of shareable physical or virtual resources with self-service provisioning and administration on-demand." While the simple way it is described for this book, "any data or process that is not in your own data center or location," is still accurate, the more technical definition would be resources, data, and/or processes that are pooled and made available for use by the customer. When the use is complete, the resources, data, and/or processes are then released for use by another customer.

As discussed earlier in the chapter, there are three service models described by NIST: SaaS, PaaS, and IaaS.

ISO includes other definitions like Compute-as-a-Service (CaaS) and Data Storage-as-a-Service (DSaaS), and the lists of types can get muddled. For the vast majority of services required for business, however, NIST breaks them down into the three categories listed. An easy way to illustrate this model is by showing the stack where SaaS is on top of the PaaS, which lies on top of the IaaS. Figure 10.1 shows how the different service models compare.

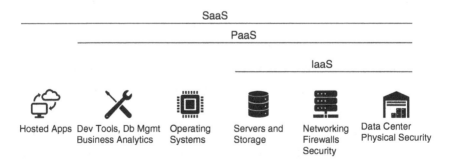

FIGURE 10.1   SaaS, PaaS, and IaaS Stacks

Cloud computing is a shared technology model that allows different organizations to manage and be responsible for different parts of the stack. The result is that the responsibilities typically owned by the customer are shared across all the organizations involved in the cloud deployment, whether it is SaaS, PaaS, or IaaS. This Shared Responsibility Model drives how the service model is managed by the different deployment types.

The SaaS model dictates that the CSP is responsible for nearly the whole stack, including security. The user generally can only manage the application and is not allowed to alter its functionality on the back end. SaaS solutions can enable the customer to manage user-level access, but the cloud provider is the owner for perimeter security, logging, monitoring, auditing, and the security of the application itself. The customer often manages the authorization and entitlements of their users and is responsible for the data located in the cloud.

PaaS dictates that the CSP owns the security of the platform (e.g., operating system) while the consumer is responsible for all services and products that are deployed on the platform. This is where the responsibilities are evenly split between the consumer and cloud provider. For example, if the customer has deployed a Database-as-a-Service, where the platform is the database running on an OS, then they are responsible for the security of the accounts and authentication methods. The cloud provider is then responsible for the security of the platform itself. Figure 10.2 illustrates the differences in the Shared Responsibility Model.

In the IaaS model, the cloud provider is responsible for the security of the underlying substructure, while the customer owns all the security controls placed on top of the infrastructure. This is the far end from the SaaS responsibilities, where most of the ownership lies with the cloud provider; in the IaaS model, nearly all of the responsibilities lie with the customer. The cloud provider monitors the perimeter for security, but the customer owns the virtual network security and all that is included with the network security.

Responsibility	On-prem	IaaS	PaaS	SaaS
Data Classification	●	●	●	●
Client & Endpoint Protections	●	●	●	◐
Identity & Access Management	●	●	◐	◐
Application Controls	●	●	◐	◐
Network Controls	●	◐	○	○
Host Infrastructure	●	◐	○	○
Physical Security	●	○	○	○

● Cloud Customer   ○ Cloud Provider   ◐ Mix of Both

FIGURE 10.2   The Shared Responsibility Model

The most important part of the security in any deployment is having a clear understanding of who is responsible for what actions at all phases of the cloud's deployment. What is provided by the CSP and when in comparison to what the consumer is responsible for and at what point in the deployment are crucial questions that can get muddy when a consumer is your third party providing this service to you as an end customer.

In the Shared Responsibility model, whether you select SaaS, PaaS, or IaaS, the customer is responsible for some key areas:

Data Security: The CSP has no insight or visibility into your data on their platform. Ensure that both you and the vendor retain control of the data, its maintenance, and use. The data's security should be the primary concern regardless of model chosen.

Application Security: Any applications the vendor or you operate on the cloud environment are not the responsibility of the cloud provider. Any malicious code, intrusion, misuse, or maintenance of the application is the responsibility of the customer.

Identity and Access Management: Any Single-Sign-On (SSO), multi-factor authentication (MFA), keys, certificates, password management, and the identity and access management (IAM) process are the responsibility of the customer. The vendor providing the service to you, as the customer, may pass some of this responsibility on to your organization; however, this is not the CSP's responsibility.

Platform, Resource, and Network Configurations: When a vendor leverages a cloud provider in their service or product to you as the end customer, the vendor controls the operating environment. This includes OS security, application hardening, maintaining the OS's patching cadence, and supporting software and security patching. In a serverless resource deployment, the cloud provider's control plane (i.e., the part of a network that controls how data is forwarded) acts as this medium for security and configuration controls.

Some gray areas in the Shared Responsibility Model need further clarification, though, as to where the demarcation happens. These areas revolve around the PaaS and IaaS deployments and how the responsibilities can be altered, depending on the services and terms of services deployed.

Operating systems in an IaaS or PaaS for patch levels fall to the customer to complete. Keeping up with the current vulnerabilities, security patches, and hardening guidance is the responsibility of the vendor providing the service to you as the customer. Be explicit in your questions to the vendor about what type of deployment it is (i.e., SaaS, PaaS, or IaaS) to determine if they are required to do the patching, then ask about their process and proof of adherence. identity and access management is the sole responsibility of the customer (i.e., vendor) in an IaaS cloud deployment because the type of identity management system is up to the customer. It can vary from an OS-level directory, such as Microsoft Active Directory or the Linux LDAP. These are managed by the customer, not the cloud provider.

Applications in a cloud deployment and their security are often the sole responsibility of the customer. In a PaaS, some of this burden may fall to the cloud provider, such as OS-level application permissions. But any application or resource in the cloud above that OS level is managed and owned by the customer. Be sure to inquire how the vendor manages this access and what might fall to you as the end customer for ownership. Network controls above the virtualization layer are the responsibility of the customer. Obtaining a network mapping with the security controls listed from the vendor will indicate any potential weaknesses.

Some areas can be described as always falling under the CSP's responsibility. The virtualization layer, where the physical resources are segmented and the processing, storage, and memory are isolated, is always owned by the CSP. In addition, the CSP also owns and is responsible for the physical hosts/servers host these virtual resource run on along with the networking resources and data center physical security.

The Shared Responsibility model is fundamental to how ownership for security and other controls are split between the CSP and the customer. When taking on a vendor who provides their service and products through a CSP, ask specifically what type of deployment they are using: SaaS, PaaS, or IaaS. Once that is known, then the types of questions to ask about how the vendor secures that environment become clear.

Inside Look: Cloud Controls Matrix by the Cloud Security Alliance

The Cloud Security Alliance (CSA) published the Cloud Controls Matrix (CCM), which provides a framework for cloud computing that can be used to assess vendor cloud security. It comes as a spreadsheet consisting of 16 domains, with each domain separated into 133 control objectives. This tool provides guidance on which controls to use, depending on the Shared Responsibility model. It aligns with the CSA's Security Guidance for Critical Areas of Focus in Cloud Computing version 4.0. In addition, it aligns with and is mapped against the following examples of industry standards, regulations, and control frameworks:

- PCI DSS
- ISO 27001/02/17/18
- ISACA COBIT
- NERC CIP
- NIST SP 800-53

CSA even recommends that the CCM be used to assess a vendor's cloud security controls, depending on if it is an IaaS, PaaS, or SaaS solution. These questions are asked from the control sets in the document and used to grade in a Request for Proposal (RFP), Intake, or Ongoing due diligence assessment. The CSA boasts that over 500 organizations currently use the CCM to perform self-assessments on the STAR registry. According to the CSA STAR website:

> The STAR registry documents the security and privacy controls provided by popular cloud computing offerings. This publicly accessible registry allows cloud customers to assess their security providers in order to make the best procurement decisions.

The domain coverage for CCM is broad but detailed in the spreadsheet, and covers the following:

Application and Interface Security
Audit and Assurance
Business Continuity and Operations Resilience
Change Control and Configuration Management
Data Security and Privacy
Data Center Security
Cryptography, Encryption, and Key Management
Governance, Risk, and Compliance
Human Resources (HR) Security
Identity and Access Management
Infrastructure and Access Management
Infrastructure and Virtualization
Interoperability and Portability
Universal Endpoint Management
Security Incident Management and Cloud Forensics
Supply-Chain Management
Threat and Vulnerability Management
Logging and Monitoring

The relevance of these controls for responsibility vary, depending upon the type of deployment (i.e., SaaS, PaaS, or IaaS). The CCM spreadsheet has columns with each of these types as a header. If the control is applicable to that specific deployment type, then an "X" is placed in the row.

Security Advisor Reports as Patterns

The big three cloud providers—AWS, Azure, and Google—all have online tools that provide guidance on how to provision and maintain best practices for security controls. These products vary in their capabilities, but they all can be leveraged as a pattern if developed properly. As each was reviewed, KC's team looked for ways to document their capabilities and to be able to produce these documents, depending on which CSP was being used. In some cases, it was discussed during the decision-making process about the pattern if they would allow all three of the CSPs or just one or two to be included.

The AWS Trusted Advisor Report (TAR) is one of the oldest of such tools deployed by a CSP, and it has a lot of default options. AWS Basic Support and Developer Support have access to six security checks:

1. S2 Bucket Permissions
2. Security Groups
3. IAM Use
4. MFA on Root Account
5. EBS Public Snapshots
6. RDS Public Snapshots

While this may be basic, it was decided that any vendor doing business with KC must use the AWS Business Support or Enterprise Support that offered access to all 115 TAR checks that include the following:

14 Cost Optimizations

17 Security Checks

24 Fault Tolerance Checks

10 Performance Checks

50 Service Limits

These add up to the 115 items in the TAR report.

The 17 security checks were added to the list for the TAR pattern. For the AWS TAR pattern, the team's guidance was listed as follows, like a vendor would read their own TAR report:

- **Security Groups:** Ensure that there are no rules that enable unrestricted access (0.0.0.0/0) to unused ports. The TAR report breaks down ports by risk where the highest risk is red and ranges down to yellow and green for the lowest risk for commonly used ports. The cloud security pattern requires no red or yellow flags.

- **Identity and Access Management (IAM):** This checks AWS IAM for any red flags. Again, no red or yellow flags are permitted in this pattern.

- **Amazon S3:** These are the Amazon Simple Storage Service (S3) and the system checks that ensure permissions are correct. Any permissions that grant upload or delete permissions are flagged and are not permitted in this pattern.

- **MFA for Root Account:** This is a Boolean checkbox that is either enabled or not. Root in this case is the ultimate privileged account; this flag is required to be enabled or it will not meet the pattern standard.

- **Amazon Relational Database Service (RDS) Security Group Risk:** Amazon's RDS is checked for overly permissive access permissions to the database. The pattern calls for access to be limited to either a specific Elastic Compute Cloud (EC2) or specific IP addresses.

- **AWS Cloudtrail Logging:** Logging is critical for finding and preventing breaches. If there is a breach, it's critical to have a log to determine the level of compromise. The requirement ensures that the CloudTrail has permissions to write to the S3 bucket.

- **Elastic Load Balancer (ELB) Security Groups:** A load balancer is important for web traffic management. This item must not indicate any alerts for a security group, which allows access to ports that are not configured on the load balancer.

- **Exposed Access Keys:** There must be no flags for exposed keys in any code repositories or any irregular use of Amazon EC2, which indicates revealed encryption keys.

- **Amazon Elastic Block Store (EBS) Public Snapshot:** This ensures that no alerts for snapshots are marked as public.

- **Amazon RDS Public Snapshot:** This is the same as above—none of the RDSs can be marked viewable by the public.

- **AWS Identity & Access Management (IAM) Password Policy:** The password policy and password content requirements increase the security by enforcing stronger passwords. There must be no warnings on this item.

- **AWS IAM Access Key Rotation:** Rotation of the keys must occur every 90 days to lower the risk of compromised keys.

The specific items in the Security section (in the AWS TAR) are listed as how a vendor can design their cloud security in a repeatable fashion. As you decide what the security settings are that you want a vendor to adhere to, then this can be provided as a set of pre-approved security controls to a vendor. If a new cloud vendor is going through an Intake assessment that uses AWS, then these security controls are output on the TAR reports that are given to them.

Azure Advisor is the security tool used to determine if any gaps need to be addressed. As with the AWS TAR, the intent here is to provide third parties going to or already in Azure a pattern to repeat for KC. Within the Advisor product, Microsoft has a Security tab that integrates with its Azure Security Center. The security items in the Azure pattern can be found in the Security Center's menu option titled "Recommendations." None of the following can have a high severity alert against them in the tool:

Remediate vulnerabilities.

Enable encryption at rest.

Remediate security configurations.

Apply system updates.

Protect against DDoS attacks.

Secure management ports.

Apply adaptive application control.

Encrypt data in transit.

Manage access and permissions.

Restrict unauthorized network access.

Enable endpoint protection.

Enable auditing and logging.

Apply data classification.

Enable Azure Defender.

Implement security best practices.

Enable MFA.

As the vendor reviews each of these items, the tool provides remediation steps. It also has a View Remediation Logic option to view the logic impacts of the change prior to application. These remediation steps are explicit enough for action to be taken in instances where there are high-severity alerts.

Google Cloud's offering for how to view security controls is Security Command Center. Google's offering is similar to AWS in that there are free and premium tiers. Given that the KC team does not view security as something to go cheap on, their vendors are required to replicate the pattern at Premium-tier features. The Security Command Center report must be clear of any high findings in order to be considered for pattern approval. The list of standard (free) scan outputs for review are:

MFA_NOT_ENFORCED: Indicates users are not using MFA verification.

NON_ORG_IAM_MEMBER: A user outside of your organization has IAM permissions on a project or organization.

OPEN_FIREWALL: Indicates the firewall is left open and not denying traffic.

OPEN_RDP_PORT: Indicates the Remote Desktop Protocol is open.

OPEN_SSH_PORT: Indicates the Secure Shell Protocol is open.

OPEN_TELNET_PORT: Indicates the Telnet protocol port is left open.

PUBLIC_BUCKET_ACL: Indicates a public Cloud Storage bucket is publicly accessible.

PUBLIC_COMPUTE_IMAGE: Indicates a Compute Engine instance is publicly accessible.

PUBLIC_IP_ADDRESS: Indicates there is a public internet address and not using a private subnet.

PUBLIC_LOG_BUCKET: Storage buckets used as log sinks are publicly open.

PUBLIC_SQL_INSTANCE: A database is open to the public.

SSL_NOT_ENFORCED: Secure Sockets Layer (SSL), which establishes authenticated and encrypted links between browser and destination, is not enforced.

WEB_UI_ENABLED: A highly privileged Kubernetes Service Account backs the Kubernetes web interface. If compromised, the service account can be abused.

Premium-tier features monitor the vendor's cloud logging and consumes logs to detect these threats:

Malware

Cryptomining

Brute-force SSH

Outgoing DoS

IAM anomalous grant

Data exfiltration

Cross-site scripting (XSS)

Flash injection

Mixed-content

Clear text passwords

Usage of insecure JavaScript libraries

All these CSPs provide security monitoring that can be leveraged as a pattern to guide vendors on cloud deployments. The KC team keeps this documentation at the ready and uses it to guide best practices whether it's during Intake, Ongoing, or other due diligence assessments.

Increased Oversight of Cloud and Cybersecurity Risks by Regulators and Governments

As governments and organizations increase their cloud footprint and the number of breaches has grown, regulators and governmental interest and oversight is increasing. There are currently almost 80 congressional committees and subcommittees who claim jurisdiction over some part of the U.S. cybersecurity policy. The agendas for these committees and subcommittees is as varied as their number, covering privacy rights, defense technology security, IoT security, cloud computing, and more.

In March of 2020, the U.S. Cyberspace Solarium Commission published its findings and recommendations for how to best secure against attacks in the coming years. It prescribes working with our allies and partners to promote responsible behavior on the internet. It includes denying access to adversaries who have long exploited the cyberspace for criminal or political ends, along with imposing costs for those who exploit it for malicious purposes. In June of 2019, the Federal Cloud Computing Strategy report was released by U.S. Federal CIO, Suzette Kent. This report details the modernization and maturity of how cloud computing is approached by the federal government. There is a broad discussion and recommendations are given on security, procurement practices, and the workforce challenges for securing the cloud.

In April of 2020, the Office of the Comptroller of the Currency (OCC) and the Federal Financial Institutions Examination Council (FFIEC) issued a joint statement titled "Security in a Cloud Computing Environment." This summary lists the primary concerns:

Security breaches involving cloud computing services highlight the importance of bank2 management's understanding of the shared responsibilities between Cloud Service Providers and bank clients. Consistent with the joint statement, the OCC expects banks to engage in effective risk management for safe and sound cloud computing.

While the joint statement did not contain new regulatory guidance or expectations, it can be expected if the two bodies do not see sufficient traction on their guidance or risk concerns.

The statement emphasized the importance of management understanding the division of responsibilities (i.e., the Shared Responsibility model), which if not understood or implemented correctly can result in security breaches or incidents. Highlights of the statement center around the risk management and due diligence for controls to ensure the safe use of cloud computing services. The document also shares a list of government and industry resources to assist financial institutions on their security in cloud deployments.

Governmental and regulatory interest and oversight in cloud computing is likely to increase in coming years, expanding beyond finance and other highly regulated industries. The compliance offices of most large companies and even smaller ones need to pay attention to the directives to ensure that nothing is missed.

Cloud Security Baselines, Benchmarks, Frameworks, and Certifications as Patterns for Third Parties There are probably hundreds of frameworks, benchmarks, and certifications for cloud security. The goal for KC Enterprises is to offer the ones most commonly used by their third parties and aligned with

KC's risk appetite, but we list a few others here to demonstrate the possibilities and provide them as patterns for cloud vendors.

ISO 27017 is a CSP security standard designed to make cloud computing more secure. This standard provides guidelines, security control recommendations, how and who implements controls, and how CSPs can support the implementations. All of the big three (and more) adhere to this standard, which provides guidance on a number of key areas: the Shared Responsibility model, removal and return of assets, protection and segmentation of the customer virtual environment, virtual machine configurations, administrative procedures, monitoring, and virtual and cloud networking. Pointing the vendor to the 27017 standard offered by one of the CSPs gives them a template or pattern to follow for lower risk.

The National Institute of Science and Technology (NIST) provides several benchmarks for use. For AWS, Azure, and Google, the Center for Internet Security (CIS) has uploaded frameworks for use. Go to the NIST National Vulnerability Database (nvd.nist.gov). At this location (nvd.nist.gov/ncp/repository) you'll find a National Checklist Program Repository. All three (and many others) are listed here. The CIS Amazon Web Services Foundations Benchmark gives the user specific guidance on configuring security for AWS IAM, CloudTrail, AWS S3, and AWS Virtual Private Container (VPC). The CIS Google Cloud Platform Foundation Benchmark provides a security configuration for designing and deploying on Google Cloud. Azure Security Benchmark is based upon the CIS framework and guides users to security and compliance controls for these deployments.

The Federal Risk and Authorization Management Program (FedRAMP) provides a standard for cloud security. It was designed to promote the adoption of secure cloud services across the U.S. government by providing a standardized approach to security and risk assessments. There are three pillars to this program. Federal agencies are the requestors for these services, FedRAMP has CSPs that are authorized to offer cloud services to government agencies, and third-party assessment organizations perform initial and periodic assessments to ensure they meet FedRAMP requirements. Within the FedRAMP website is a security controls baseline based upon the high, moderate, and low risks.

KC Enterprises determined that if a vendor could meet FedRAMP moderate risk, then that was the level of risk reduction required for their business. The moderate category covers many of the cloud controls discussed earlier and comes in a spreadsheet that can be easily shared with vendors and internal stakeholders. While ideally the vendor would be FedRAMP certified, the vendor could use this as a pattern and then provide physical validation of implementation (during both Intake and Ongoing assessment monitoring).

While KC Enterprises did not have any business that directly performed medical services, nurse's offices were located at several of its production plants and the two large offices. These provided a number of services and were contracted through a third party. In addition, other vendors had access to medical records of the employees. In order to provide a pattern for these, KC decided on Health Information Trust (HITRUST) Alliance, which published a Common Security Framework (CSF). This organization allowed for a certifiable framework to ensure that healthcare providers and organizations demonstrate security and compliance. The HITRUST-CSF has 19 domains ranging from endpoint protection to mobile device security. The three CSPs that were supported all had HITRUST-CSF deployments available and provided a consistent method for due diligence by Cyber Third-Party Risk.

The Cloud Security Alliance (CSA), of which KC Enterprises is a member, published a Cloud Controls Matrix (CCM). This CCM provides an ideal pattern or guide for vendors to follow. The CCM is a framework of the security controls for the cloud mapped to standards, best practices, and regulation. This mapping is ideal for structure and clarity on what is driving the requirement. The CSA also offers a verification program called CSA Security Trust and Assurance Risk (STAR). STAR provides CSPs the ability to validate to their customers that their cloud security offerings are secure. It also allows cloud customers—in this case, vendors who offer cloud solutions to KC—to be certified that they are following this guidance. While the preference is to have vendors who are STAR certified with an approved STAR assessment firm, the STAR CCM provides the guidance needed for a third party to use it as a pattern.

Lastly, all of the major CSPs offer security baselines to all their customers. On Azure, there are baselines on everything from API Management Security Baseline to VPN Gateway Security Baseline. AWS has similar guidelines as well as Google Cloud. The focus has been on the three options that cover the CSPs KC has decided to support. In fact, this focus was part of a decision to form a "pattern" or standard: Vendors wanted to do business with the company which involved taking sensitive data to the cloud, and only the big three were supported as options. However, the firm went to great lengths to offer ways to meet standards and perform due diligence.

This pattern approach, mimicked from the Security Architecture space, provides a number of advantages in almost every step of the process of being a vendor. During Intake, the patterns and only supporting three common CSPs (AWS, Azure, and Google) make it possible to assess risk quicker and more transparently. The Ongoing due diligence benefits because you are able to ask a standard set of questions with expected answers to avoid having to analyze a larger set of potential alternatives. The on-site process enables the assessor to obtain much of the data by requesting data about their patterns through the Cloud Security Report from the CSP through the vendor. Similarly, the Continuous Monitoring team is able to request a CSR from a vendor in order to confirm IP ranges and potential risks related to any alerts they are chasing.

Vendors and internal customers/stakeholders benefit because of how efficient using a pattern makes the cybersecurity due diligence process. Internal stakeholders who request new services that require sensitive data have clear options and the requirements are more transparent. As a vendor goes through either an RFP or Intake Risk Questionnaire (IRQ), they have the ability to screen that they only used one of the approved CSPs. Once through that process and Intake begins, the Cybersecurity due diligence team can provide the vendor with a few options to conform to KC vendor cloud security standards via the chosen patterns, enabling quicker discussions between the vendor and customer's Cybersecurity teams.

The third party also realized benefits any time the subsequent due diligence efforts were required. During the Ongoing assessment, if the vendor stuck to the pattern, then the act of revalidation each year on the secure vendor portal was a known straightforward activity. Benefits included increasing transparency, speed to complete due diligence processes, and a repeatable scalable solution, but the team still was concerned about high-risk vendors and how their cloud deployments presented risk at levels that this effort did not cover fully. There needed to be a more real-time, physical validation for cloud security controls at this heightened security risk level.

A CSP's APIs   The top CSPs offer programmatic ways, via an API, to monitor in near real-time the health of a customer's instance. Originally, these tools were designed to allow direct customers (not a service to another customer) to connect their internal monitoring software to the data in a CSP. These APIs can be leveraged by a vendor to give the customer the same view into the health of the specific instances used.

Amazon's API Gateway enables developers to create and deploy the Representational State Transfer (or REST, which is far easier to say and type) and WebSocket APIs on AWS. From these APIs, a developer can create a number of automated monitoring alerts that can either automatically take action or require manual intervention. Given that the customer, KC Enterprises, is not the direct customer of AWS, the alerting would be for manual intervention unless otherwise agreed to and contractual changes were made if required.

Amazon CloudWatch Alarms, Logs, and Events are all accessible via this API. These can monitor almost everything on the instance, so there is a need to narrow to the most critical security controls. MFA for Root Access is a top alert as well as any encryption state change alerts. The idea isn't to monitor logs at a level that would be performing cyber operations threat hunting, but to have a key few items let the KC cyber team know that something needs to be investigated.

Microsoft Azure Defender (this name changed during the writing of this book and this will happen as vendors change names of offerings over time) allows for continual export of data. Azure allows for a direct export from the Security Center, using a REST API or using Azure Policy. The last one, Azure Policy, is designed to export huge amounts of log data and does not fit most scenarios for use. The automated export from Azure allows the selection of what data types will have alerts being sent; again, the scope for these use cases is for critical security control alerts: MFA for privileged accounts, encryption state changes, and vulnerability assessments of any databases.

The REST API approach is the preferred method because it is a common language between the two teams: vendor and customer. Security alerts and recommendations in Azure are stored in *SecurityAlert* and *SecurityRecommendations* tables in the logs. Also, there is a *SecurityBaseline* table, too, if the team wants to do a comparison of the KC Azure baseline for vendors to see what is actually in production logs.

This ability to see and even take action if a setting is changed gets vendor cloud security to where KC Enterprises would ultimately prefer to see any vendor who uses a CSP. Getting 100-percent adoption of this is not the goal but an aspiration. KC's decision was made by the risk team, focusing on the critical vendors first to find partners willing to collaborate. There had to be an incentive for the third party to want to participate, and the team knew that this would be viewed as a little concerning by many of their suppliers.

The first vendor approached with the initial pitch was offered, if they participated, then other due diligence efforts would be reduced on the cloud security controls. This required some high-level discussions to determine specifically how much due diligence would be reduced but also to get more clarity for the vendor on what security events would be alerted. At KC Enterprises, the team was able to get nearly all of the critical vendors into the program after working with them each individually to find what incentive worked best to encourage them to participate in the API program.

All the CSP APIs, like any API, can be pointed at any data source internally, and the team used this data in their reporting and predictive modeling. Each of the security controls the APIs were polling fed back into the database and business intelligence reporting to provide a single review. The data was also included in any emergency paging system for the team: Because these are critical vendors, any of these monitored security controls (MFA and Encryption) were serious enough to warrant immediate action.

Inside Look: The Capital One Breach

On July 29th, 2019, a former Amazon cloud employee was arrested on charges of stealing more than 100 million applications for credit from AWS customer Capital One (known as CapOne). CapOne had swung hard to the cloud in recent years, transferring much of its technology workload to AWS. The breach was accomplished via a misconfigured Web Application Firewall (WAF) that CapOne used for hosting on AWS. The WAF was designed to work on an Apache Web Server to protect against known classes of vulnerabilities.

The class of vulnerability that was exploited is called a Server Side Request Forgery (SSRF), and is where the system is tricked into running commands and services that it should not be able to run. SSRF attacks are hard to detect, and the detection rules are not part of the default configuration of the WAF. It isn't a common exploit because knowing how to do it takes a good deal of inside knowledge on AWS and the technology stack.

AWS took a different view of the cause of the breach, placing much of the blame on how CapOne misconfigured the WAF. This goes back to the Shared Responsibility model, and what was CapOne's responsibility for the security and how much rested on AWS. The public came to know it as the CapOne breach, but to the business community cybersecurity and cloud teams, it pointed to some flaws in the Shared Responsibility model. AWS offered some additional security features that could have lowered the risk, but had they done a better job at preventing a rogue employee, it is unlikely the event would have occurred.

The situation may also have been avoided with a periodic or automated review of the cloud configuration as part of the process to ensure ongoing cloud governance.

Conclusion

While cloud due diligence is part of the overall cybersecurity process, having a more expansive and deeper program on cloud security is warranted because of the risks associated with the Shared Responsibility model. Borrowing from another cybersecurity discipline, Security Architecture, the use of patterns produces repeatable and clear guidelines for vendors going to or using the cloud. In addition, there are a number of ways to perform this task: Cloud security reports, frameworks, certifications, baselines, and benchmarks are all opportunities to provide guidance both internally and externally on cloud security control requirements.

The CSA's CCM is an excellent tool for assessing a vendor's cloud security controls and it maps to most frameworks. It comes in a lot of languages and is also localized for the regulatory mappings.

Cybersecurity
and Legal Protections

Cybersecurity third-party risk is not confined to due diligence efforts and security evaluations. One of the key components of lowering cybersecurity risk as a company is to use contract language that addresses this risk. This is not to say that cybersecurity professionals need to be attorneys as well to their respective firms; rather a cybersecurity team must be prescriptive to the legal team about what security controls need to be met by vendors prior to contract signatures and execution. Cybersecurity begins with defining the security standards for third parties—the criteria for when cybersecurity language is appropriate. Then, those definitions are taken further by defining criteria of when cybersecurity is engaged for legal terms and conditions; there must be a clear definition of how the process is completed, and the process defined for when there is a Risk Acceptance (RA) for any item(s) that presents a risk to the organization.

Legal Terms and Protections

Starting with a Security Standard or Policy, the cybersecurity team lays out exactly what a vendor is required to meet. While the actions surrounding this have been covered in previous chapters, this chapter discusses the legal terms and protections that cover the domains of access management, encryption, vulnerability management, patching cadence, right to perform audits/assessments, privacy, data center security, and so on. As the standards are written, they are linked to the terms and conditions (T&Cs) that should be present in contracts where the criteria to require them is present.

These criteria are the same as the triggers for when a vendor requires due diligence from cybersecurity: A vendor has sensitive data or a connection to your company's network. The criteria can be risk-based, meaning the number of controls and ability to grant RAs is based upon the risk the vendor presents. For example, if your vendor is considered low risk, your company could take the approach of having "thin" T&Cs that focus only on critical controls such as encryption, right to audit, access management, and breach notifications. A high-risk supplier would be required to have a full T&Cs document of security controls, and few, if any, avenues for Risk Acceptance.

At KC Enterprises, there is a different Master Services Agreement (MSA) for vendors who meet the criteria of the top three data classifications or a connection to the network. As a vendor is going through an Intake Risk Questionnaire (IRQ), if they trigger security, then they almost instantly get a copy of the MSA. KC's Cybersecurity team has learned from experience that legal negotiations can take ages if the parties involved have opposing views. The sourcing manager who is managing them through the process insists on two things up front from the vendor: 1) That they assign an attorney within two weeks or less of starting negotiations, and 2) that they find the appropriate subject-matter experts (SMEs) in the third-party's cybersecurity within the same time frame. Once KC receives the contacts, a meeting is scheduled to introduce and review the cybersecurity terms and conditions at a high level. It is not a long meeting, but designed to let vendors know it's considered the standard document for doing business with KC per policy. Also, it allows for some discussion of why certain areas are really important and non-negotiable (if the IRQ process did not pick this up and flag it already). Whether a follow-up is scheduled is up to the team, but the process states that requests for any *markups* (also known as *redlines* due to the old days when a red pen was used to strikethrough disagreeable language) were helped by having the KC Cybersecurity team and the vendor SMEs discuss the expectations openly.

The next steps depend on which fork in the road the vendor takes: Perhaps they take a left to where they accept the terms with no material changes. *Material changes* are defined as any strikethrough or change sufficient to edit out the intent of the language that was original or acceptable to KC Enterprises. At the first meeting, it is explained to vendors how long it can take if they take the hard right fork to Dante's Peak of making material changes, which can be a long uphill climb that does not always end well. Sometimes, they arrive at the top of the peak and it's a majestic sleeping volcano. Negotiations can work out between the two parties enough where all the terms are acceptable. Often, however, they can arrive at the top and find that it's an active nasty volcano which spews hot lava all over the participants—where after all the work done there's still some very important risk item that cannot be bridged. This is when escalations happen, and the internal sponsors start panicking because it could all go up in flames due to those nasty lawyers and the mean cybersecurity folks who always say "no."

A company can avoid the nasty Dante's Peak by marking a very clear trail *before* they get to the fork decision. There must be a discussion and agreement about what the non-negotiables are, and those must be discussed early and often. *Everything is negotiable.* If a deal is big enough and there can be sufficient acceptance or transfer of the risk, then even the acceptance of the most hardened non-negotiable can occur. However, your company should not advertise that it's willing to do this, nor do it too often, or the secret will be out. Ensure that the acceptance of these few non-negotiables requires a higher level of executive signature to accept the risk. Plus, your company should instigate a rule that there can be no RAs filed with an executive signatory that provide for less than 14 business days for the executive to consider the risk properly. Many internal stakeholders have lobbied an executive by stating that if an RA is not signed by the end of that very day, then the business will cease to operate. Take the 14 business days.

Assuming that there are checks in the IRQ and intake system to prevent non-negotiables from appearing as issues during discussions on cybersecurity terms, there could be some instances where other items are different than what the vendor can agree to initially. Some common terms and conditions to be included are discussed soon. The specific levels of items, such as encryption or password complexity, are determined by your third-party cybersecurity standards and policies.

About Negotiations and Conflict

It is expected that vendors will push back on the legal terms at times. Their own legal team can have objections to terms they find add undue risk to their organization. There may be technical or physical challenges to achieving the level of requirements that the cybersecurity, privacy, offshore, or other terms and conditions place upon a supplier. Part of arming yourself for these inevitable conflicts is determining the non-negotiables for each addendum or controls document. This helps clarify which items your organization really is not comfortable budging on, or if an RA gets the necessary escalation for an appropriate review when it is done.

As cybersecurity professionals, it is often thought that our role is just to say "no." However, the view should more often be "how," as in "how this will work securely and safely" instead. This approach can be helpful in negotiations for both internal and external discussions. Internally, it may be that a business sponsor is really eager to sign this vendor up for the service because it will save the company millions of dollars or generate huge sales. If the vendor is refusing to meet the requirements on an important security control, then explaining some options to them can indicate that it's not simply a "no" coming from the information security teams.

Externally, discussing with a vendor how they can accomplish the required security controls can produce results. This can range from discussing compensating controls that reduce the risk of the missing or deficient control to how they can accomplish the requirement using other methods. For example, if a vendor refuses to agree to an on-site assessment, explain to them why this is an important due diligence task, required by your own internal policies, and take some time to detail how an on-site assessment is designed to be relatively quick when performed. If the vendor continues to push back, then offer a virtual assessment, with the physical security being attestation provided by another acceptable third party; for example, a Security Operations Center (SOC), International Organization for Standardization (ISO), or some other certification.

In the end, remember that you are the customer and the requirements agreed to internally as the third-party security control standards are part of doing business with your company.

Cybersecurity Terms and Conditions

Whether the T&Cs are in an MSA or a separate addendum depends on what works best for your team. However, the actual items should cover some of the following key areas:

- **Encryption:** Explicitly detail what the minimum acceptable encryption should be (e.g., AES-256).

- **MFA for Privileged Accounts:** Spell this out and provide a definition of Privileged Account in the document so there's no ambiguity.

- **Data Segregation:** If in a cloud environment, include language indicating that your company data is separated logically from other customers. If required by policy, it's good to list separate encryption keys as well.

- **Right for On-site Audit:** Should a vendor meet the criteria to warrant this level of due diligence, explicitly state what the activity entails and what is expected of the vendor for cooperation.

- **Malware:** Install guarantees that no malware or backdoors are present in the code.

- **Data Location:** Detail if it is acceptable to have customer data located outside your country's borders; if not, list it explicitly.

- **Password Management:** Include complexity and detail the process for changing/resetting passwords with an identity verification process for your vendor.

- **Vulnerability Management:** List some requirements for how you expect vendors to triage and apply patches.

- **Network Segmentation:** Discuss items such as firewalls, Intrusion Detection/Prevention Systems (IDS/IPS), Data Loss Prevention (DLP), and other defense-in-depth items.

- **Connectivity Security:** If the vendor is connected, make sure the requirements for due care and due diligence by them and your company are very clear.

- **Web Application Firewall (WAF):** If there is a web-facing product from the vendor, require a WAF to be scanned and remediated.

- **Employee Security Awareness and Training:** Hold the vendor to best practices of educating their employees and contractors.

- **Data in Lower Environments:** Insist that the third party does not store production sensitive data in test or development environments without prior consent of your company's cybersecurity and/or data privacy teams.

- **Incident Response:** Provide the vendor with expectations on when they are required to notify customers in case of a breach. Preference to contract language should be given to "confirmed" breach.

- **Backup and Disaster Recovery:** Ensure that the standards on this topic match business expectations internally.

- **Physical Security:** Hold the vendor to physical security standards to protect your data at the same level as logical controls.

- **Key Management and Segregation:** Specify that encryption keys are rotated at least every 24 months or less; if possible or offered by the vendor, require separate encryption keys for your company's data.

- **Bring Your Own Keys (BYOK):** Encryption keys can be provided in this case by your organization, but there needs to be language around management of them.

- **Definitions:** Ensure that key terms requiring a clear understanding between the two parties are part of the agreement.

The cybersecurity terms and conditions should be specific and clear with any legal wording left to the attorneys or legal staff. While the temptation is to throw everything into the document, there must be a balanced approach. More items and terms raise the odds that suppliers will push back. Pick the T&Cs that are important to securing the data and/or connection, along with security controls that the vendor's enterprise cybersecurity requires to lower risk.

Offshore Terms and Conditions

KC Enterprises has vendors who perform services offshore from the United States. If the core of your business does not involve offshore work, then having an addendum to deal with these instances is the best option. Ensure they cover these key areas: company data, resources, right to audit, and definitions.

Company Data   The use of an offshore vendor that has access to sensitive data requires very specific instructions on how to protect that data. When it is accessed from outside your home country, that distance makes assessments and validations challenging. During a pandemic event where there are travel restrictions, trusting vendors is more important, which creates legal obligations and boundaries. KC requires that the vendor maintains a certification equivalent to ISO 27001 and provides proof of that certification when requested. Personnel may only connect to the company network from the Offshore Development Center (ODC). This requirement to have the personnel work only from a vendor-managed location ensures that physical and logical security controls are centrally managed and ensures that it maintains the segregation of data.

Any paper documentation on protected data must be maintained in a locked room or container in the ODC when not being utilized in a continuous, uninterrupted way. When no longer needed for business purposes, these documents must be placed in a locked container designated for being cross-shredded to a degree they cannot be reassembled. This destruction must take place within the ODC and in the presence of a vendor's employee.

The vendor must agree to adhere to the best practice regarding a Clean Desk Policy to prevent the unintentional disclosure of protected data. Any computer with access to such data must have a logoff and screen saver that locks the computer after 15 minutes of inactivity. Workspaces must be clean of any protected data when the users are not at their desks, and all other data transmission mediums (e.g., interoffice mail, fax machines, printers, etc.) must adhere to the Clean Desk Policy.

There must be physical controlled access to the ODC. The security process for entry must include a search of bags, backpacks, purses, or other storage devices that are not permitted in the production area (where protected data is accessed). Such devices are permitted in areas with Test or Development access, provided that the data at that level has been anonymized sufficiently as prescribed by KC Enterprises. Vendors will not permit any recording devices (e.g., cell phones, smartphones, tablets, cameras, etc.) in the ODC's production area at any time. A physical separation between the non-production and production work areas must exist at all times. This physical separation must meet the intent of not allowing non-production staff to in any way view or infer the content of production data.

Continuous Monitoring of all locations at the ODC where work is performed for the company must be done by closed-circuit cameras that proactively monitor the activities for potential security violations of protected data. Recordings must be kept for no less than 90 days. Vendors may not use any keystroke monitoring or logging tools unless previously agreed to in writing by KC Enterprises. Any hardware used to store protected data may not be reused by the company but must be destroyed.

A designated workspace is required for all work done by the offshore vendor to ensure that the data is protected. All data connections must be done over an encrypted connection first to the offshore vendor's U.S.-based location, then to KC's network. This connection is only permitted with a virtual desktop that prevents access to the internet, does not allow for the copying of data out of the virtual desktop, and logs all the user's activities, with the logs retained for no less than 90 days. A dedicated network can be used with a separate virtual local area network (VLAN) to isolate any protected data from the other network traffic.

Any access to the internet or company email while on this virtual desktop is limited to the functions needed to perform the job. If there is any communication software running on the vendor's desktop that is used by the staff, a Data Loss Prevention tool must be running as well. Any visitors to the designated workspace must log in at the security desk and be escorted at all times. No competitors of KC Enterprises are allowed into the designated workspace at any time. Emergency personnel (e.g., medical, fire, other emergency staff) may be permitted for the duration of the emergency and must be logged in by the vendor's physical security staff. Any emergency personnel entry logs must be kept for no less than one year in case of review.

Resources   When using dedicated resources for the processing of KC Enterprises' protected data, the vendor resources are required to have a background check performed before work can begin. Personnel must have a photo and copy of their fingerprints on file with the vendor. Employees must go through an annual Security and Awareness Training program, and read and accept the Code of Ethics and all appropriate vendor policies applicable to their job role and functions. All correspondence with the vendor and KC Enterprises must take place using already approved and agreed-upon communication software (e.g., email, chat, fax, and so on).

Right to Audit KC Enterprises reserves the right to perform a physical on-site security assessment of all offshore facilities where work is performed for them. This right to audit can be performed at least once a year or within 90 days of notification of a security breach.

Definitions Within the vendor's contract, ensure that a section is included that defines and clarifies all terms and conditions within the contract for that the vendor and company as related to offshore terms and conditions. Terms typically defined in this section include protected data, destruction of data specifics, vendor, services, offshore, ODC, and personnel.

Hosted/Cloud Terms and Conditions

At KC Enterprises, when a vendor goes through the IRQ and is flagged as having a cloud-based solution, then the Legal and Cybersecurity teams also include a Cloud Terms and Conditions addendum to address those specific security risks. It may overlap with other addendums, but the desire is to ensure that the vendor understands and commits to them.

Data Ownership, Use, and Retention Within the vendor contract, it's important that you specify that the use of data by the vendor is limited non-transferable for use within the data centers. At KC Enterprises, the contract also states that the data must never leave the United States, to avoid any entanglements with foreign data security or privacy laws. Directions should be given that the data must be used solely for the purposes of the service/product provided to the company, and that it must be encrypted at-rest, in-transit, and in-use. Data is owned by the company, not the vendor or CSP. Vendors must also return the data upon completion of the contract.

Vendors must have sufficient data backup and retention methods to meet the service-level agreement (SLA) commitments to the company. Upon the termination notification of the contract, the vendor has 90 days to provide copies of the data. Within 90 days of contract termination, the vendor must provide a digital certificate of destruction (COD) of the data. Hardware may be reused, but it must go through an overwrite process no less than five times.

Data Center Security   Specific directions and requirements for the physical security at the data center are for security 24 hours a day, 7 days a week, 365 days a year. Stipulate in the contract that there is no public access to the facility, in addition to having only minimal or no signage posted as to the facility's purpose. A monument sign that gives the company name, but nothing that indicates it is a data center, is allowed. Personnel must be company employees, or if outsourced, they must meet or exceed the background checks and training for the vendor's personnel.

Data centers used by KC Enterprises or its vendors must meet at least a Tier 3 rating. Tier 3 data centers have multiple avenues for electrical, HVAC, and other systems in place to update and maintain them without taking them offline. They should have an expected uptime of 99.982 percent (or 1.6 hours of downtime annually).

Application Security   Similar to the requirements surrounding secure coding and software delivery, application security should be spelled out in the contract, given the risk of cloud applications. A warranty in the contract addendum for ensuring that no viruses, trojans, time bombs, backdoors, or other malware are included in software must be provided. A contingency plan must be included in the language in case any illicit code is found: If malware or other security risks are found in the code, the vendor must notify the company within 24 hours. They must take remedial action and provide a patch at the earliest possible moment along with any steps that can be taken by KC Enterprises to mitigate the risk until the updated code is ready. The contract should specify that any damages resulting from the illicit code, intentional or unintentional, are the responsibility of the vendor and not the company.

Support   If the vendor uses another provider for the data center (a co-location or CSP), then support can be multi-tiered, depending what actions need to be taken. Within the contract, define support terms (e.g., support is available 5 or 7 days a week) and who performs it during this period. Include which time zones are expected for support hours. Specify how fast the calls must be answered and the percentage of calls expected to be answered within a certain number of rings or elapsed time.

Incident Notification   The contract should also include specific language that defines what constitutes an actual or suspected breach or compromise of security. This breach should not be confined to the services/products provided to the company, but to any other customer or the vendor as a whole. The notice of a suspected breach can be challenging to get agreement on, but it can be added to the contract's Definitions section if it is unclear. Breach notification includes both physical and logical security, and the vendor must notify within 24 hours of the breach occurring. You can negotiate up to 48 hours, but target it at 24 hours if possible. Tie the notification and breach to the contract's termination if the company determines that the scope of the incident warrants severing the relationship.

Definitions   In the context of hosted/cloud terms and conditions, the contract should define terms that are likely to produce conflict or risk. Such terms include best practices, destruction of data, personnel, contractors, breaches, suspected breaches, and notification methods.

Data Center Tiers

Data centers are systems that can vary from simple to complex. An accepted tiering of them can assist in deciding what type of data center best fits a customer's needs. The international standards from EN50600 and ISO 22237 for data center infrastructures lists four tiers. The Telecommunications Industry Association (TIA) and the Uptime Institute also provide standards for data centers and list four tiers.

Tier 1 data centers have one power and cooling system and few redundant backup components located in them. These data centers are basic and would not be acceptable for business or corporate use. They have an expected uptime of 99.671 percent, which translates into almost 29 hours of downtime annually.

Tier 2 data centers also only have one power and cooling system, but they have some redundancy and backup systems within them. Their uptime expectation is 99.741 percent annually, which provides for up to 22 hours of downtime annually.

Tier 3 data centers have multiple paths for power, HVAC, and other systems in place to ensure that there's no time offline. These data centers have a 99.982 percent of uptime and allow for 16 hours of downtime annually.

Tier 4 data centers are built to be completely fault tolerant and redundant for all systems and parts, resulting in an uptime of 99.995 percent, which allows only 26.3 minutes of downtime annually.

Privacy Terms and Conditions

As stated earlier, data security is not the same as data privacy. *Data privacy* is the proper use, collection, retention, storage, and deletion of data. *Data security* is the process, policies, methods, and means to secure sensitive protected data. These details can be found in your Master Services Agreement (MSA) or in a separate exhibit, but they should cover the vendor's privacy program, data ownership, data use, data collection, compliance, and fourth parties.

The Privacy Program   Stipulate in the privacy addendum that the vendor will maintain a privacy program of its own that manages handling personal identifiable information (PII) and documents how it will respond in the event of a breach. Any work needed as a result of a breach, such as privacy impact analysis, consultations, and reporting to any supervisory organizations, must be done with the assistance of the vendor.

Data Ownership   All data is the property of the company, irrespective of which party has custody of it. Ownership is important for several reasons: Ownership equals access, and specification of the ownership ensures that the company will retain that access. Managing data integrity is dependent upon the data's ownership resting with the company. The ability to inspect and examine the data first-hand on demand rests on who has ownership of the data.

Data Use   As one of the core tenets of data privacy, be specific in your contract about how the vendor is allowed to use the data. Verbiage may need to be generic in approach, such as "vendor will only use data and information provided as directed by the company" or it may need to be specified at an application level.

Ensure that the vendor knows your data's limitations (i.e., how any data collected from your customers or employees is used as intended).

Data Collection   Terms and conditions limits must be placed on the vendor's collection of personal data gathered on the company's behalf. A vendor should only be allowed to collect the PII necessary to perform the services required. Specify in the contract that there will be no data collection done anyone under 16 years old or provide this information knowingly to the company performing the collection of data. The age limit is driven by the General Data Protection Regulation (GDPR) that sets the age of consent at 16; anyone 15 and younger requires the permission from a parent or guardian. The law is different in the United States, but GDPR is one of the most stringent so adhering to it is always a good baseline. The language for compliance is using "reasonable efforts" to verify that the age of the minor is the age of consent or below.

Vendors must notify the company about the methods used and operation of the data collection for cookies, pixel, beacon, JavaScript, UDID, or any other mechanisms used for tracking users. Any tracking technology must be previously approved by the company; it may not use local shared objects, be deployed on behalf of fourth parties, circumvent user preferences contained in browser settings, or fail to provide users with an opt-out option.

Data Location   Much like the other parts of an agreement about data, the data should be confined to areas where it is only needed and used. At KC Enterprises, the contract stipulates that the data must not reside or be transmitted at any time outside the United States. This limits the risk that it might become subject to another privacy or security regulatory body or organization, such as GDPR.

Compliance   Depending upon the location of your business, there may be specific laws and regulations stipulated to ensure that the vendor does not present a risk to your company, such as the California Consumer Privacy Act (CCPA) or GDPR. If the data is Personal Health Information (PHI), then the contract should list any applicable regulations they must adhere to as well.

Fourth Parties   Often called piggy-back or fourth-party tracking parties, *fourth parties* are parties who leverage your data for their own use. Piggybacking tags are dangerous because another party, not your third party, can potentially obtain access to the data, slow the loading times at websites resulting in customer issues, and create non-compliance with regulations like GDPR or CCPA.

A Note on Risk Acceptances

Risk Acceptance (RA) is a perfectly acceptable outcome in some situations. Non-negotiables are high-risk items, such as encryption, MFA on privileged accounts, and the right to perform on-site security assessments. In large or medium companies, RAs can be limited within business silos; if the vendor is going to service the Finance department and they are seeking the RA, then very often the policy will state the executive for that unit can perform RA.

The issue with this approach is that a lone business unit accepting an RA for one or more of the non-negotiables is taking on the risk that actually exposes the whole company. If there is a risk that rises to the seriousness of no encryption or MFA for privileged accounts and there is a breach, the whole company loses, not just Finance. RA can happen for non-negotiables, but it must be done at the corporate level,

(Continued)

(Continued)

not at the business-unit level to ensure that an executive sees the whole picture in order to safeguard against accepting too much risk. At the corporate level, a CEO, CISO, or CIO would understand and appreciate the risk this presents to the entire organization. They are the ones who are best to perform these risk reviews and acceptances.

Make sure to document the risk in a risk registry and review it on a regular basis and get signed off by the business, CIO, CISO or CEO, depending on the risk being accepted.

Inside Look: Heritage Valley Health vs. Nuance

We begin this Inside Look with the admission that in 2020, a judge dismissed the case by Heritage Valley Health vs. Nuance. However, the damage was, in many ways, done to further the punishment of Nuance for their breach. The case was around the damages Heritage Valley Health was seeking due to having a network connection to Nuance. The case was filed in 2019, after Nuance was breached by the NotPetya malware in 2017. This was year upon year of bad press, reminding readers of the hack three years ago, the wasted energy having to fight it, and all the court fees and attorney's fees.

The case against Nuance by Heritage Valley Health held that it was responsible for Nuance's systems getting Heritage Valley Health's systems also infected. Nuance had a VPN connection to Heritage Valley Health. Heritage Valley had to cancel patient visits for a week, and the damage to its systems ran in the millions. Heritage Valley stated:

> Nuance is liable for any contractual obligations and tort liability arising from the plaintiff's use of the products

acquired from Dictaphone, and Nuance should be held liable for poor security practices and governance oversight as it had a broader duty to prevent the cyberattack.

More importantly, to the legal risks raised in this chapter, this is why the case was dismissed. The judge accepted Heritage Valley Health's arguments and stated that the facts were not in dispute. However, the contract that was for the service was with Dictaphone, which was acquired by Nuance in 2006. That meant Heritage Valley Health's legal and third-party management team had not updated any contract in over 10 years. Because the contract was with Dictaphone, the judge held that there was no product liability for Nuance.

As hard as that might be for them to hear and placing the legal logic aside for a second: When Nuance bought Dictaphone, there should have been a new contract created and set into place immediately. Secondly, parts of the information security language should not be more than 3 years old or the risk of it being outdated grows. The industry and threats move too fast, and if contracts automatically renew with no review or brand-new contract, then it is a ticking time bomb.

Conclusion

To secure your data and connections, you must have contractual requirements listed for the third party. The terms and conditions for vendors on items such as encryption, access management, vulnerability management, and other controls, provide a clear list of expectations. When the supplier starts negotiating on the specific terms, keep a list of items that your organization defines as non-negotiable, such as encryption, access management, and vulnerability management (depending on your risk appetite). If the supplier pushes back on them, the question on whether or not the relationship should continue is a legitimate one. The number and types of contractual addendums and terms will vary based upon your vendors and types of risks. If private customer data is to be shared with a vendor, a Privacy Addendum (or Privacy language in your base contract) is a must-have in order to meet today's privacy regulations.

12

Software
Due Diligence

Third-party software is located everywhere in an enterprise. From the common desktop productivity software, backend server operating systems, mobile apps, and hundreds of others, they are often acquired, installed, and updated with little to no testing performed at any stage of the process or lifecycle. While testing Microsoft Word is possible, the approach should be risk-based. If all a customer's private data is stored in a Microsoft Word document, then yes, testing that document then would become important because that is where the risk resides. However, most of the riskiest software goes unnoticed. Recent examples are the SolarWinds attack in December 2020, OpenSSL/Heartbleed in 2014, and the large complex supply-chain hack on Vietnam's government portal that runs the country's e-signature program in late 2020. All of these were ubiquitous software in their space.

The SolarWinds software was one of the most widely used network monitoring tools on the planet. Nearly every Fortune 500 company used it, and in many cases, had APIs connecting it to other tools, making it an interdependency risk. OpenSSL was the software with an open security flaw that became known as Heartbleed. OpenSSL was the key open source software many developers used when requiring a secure connection with another. More critically, there was no tracking of where the code was or its owner, so if an issue required a code update, it took a long time to find all the locations of OpenSSL. In Vietnam, if anyone (e.g., a company, citizen, or other government agency) needed to submit files to the government, the e-signature was the required method. This flaw was exploited by the developer's toolkit that enables users to automate the e-signature process.

Again, the software was widely used, and more often used with no testing prior in areas with sensitive data or connections.

Methods and tools exist for businesses to perform due diligence on third-party software. It can be as simple as asking a vendor to supply vulnerability scans, industry-standard compliance reports, and working with them to understand open risks with remediation dates. The questions asked of a vendor during the intake, ongoing, and on-site due diligence assessment visits should address how they approach the secure development lifecycle, whether they have an open source tracking process or system, and how they perform their cloud development testing.

The Secure Software Development Lifecycle

The Secure Software Development Lifecycle (SSDLC) is a process that places security directly into the development of the software or hardware. It can be a waterfall or agile project process, or whatever process is defined by the vendor; vendors should just confirm they are following it and have a process for improvement. There are tangible rewards for both the third party and customer: Companies that have a documented SSDLC process lower their risk of critical vulnerabilities by 80 percent, which in turn lowers their time to market and lowers the risk of a bug or security flaw. Furthermore, customers who purchase software that goes through a documented SSDLC process are rewarded with an average 75-percent reduction in Incident Response and configuration management costs, which equals real money and lower risk.

KC Enterprises uses a waterfall approach that takes five steps: Requirements, Design, Test Planning, Coding, and Testing. Numerous substeps exist within these five, but the point is that they have it documented, and the process itself gets tested by internal audit teams yearly to ensure they are following it. The Cyber Third-Party Risk team takes the same approach on any assessment: Does the vendor have a process, do they test that process, and can they demonstrate both to us via our due diligence questions?

When performing due diligence on an intake assessment, the questions generally didn't rely on proof of activity. However, the intake questions and any conference calls focused on confirming the vendor had an SSDLC or Software Design Lifecycle (SDLC) process published. At the on-site assessment, there are a few areas that the analyst should delve into for clarity on how well they perform this critical process.

Request to view the policy, standards, and process documents that describe how secure software design is performed. An owner or stakeholder must be designated for these documents, and updates or reviews should be performed at regular intervals. The responsibilities for all members of development (i.e., developers, testers, managers, and quality assurance [QA]) are clearly defined. Is there a process where owners describe how bugs are triaged, risk-rated, and fixed? Do they have clear segregation between roles and environments that prevents escalated privileges and data leakage?

Several types of testing must be performed during development. Static analysis does not run or execute the software, but can locate defects to prevent them from getting into the broader code base. Inquire what type of static-testing tools and processes are executed and how bugs are logged and resolved for it. Once the code is in an executable, dynamic analysis testing should be done to locate any bugs at that point in development. Find out how the team performs the testing that identifies vulnerabilities at runtime and validates static code testing.

The last option is *fuzz testing* (or known as *fuzzing*), which is automated software testing that finds software bugs that are common hacking targets. It tests for invalid data inputs, unexpected or random data, memory leaks, crashes, and code logic failure. All testing is important, but this particular one directly tests against security flaws most commonly associated with cybersecurity risks. Fuzzing can be a complex subject, but due diligence efforts can focus on a documented process that clearly defines the types of fuzzers deployed, their uses (e.g., exposing bugs, static analysis validation, and browsers), and their toolchain. Lastly, confirm that fuzz testing is being done at the vendor by viewing logs and evidence of findings that are resolved.

Upon intake, after the IRQ flags this as software (as being on-premises, cloud, open source, or mobile), there will be some sorting on the risk of that application. If it is cloud-based, at KC Enterprises, their risk-based approach dictates that it will get a lot of attention to its risk assessment of cloud. Soon, we will discuss how to test cloud-based software. If it is mobile or open source, there is another set of questions that address that risk area. On-premises software does not get tested at KC Enterprises, as with most companies. After SolarWinds, the Vietnam Supply-Chain Hack, and Heartbleed, the risks made it clear that it needed to be re-examined.

Lessons from SolarWinds and Critical Software

Prior to the process changes enacted after SolarWinds, KC Enterprises did not perform due diligence on on-premises software. After SolarWinds, cybersecurity leadership and Third-Party Risk Management (TPRM) had learned lessons from their efforts to mitigate any damage caused by the attack, and raised concerns about other on-premises software vulnerabilities that necessitated further examination.

KC Enterprises ran SolarWinds, like thousands of other companies worldwide, but luckily, they had not installed the product that contained the exploit. Nonetheless, out of an abundance of caution, they disabled SolarWinds until investigations could be completed, which caused some operational issues as it was used to monitor and alert on thresholds. When the systems, which would normally alert administrators of an impending issue (e.g., a disk full, log full, power loss, network not replying, and so on), were not operating, they had to work quickly to find alternate products and rush them through onboarding. This level of activity across nearly every segment of the company required a rethink.

In response, a process was developed to risk-rate the third-party software that was run internally. While the usual criteria of having protected data or a connection to the company were triggers, there needed to be some due diligence on this software. The criteria is the tricky part, and it can make that universe of what to review either manageable or scary. KC's leadership believed the best approach was to start with a small universe and work outwardly as that process was completed. The starting risk scope would be software identified as "systemically critical." This definition took some work to agree upon to ensure that the list wasn't too big for a first bite (i.e., to take an approach that allows for easier initial adoption and success, then build upon that as needed).

The description of *systemically critical* for a vendor means if said vendor becomes unavailable (e.g., due to going out of business, a system outage, or being hacked and unusable), business operations would cease within a business week or less. Systemically critical software is defined as any suddenly unusable application or code that impacts a business to a degree that operations would cease in a business week or less.

Once the work to find candidates that fit this definition was completed, KC Enterprises quickly followed up by ranking them by risk. Rather than try to test all these on their own, they decided to perform some further due diligence on how these vendors perform their SSDLC. And, as gaps were identified, they were logged as findings, and remediation steps were developed as with any other due diligence effort.

The SolarWinds attack will take years to unravel. At this time, many unsolved issues and suspicions still exist about whether other attack vectors were used but have yet to be discovered. In December 2019, there was a zero-day alert for VMWare that potentially was an initial attack vector. "We don't fully understand all of the different vectors or scope of this compromise," stated Costin Raiu, director of Kaspersky's global research and analysis team. According to Gregory Rattray, former global CISO of JP Morgan Chase and White House cybersecurity director during the George W. Bush administration, "I see SolarWinds [the attack] as a very natural element of an ecosystem that has existed" in cyber espionage for some time. Rattray, who is credited with creating the terms *nation-state hackers* and *Advanced Persistent Threat (APT)* while serving in the U.S. Air Force, indicates that the SolarWinds attack is one of many comparable supply-chain attacks by these APT groups and "We're only seeing the tip of the iceberg. . . . There's a whole lot more of this."

Inside Look: Juniper

In late 2015, two security flaws were found during an internal code review by Juniper. These two flaws were identified as "unauthorized code" that would allow hackers to decrypt information going through their equipment. It provided the attackers with access to all their VPN traffic, and had been there as early as 2008. This backdoor code took advantage of a weakness in the password algorithm used called "Dual_EC." The National Security Association (NSA) is reported to have engineered this algorithm and promoted its use as a standard. "Juniper discovered unauthorized code in ScreenOS that could allow a knowledge-able attacker to gain administrative access to NetScreen devices and to decrypt VPN connections," stated Bob Worrall, CIO at Juniper Networks, who continued on:

> Once we identified these vulnerabilities, we launched an investigation into the matter, and worked to develop and issue patched releases for the latest versions of ScreenOS. At this time, we have not received any reports of these vulner-abilities being exploited; however, we strongly recommend that customers update their systems and apply the patched releases with the highest priority.

The hack was so stealthy that any signs of the system login were erased.

Juniper has never explained why it used Dual_EC as its encryption algorithm, despite warnings about its security weak-nesses. Juniper insisted that any weakness in Dual_EC was coun-terbalanced by a second random-number generator called ANSI X9.31. Their assertion was this would *cancel* out any security gaps in the first product. Unfortunately, that turned out to be wrong, and if and how they tested that assertion has never been answered. Once the flaw in Dual_EC was exploited, the second product did not matter—the timing of which product was added when raises further suspicions. Dual_EC was added after ANSI X9.31 was already a working product in the Juniper product. The question remains: Why add known-vulnerable code into the product?

Other research shows Juniper changed settings on the Dual_EC implementation to further lower the security of an already flawed product. A month after the backdoor was revealed, Juniper released a patch that solely focused on eliminating the unauthorized code placed in there to exploit the Dual_EC back-door. However, it did not release code that removed the flawed algorithm itself or the bug that allowed the attackers to avoid the second random-number generator and only get data from the Dual_EC until the following year.

The problem did not go away for Juniper. In June 2020, three U.S. Senators and 13 House members sent a letter to Juniper asking it to disclose what its own internal investigations had found out, as there were allegations of "secret government backdoors." Whether this was placed there intentionally or was an extreme coincidence has not been confirmed, but for any company that used Juniper Networks during this period, it had a very chilling effect on their sense of security for their networking equipment.

On-Premises Software

On-premises software (known as on-prem software) is any code or application that runs internally in your network. As stated earlier, there are potentially thousands of candidates for this software type at any medium to large business. Picking which ones that an organization would benefit from testing depends on size, market, industry, and dozens of other factors. In manufacturing, it could be the software that runs the factories; in finance, the applications that move money around; in the software industry, they could chose anything that handles their code. Once that criteria has been established, there are ways to test this third-party software on your own for risks and bugs.

First, you should examine the service accounts or privileged access that the software requires. The principle of least-privilege applies to applications as well, where the applications only have the least privilege necessary in order to operate. No service should require full administrator or root privileges. If the application requires read/write access to the database to perform its function but does not delete any data, then it should only have read/write access. Also, examine any high-level designs vendors are willing to share so that the information flow can be examined for any weak spots.

Application Security Testing (AST) tools, and there are many, can provide valuable information on bugs and weaknesses in a vendor's software. There are a number of AST tools, and each has various ways in which they can best help you discover hidden flaws. For testing software where access to source code is not available (as in third-party software), Dynamic Application Security Testing (DAST) is most effective, but using Software Composition Analysis (SCA) tools will provide clues on other third-party and open source code found in the application. Often, SCA tools will run with DAST tools, but if there is no budget for both, SCA may be viewed as being more helpful because it provides a list of vulnerabilities that are already widely known.

In DAST, the tools act like the software is a black box (where nothing is known about what is inside). These test tools detect conditions that would make the software vulnerable in a running state. DAST runs at the operating system level and spots problems with how the software acts on any number of functions (e.g., authentication, scripting, API calls, requests to the CPU and memory, and so on). These tools use invalid and unexpected values in the software while looking for flaws in the response.

SCA examines all the components and system libraries to find their origins. These tools are great at finding known vulnerabilities for common components, particularly in open source software, but they will not find vulnerabilities in customer code made by the vendor. However, because SCA tools will not discover this custom code does not diminish this tool's usefulness. If the SCA tool is run along with the DAST tool, it should give you a very complete picture of security vulnerabilities for third-party software.

Once the testing has been performed by your team, a discussion must be held with the vendor about the results and next steps. Focus on any high or severe risks first, by providing vendors the data gathered using the tools. They might or might not be aware of an issue, and some discussions could be required to get to closure. (It will likely take more than one email request.) If the vendor is receptive to the feedback, inquire if they have a similar finding and what their plan for a patch is. If they insist it is a false positive (meaning, it is not really an issue but a mistake in the testing), one option is to request a walkthrough of the code in question with their development team. Having an active relationship with these vendors will prove beneficial and allow for transparency on this potentially sensitive subject.

Testing on-premises software is not without its challenges, but the rewards for high-risk applications and code can be well worth the effort. There are plenty of examples where untested third-party software caused a breach (or a suspected breach in the case of Juniper, as no one has ever shown leaked information as a result of the backdoor). On-site testing should be risk-based and targeted at the vendor's software that poses the risk to operations and security.

Cloud Software

Cloud software, which is generally offered as Software-as-a-Service (SaaS), is often the solution of choice given that it is fast to deploy and requires minimal internal support. What SaaS customers often don't know is that they are able to perform their own testing using static and dynamic analysis if it is performed properly. It does require a different method than using on-premises software and collaborating with the vendor. If using cloud software is a requirement for your firm, it is ideal to place this need into the terms and conditions of the Cybersecurity section in any Master Services Agreement (MSA) or statement of work.

The first step to testing cloud software is working with the vendor to set up a test or sandbox area (except without production data). A sandbox is similar to a test area and is open to testing and fast reconfiguration. Be sure to use anonymized data that cannot be reverse-engineered into personal identifiable information (PII). The vendor should be able to provide the sandbox and collaborate on the testing if desired. They could even have a set of clean data for testing to be performed. Testing cloud software must be done in cooperation with the third party, but there should be a process in place already at the vendor that deploys to the cloud.

There are three focus areas in static analysis for cloud applications: application programming interfaces (APIs), signatures, and strings. The use of APIs is extremely common and is important to allow interoperability and communication with other software. Running static analysis against the APIs performs input validation. Checking to verify that the API rejects input values of null or unacceptable data, as well as ensuring the output from the API, is the expected value.

Your company should perform input validation, where the testing involves determining if the software will allow unexpected, malformed, or unallowed data input. There must be a rejection of null values and a test that the output from the API is as anticipated. Signature testing looks at the digital signatures that validate if a software package is authentic and not tampered with. Static analysis of strings, using the command-line in Unix, produces this type of information, which could make the application vulnerable to an inference attack. An inference attack is akin to listening through the walls of your apartment complex to hear what your neighbors are talking about. The less insulation in the walls, the more you can infer about what is going on next door.

Dynamic testing for cloud software focuses on three areas: memory, registry, and network. Memory data is accessed during testing to view if any sensitive data leakage is occurring. Registry keys and modifications to the registry in dynamic analysis will alert if there is unexpected behavior. Network traffic testing can view if the username that is sent to the cloud can be changed. This name alteration could escalate the user's privilege level and allow them to view and possibly exfiltrate sensitive data.

Some very straightforward dynamic and static analysis can be performed on third-party cloud-based applications. Use clean data sets, work with the vendor for the sandbox environment, and engage with them for any items found in the testing.

Open Web Application Security Project Explained

The Open Web Application Security Project (OWASP) is an online group that publishes free articles, methodologies, documentation, tools, and technologies for web application security. It is a non-profit 501c that takes donations and memberships. It has chapters around the globe for folks to network and learn from their local peers.

OWASP Top 10

A number of excellent resources for developers and Cyber Third-Party Risk teams are available. One of them is known as the OWASP Top 10 Web Application Security Risks, which is a dynamic list that changes periodically as the threats change. The list includes the following items:

- **Injection:** When untrusted data is sent to an interpreter as part of a command or query, this can allow the attacker to trick the interpreter into executing commands or accessing the data.

- **Broken Authentication:** If the authentication and session management are implemented improperly, it can allow the hacker access to passwords, keys, or session tokens, or to assume another user's identity.

- **Sensitive Data Exposure:** Leaving sensitive data unprotected (without encryption) as it passes through on a website can leads to data breaches.

- **XML External Entities:** eXtensible Markup Language (XML) is designed to store and transport data. If it is misconfigured or an older version, it can lead to data loss, remote code execution, internal port scanning, and denial-of-service attacks.

- **Broken Access Control:** When restrictions on what actions authenticated users cannot perform and data viewed are poorly or not enforced, hackers can misuse it to gain access to data or unintended functionality.

- **Security Misconfiguration:** Reported as the most commonly seen vulnerability, this is a result of users not properly configuring security controls as best practices recommend, which leads to breaches and security incidents.

- **Cross-site Scripting (XSS):** When an application includes untrusted data in a web page without validation or ability to escape (going around), it can allow a remote script execution to hijack browser sessions, redirect users or traffic to malicious sites, or alter websites.

- **Insecure Deserialization:** Deserialization is the process of taking data from another format and rebuilding it into an object. It can lead to remote code execution, replay attacks, injection, and privilege escalation attacks.

- **Using Components with Known Vulnerabilities:** Libraries, frameworks, and other software modules often run with the same level of privileges as the application. Using these items when there are known vulnerabilities is an obvious invitation for an attacker.

- **Insufficient Logging and Monitoring:** Lack of this key piece results in the inability to track or view suspicious behavior, and if a breach occurs, to determine what took place.

OWASP Web Security Testing Guide

The OWASP Testing Guide has a best-practice penetration testing framework for developers and security professionals. The guide is a complete document on testing the security of web applications. It includes threat modeling, testing techniques, source code review, and how to derive security testing requirements. There are five phases of the testing framework:

1. **Phase 1:** Before Development Begins
2. **Phase 2:** During Definition and Design
3. **Phase 3:** During Development
4. **Phase 4:** During Deployment
5. **Phase 5:** During Maintenance and Operations

In addition, there are detailed plans and guidance for web application security, authentication, authorization, session management, input validation, error handling, business logic, cryptography, and numerous other tests.

This guide provides details about the security testing performed on due diligence for web applications, and can be a source of testing used by vendors.

OWASP also has many other tools and documentation that are useful for the developers and security communities. In addition, guide creators are also constantly looking for contributors to the data they already have collected as updates are required.

Open Source Software

Open source software (OSS) is a type of code or software where the source code is available under a license that the copyright holder grants other users the right to study, use, change, and distribute for any use by anyone. These actions can be performed via a collaborative effort by numerous people and organizations or by a sole license holder. This software is often thought of as being free, but that is not accurate. Its use is often (though not exclusively) free, but the use of it does come with certain costs, such as maintenance and patching. It does have some great advantages due to its ease of development, flexibility, and quick innovation. Some OSS examples include the Apache Web Server, Mozilla Firefox, and Libre Office.

The costs of maintenance and patching of open source software are overlooked by some development teams, which can become the point of entry for a due diligence effort. This effort can be performed on two main areas: 1) on any vendor's existing security examination (i.e., intake, ongoing, on-site assessments; find out more about how they maintain their OSS records and test against them), and 2) to test software for open source vulnerabilities, using some of the tools discussed earlier in the chapter.

Commercial off the shelf software may contain references to some open source libraries. Ensure these are reviewed and agreed to, either during the contract negotiations (by adding a clause to protect your company from any open source–related incidents) or later during the normal operations or during contract renewal.

Open source code is most often used in development much as the OpenSSL code is used: When a developer requires a way for the program they're creating to securely communicate with another program, they drop in the OpenSSL code. While there is a bit more to it than just "dropping in the code," for this book that's as deep into coding as we'll go. Many applications contain thousands to millions of lines of code, so the challenge is to ensure that an owner knows where the data was dropped and what version it was dropped in.

Automated software tools can fulfill much of this activity and automagically store that information (e.g., code, version, location, etc.) so it is searchable and can create alerts. Some of the more sophisticated applications will even alert when there is a new vulnerability about the code it knows is in your application(s). This can be done manually, with a spreadsheet and updates done by developers as they code. Obviously, this method has its shortcomings and challenges, but if a firm can't afford the automated software packages, it is a perfectly acceptable solution.

The goal is to track and identify open source code in an application. In a large application, this can mean you have a lot of OSS to track. Using an automated software package enables the due diligence effort as a vendor to be much simpler. Confirm it is being used per process by requesting to see evidence that OSS has been flagged as having a vulnerability, then assigned an owner, and being updated or patched to close the risk. Physical validation on the manual process is as challenging as the manual process itself. You should view the log or tracking artifact that the development team is using for your application, then pick a sample or two (or more, depending on risk) from the tracking log to see how the vendor locates the code.

If any gaps are observed, this exercise with a manual OSS-tracking method should involve some discussions with the vendor. If the application is a higher risk to your company (e.g., it's systemically critical or it traverses business operations that move funds) and the revenue they receive from it is sufficient, it is reasonable that the lack of automated OSS tools is declared a security gap. Check out the example of Heartbleed in the following section. The damage that was done stemmed largely from the Herculean effort to find and fix the vulnerable OpenSSL code.

Software Composition Analysis

Software Composition Analysis (SCA) is another method that tests open source software. As your own testing is performed using these tools, it will identify some of the open source software by identifying any with known vulnerabilities. This testing can be combined with the vendors' due diligence using OSS to provide a better picture, in particular with high-risk vendors, on their adherence to best practices in this space.

Inside Look: Heartbleed

In April 2014, the Heartbleed vulnerability hit the internet by surprise. Heartbleed was the name given to CVE-2014-0160, which was an exploit in OpenSSL that allowed attackers to view cryptographic keys, login credentials, and other private data. OpenSSL was one of the most widely used secure (supposedly) transports on Apache and Nginx web servers.

It is estimated that up to 55 percent of the Alexa Top 1 Million HTTPS-enabled websites were open to the vulnerability at the time of its announcement. This software security flaw affected Bitcoin clients and exchanges, Android devices, email servers, firewalls made by big names like Cisco and Barracuda, and millions of websites. How was this bug found? By Google and Codenomicon security engineers running scans and testing OpenSSL.

The Heartbleed bug in testing was shown to be able to steal encryption keys, user names, passwords, instant messages, documents, and any data passing through what was supposed to be an encrypted medium. The worst part was that this exploited bug left no trace of any data leakage. There will never be a way to forensically determine if, when, and where the data went. There have been some unnamed government sources that reported the NSA knew of the bug near the time of availability but kept it secret to exploit it, yet the NSA has publicly denied this claim.

A few instances were reported of the Heartbleed exploitation. Mumsent.com, a U.K. parenting website, had its user accounts hijacked and its CEO was impersonated. The Canada Revenue Agency disclosed a theft of Social Insurance Numbers for 900 citizens. The Royal Canadian Mounted Police charged a Canadian citizen who was a computer science student with the crime. Community Health Systems, at the time the second largest for-profit U.S. hospital chain, disclosed in August 2014 that the Heartbleed exploit was used by an attacker to steal encryption keys. The healthcare provider's lack of updating with a patch exposed the Personal Health Information (PHI) records of their 4.5 million patients and employees.

The exploit was discovered by a Google security team on April 1, 2014. (Yes, ironically that is known as April Fool's Day in many countries.) The vulnerable version of OpenSSL was released with version 1.0.1 in mid-March of 2012. Any subsequent versions for the next two years included the bug. The use of OpenSSL in Apache Web Server—one of the most widely used on the internet—for two years with no testing performed seems surprising in retrospect.

The consequences of this lack of testing upon release and by customers led to a huge effort globally. Cisco relied heavily on this code in its products and had to expend a huge resource effort to find and update it, then release patches. In fact, Cisco decided to produce a version of OpenSSL on its own that ensures it is never out-of-date with security patches. The list of other affected systems would span the size of this book. Oracle, Juniper, HP, VMWare, Android, AirPort, Western Digital, Red Hat, and many other big-name companies and products are just a few that were impacted.

Mobile Software

Mobile software is defined as any application that runs on a *low compute device*, which refers to a device such as a tablet or smartphone. A high compute device would be a computer. The difference of compute power between the two is getting smaller, but it does still exist. While the newer tablets and smartphones have significant compute power, they are used and managed differently than a typical corporate-issued device, such as a laptop or desktop. If using a third-party mobile application, ensure that data storage and backups are appropriately protected (i.e., encrypted).

There are some key vulnerable areas in mobile applications to know so that testing and its validation purpose is understood. First is the issue of the data on the mobile device. The protection of sensitive data, whether it's credentials or PII, is one not often well implemented. Data leakage is a concern if the software is using the operating system's APIs to leak data by communicating insecurely with other applications. Many users do not set their phone to wipe it if a certain number of unauthorized attempts are made at unlocking it, making it a treasure trove of information. In addition, the number of Android versions by phone manufacturers makes how encryption and secure communications are handled very fragmented. Older Android versions are less secure, but many developers want to ensure broad adoption so this presents a unique risk. Solid encryption algorithms, key storage, and ensuring the application is using the latest security features in the operating systems are key controls. Also, the method of secure communications is a weak point if the development is using or allows earlier versions of Transport Layer Security (TLS, which encrypts traffic), for example.

Authentication methods on mobiles are typically done less securely. They have long-term session tokens to allow users more convenience. In addition, the logins can have a very low bar for authentication. A four-digit PIN is not going to deter a determined hacker from breaking into a lost or stolen cell phone. Hackers will log in to a mobile application on the device, which provides the hackers with access to backend sensitive data with such a low bar for entry to the device. It's a known area of exploit too often overlooked in mobile development.

Due to the way mobile software works with the operating systems and other differences (from web applications), they are not as susceptible to typical attacks like cross-site scripting (XSS) or buffer overflows. However, sloppy coding will leave a phone or tablet application vulnerable to exploitation by an attacker. Using best practices for software development should still be followed.

Testing Mobile Applications

Testing the strength of authentication and authorization tests is a key concern in how mobile applications perform and grant access. Using static analysis to test the password complexity (i.e., minimum and maximum length, character requirements) in the code ensures that a verification check is performed on each step. Along with this is testing for login throttling, which is a counter for how many attempts have been made to log into a device during a given time period. There are dynamic testing tools that can simulate an automated password guesser to test for validating some of these authentication weaknesses.

Some common areas to look for when performing the testing on authentication and authorization are to ensure that the mobile software does not store session IDs permanently, the session IDs are generated randomly on the server, any ID exchange is done over a secure connection, IDs are of proper length, and entropy is too difficult so as to not be guessed; and all sessions are terminated on the server and all information deleted on the mobile device when completed. There are common frameworks by development tools that should be leveraged that provide established security integration.

Testing for secure encrypted communications involves viewing how the software manages the traffic and performing some common attack types. Using a network security tool or sniffer to view outbound traffic can provide a look at whether the traffic is passing in the clear or is encrypted. Ensure that the code is using TLS versions v1.2 or higher. (SSL is deprecated and should not be used.) A common attack in this area is a man-in-the-middle attack (which is literally an attacker getting between the communications and redirecting or stealing data). In an insecure Wi-Fi environment, attackers can use this to snoop in on what the mobile user is doing. A dynamic analysis will find much of this risk, but if the test tool allows for ARP poisoning (a type of man-in-the-middle attack), it will locate a man-in-the-middle attack vulnerability in the source code.

Encryption testing focuses on some common areas of weakness on mobile devices. Weak key generation, weak random-number generators, insufficient key length, hardcoded encryption keys, deprecated encryption algorithms, custom encryption, and keys stored in memory and their protection are the high-risk categories for validation. Ensure that the validation results match the policies set out by the development team and best practices on mobile device encryption.

Static and dynamic analysis testing can also reveal slack coding techniques. As discussed, these types of applications are less susceptible to typical browser-side attacks but are not immune from them. SQL Injection, XML Injection, or Inter-Process Communications (IPCs) Injections are areas to watch from in the output from this validation. Buffer overflows are a common attack point in mobile applications, and fuzzing is a great way to find this type of vulnerability.

Code Storage

Code storage can be a source of security gaps if not managed properly. There are procedures and methods for securing code repositories (i.e., where code for applications is stored), but the challenge can be misconfigured security or developers who attempt to shortcut security in exchange for ease of use. Hard-coding credentials into code or not ensuring that the code repository has adequate access controls are two of the biggest gaps. Ask your vendor to see where they store the code to ensure that it is not a public space, but is private and access is controlled. GitHub is a very popular code storage provider, and there have been numerous instances of code and data being leaked due to its improper security settings. An internet search can reveal the scope of the problem, which is not confined to GitHub but also to many other code repository products.

Common Vulnerabilities and Exposures Explained

Common Vulnerabilities and Exposures (CVE) is a public list of known cybersecurity vulnerabilities for software and hardware. As described on the list's website: "CVE is a list of entries—each containing an identification number, a description, and at least one public reference—for publicly known cybersecurity vulnerabilities." The term *CVE* has become an acceptable term used by security professionals to describe an item on this list. CVEs are listed in the form of CVE-Year-ID, so the Heartbleed CVE is CVE-2014-0160. Heartbleed was discovered in 2014, and the four-digit number was randomly generated at the end. Scores are listed in terms of severity in Table 11.1. Note, CVSS stands for Common Vulnerability Scoring System, which is a vendor-agnostic scoring system for vulnerability severity.

TABLE 11.1 CVE/CVSS SCORES

Severity	Base Score
Critical	9.0–10.0
High	7.0–8.9
Medium	4.0–6.9
Low	0.1–3.9
None	0

The main benefit of CVEs is the ability to prioritize scores based upon their rating. There are thousands of CVEs published each year on top of the existing millions that are already historically listed. Being able to look at the

(Continued)

(Continued)

Severity or Base Score relative to the other vulnerabilities listed can help prioritize the remediation of them. Matching up the CVSS scores with critical systems and infrastructure further refines the focus into a risk-based approach. Many organizations have hundreds, thousands, or millions of open vulnerabilities. CVE scores aligned with the risk of the system is a key tool in prioritization.

The list is not a comprehensive list of all security threats, as it only lists those vulnerabilities that are known and published. These undisclosed vulnerabilities (such as zero-day and unknown) are a serious threat to security; the CVE is an important list, but do not mistake it for all security exposures in the wild. The other security controls in place for software, such as the testing described in this chapter and the SSDLC, are intended to mitigate some of these unknown or undisclosed weaknesses.

Some automation tools are available to ingest the CVE lists and match them to software and hardware kept on an internal Configuration Management Database (CMDB), where assets are tracked through their lifecycle at companies. If available as a budget item, the automation tools can greatly ease the burden of managing the large numbers of vulnerabilities possible at medium and larger organizations.

Conclusion

The world of business, personal use, and government runs on software. Whether it is cloud-based, on-premises, on a smartphone, or leveraging open source, it must follow a secure design lifecycle. This process must be documented and validated as being followed and internally tested. Lastly, as a consumer of third-party applications, you should risk-rate the software used at your organization, then decide which meet the criteria and have your own internal testing performed. Each type requires some difference in approach and analysis, given the differences in how they are developed, used, and maintained.

The examples of how third-party software has been exploited by malicious actors has been clearly established. From Heartbleed to SolarWinds, there is a track record of how firms do not perform adequate testing, have inadequate secure design and validation, and follow an inconsistent approach on how customers test third-party software. There is a term in business called *caveat emptor*, which translates into "buyer beware." However, it is part of a larger warning: *Caveat emptor, quia ignorare non debuit quod jus alienum emit*, which means "Let a purchaser beware, for they ought not to be ignorant of the nature of the property which he is buying from another party." This more complete declaration captures the approach organizations need to be taking regarding third-party software: To ensure they make this software secure, they must test and validate its security and hold a vendor legally responsible for the products they provide.

13

Network
Due Diligence

Verifying that data in transit is protected involves a number of controls, tools, and risks entailing some particular due diligence efforts. This work is not isolated to determining if the data is encrypted in transit but includes systems such as Intrusion Detection/Prevention System (IPS/IDS), Secure Web Gateway (SWG), Data Loss Prevention (DLP), Cloud Access Security Broker (CASB), and Security Information and Event Management (SIEM) tools to detect and prevent data exposure. Network attack surfaces have evolved in the last few years as virtual private network (VPN) use has expanded. However, the number of these surfaces exploded after the pandemic sent nearly 30 percent of the American workforce home in a matter of days (according to Pew Research: `www.pewresearch.org/social-trends/2020/12/09/how-the-coronavirus-outbreak-has-and-hasnt-changed-the-way-americans-work`). VPNs are an extension of corporate networks, and another entry point that multiplied by the hundreds or thousands during the pandemic.

While earlier chapters have covered some of this security effort, more examination of how vendors connect to customer networks and the heightened risk it entails is necessary. Nearly 100 percent of these connections are done over hardware supplied and managed by a vendor, leaving the customer with no direct access to understand vulnerable software operating systems (OSs) or configurations. The risks such devices present as unmanaged and unmonitored gaps into the network can be lowered.

Third-Party Connections

Third-party connection due diligence can divided into these main categories:

- Personnel physical security
- Hardware security
- Software security
- Out-of-band security
- Cloud connections

Next, we will break down these categories into what they are and how to protect them.

Personnel Physical Security

Connectivity between a vendor and a customer can involve physical installation of hardware at a data center or another location. This physical access by a vendor employee or contractor (or even a fourth party) needs to be clearly understood during the intake process, documented in legal documentation, then monitored at regular intervals. Vendors are important partners; however, most of the locations at which this hardware is placed and maintained are highly sensitive, controlled access locations at companies.

During the intake process when a connection requirement is triggered, a discussion must occur about what the expectations are for connecting to the network. A business needs to know exactly where equipment must be located in its data center or network closet. They must also understand if their business's requirements also necessitate a connection to a backup or DR location that exposes another location to physical access. Businesses must inquire if their vendors use a third party to contract this installation and maintenance instead of doing it themselves. This will lead to questions about how vendors perform their own third-party cybersecurity reviews and what questions they ask of these fourth-party vendors regarding personnel.

If the vendor is performing the installation, businesses should refer to the answered questions located in the Human Resources (HR) Security section of their due diligence questionnaire to ensure that background and criminal checks are performed on personnel who perform these installations. These personnel must be rechecked at least annually, or as new personnel are rotated. It's important to note how often personnel are rechecked for any new arrests or issues since hiring and if there's a termination policy when such a violation occurs. If the vendor does not check its personnel's security status at regular intervals after hiring, it must be a requirement in HR's policy that an employee must report if they've been convicted of a crime.

Some industries, regional requirements, or sectors might have additional security requirements (e.g., perhaps only personnel with citizenship in the country where the data center is located could be allowed entrance). Ensure that this type of requirement is clear on the intake assessment and insert it into any legal contracts. The expectations on how a vendor performs due diligence on physical access, HR screening, and the ability to use a subcontractor for installation and maintenance needs to be negotiated and written into the contract. If your company has concrete requirements for physical access (items that are non-negotiable), and rules that a vendor cannot subcontract any of the services, be prepared to include them in the contract as non-negotiable: items that cannot be redlined out. Lastly, if there are DR or uptime requirements from your business, clearly include this information in the service-level agreement (SLA) for how quickly they can service the hardware.

Hardware Security

Hardware is almost always provided by a vendor for any connectivity. Every manufacturer or type is a new attack surface on the network and multiplies the risks. Most often, a customer implicitly trusts these vendors to properly manage their hardware. Hardware security does not apply to updating the operating system with the latest patches; it refers to how the chosen equipment's risks are managed for how it secures secrets, performs encryption and decryption, and manages the keys.

One way to lower hardware security risk is to have an approved list of devices that a vendor can use. When the Intake Risk Questionnaire (IRQ) alerts to a connectivity requirement, the next prompt is the provision of a list of hardware that the company supports. A vendor's choice of hardware can be reviewed against this list of acceptable devices or what can be supported by your internal standards. For example, the hardware could require special power supplies in case of failure or rack space that needs evaluation.

This list of approved or supported hardware must be periodically reviewed as it nears its end of life and end of support. This is especially important as advances in hardware security lower the risk of a breach, and because older devices must be deprecated from any hardware-approved list. Inform your vendors of these changes, which should be linked to an internal database where the hardware-level records are tied to the vendor's record. This data must be tracked with the same due diligence and due care as a Security team that looks for hardware vulnerabilities internally. The data may be located in a Demilitarized Zone (DMZ) area logically, or in enclaves, to lower its security risk. (More information about this will be provided later in the "Zero Trust for Third Parties" section.) However, this data should be tracked for vulnerabilities in case the vendor does not track them.

Instead of having a specific list of hardware gear to lower risk, it can be lowered by making decisions focused on capabilities. For example, criteria could include the level of encryption supported, onboard Trusted Platform Module (TPM) capabilities, or how the vendor performs on supply-chain security. Including definitions on power and size limits can also add more clarity to the list for vendors for comparison of hardware options.

Software Security

The software running on the hardware is the attack surface that will most often be leveraged for an intrusion. The attacker might use a hardware flaw (e.g., low entropy on a TPM), but chances are the avenue used to perform the intrusion came via an OS flaw. If you look at the Common Vulnerabilities and Exposures (CVE) page at any particular hardware manufacturer, the list of security vulnerabilities seems endless. Sort the same list by a CVE rating score of 7.0 or higher (7.0–8.9 is high severity, and 9.0–10.0 is critical, according to v 3.1 of CVSS). The number of vulnerabilities found at the major manufacturers (e.g., Cisco, Juniper, ZTE, Huawei, Netgear, Belkin, and so on) still is in the hundreds to thousands.

Managing software vulnerabilities has become so time-consuming that the information technology (IT) and cybersecurity professions have developed teams and disciplines surrounding it. Look internally at your own company, and they'll likely admit it can be like the kid trying to plug all the holes in the dam (holding back the flood of vulnerabilities) with only two hands. Any medium to large enterprise like the ones just listed are likely dealing with the same huge number of vulnerabilities as they manage all the servers, routers, switches, endpoints, and countless other devices on a modern network that requires patching. Because this universe of connections is known and the risks are managed by the Cybersecurity Third-Party Risk team, it reduces the risk that a vendor will miss something, depending on the vendor's transparency and the Cybersecurity Third-Party Risk team performing its responsibilities.

As described in the earlier due diligence sections, the IRQ and intake processes should clarify that vendors who need to connect are required to provide some level of transparency on software versions running on the hardware and their patch management process. This lack of visibility into network connections is a risk that does not need to be taken if the expectation is set early on during a company's vendor selection and vetting.

If this level of openness is not available from a vendor for any of a variety of reasons and the decision still is to move forward, then holding the vendor to an annual attestation that the software has no CVEs that remain unpatched above a CVE score of 7.0 can provide a reasonable risk reduction. Place this expectation into any contract to ensure that such a request does not become problematic at whatever agreed-upon period.

For vendors that meet an Enhanced Continuous Monitoring (ECM) level of transparency, the knowledge of what hardware and software is running on this connection greatly reduces the risk potential by monitoring these vulnerabilities directly.

Out-of-Band Security

Out-of-band (OOB) connections are defined as ways to communicate to the hardware remotely, regardless of whether a machine is powered on or functional. These hardware types are often used in situations where some expectation of availability meets higher requirements. In case of hardware failure or unavailability, the remote operator will have another means to connect and potentially correct the issue. There are in-band management systems, for example Remote Desktop Connection (such as Virtual Network Computing [VNC] or secure shell [SSH]), but if that primary connectivity is unavailable due to its root cause, then out-of-band communications are a reasonable backdoor for uptime requirements. However, the use of this backdoor means that some other security controls should be required for vendors. Another big area of risk is that these devices, because they are out of band, are not monitoring to detect access like other connectivity.

KC Enterprises tackled this issue by providing strict guidelines on connectivity that require out-of-band connections. First, the vendor had to provide justification for requiring the OOB connection. It was not a checkbox on a questionnaire; instead, some logic had to be provided for requiring the OOB for uptime, as well as an SLA with a business impact assessment. This process was to avoid some vendors who added them as a default for each new customer. If it could be established that there was no real business need, then cybersecurity could deny the request.

Once the business's need was validated, the business sponsor and vendor were provided with a list of controls and best practices that were required for the OOB to be installed and maintained. The list is used as a pre-check for the network security team as the connection and OOB hardware are installed. The pre-check covered the following:

- All default accounts must be disabled, renamed, or removed. Any default passwords must be changed.
- All management ports must have an authentication system or device.

- Modems can only be used when no other connectivity is available for out-of-band connections. If the a modem is used, separate controls are required:
  - Management ports must require a touch-tone password before a synchronization tone is offered.
  - Caller-ID service with designated phone numbers are only allowed.
  - Hardware encryption modems must be used at both ends.
- Access logs must be reviewed no less than quarterly for anomalous behavior, and the vendor is required to report any anomalies within 24 hours of discovery.

Due to the high risk associated with connections, then compounded by the higher risk of OOB communication devices, it was viewed as reasonable at KC to become this prescriptive as there is a legitimate business reason for having them. Cybersecurity can explain the risk while providing options and controls needed to do OOB securely.

Cloud Connections

Cloud connections, which are connections over a leased line or via a web connection from your internal network to a Cloud Service Provider, come in two main varieties for a third-party risk: First is a direct connection from the cloud provider to the corporate network. These are treated the same as other network connectivity because they require hardware at the customer site and where the connection's nearest hop to the cloud. The other variety is over the internet to and from a corporate network. This type flows as usual HTTP (port 80) or HTTPS (port 443) traffic for vendor connectivity from and to the network. Oftentimes, this connection type is not known or advertised because it is considered "normal," non-risky by the users, or it can be part of a *shadow IT*. Shadow IT is a term used to describe people or teams in an organization who deploy information technology solutions outside the knowledge or process of the established IT team.

While not a Cybersecurity Third-Party Risk activity, having your organization deploy a Cloud Access Security Broker (CASB) on internet traffic can find these unknown, and previously undetected, traffic patterns. A CASB sits between the cloud services and the users and monitors all traffic; when fully configured, it can also enforce policy to shape and prevent traffic when necessary. CASBs can be deployed as agents on computers, but they can be challenging to deploy and might miss any device that is not corporate-managed (such as in a Bring Your Own Device environment). Agentless deployments can be deployed rapidly and are better suited at detecting all traffic.

If your organization has a CASB deployed, work with that team to perform scans for any shadow IT or unknown traffic for cloud-based vendors. This communication can result in data leakage or a breach if not discovered and managed as cybersecurity policy and best practices would recommend.

Vendor Connectivity Lifecycle Management

Third-party connections are placed in the high-risk category in most organizations. A link from a supplier presents the possibility of an attack upon the vendor to traverse into your company's network. Ensure these connections are passed through a set of defense-in-depth controls. Oftentimes, if it's a VPN connection, once the VPN is terminated there are no additional controls placed on the incoming connections. The life of a connection from the initial vendor specifications, design, implementation, maintenance, patching, and termination must be documented, as automated as possible, and with logical and physical security validation throughout the entire process. Although some of this was covered earlier, it's worth mentioning again that the vendor's full lifecycle of connectivity must be documented.

Intake and Connectivity When a vendor begins an intake process, whether at IRQ or intake assessment, flags for engagements will pop up that require connectivity. The process notifies the network security, Cybersecurity Third-Party Risk, and the architecture teams. The subject-matter experts (SMEs) from these teams will meet several times with the vendor and business sponsor to understand the requirements and to ensure that they meet the vendor's connectivity requirements.

Security architecture staff will develop both a high-level design (HLD) and traffic flows. These designs must include key control elements and where the network traffic is expected to route. In addition, they will also indicate into which enclave (in a Zero Trust deployment) the vendor will be deployed. Security architecture has the HLD reviewed by any appropriate approval bodies and then provides it to the engineering and operations team who will use it for deployment and maintenance.

Cybersecurity Third-Party Risk performs the due diligence on the vendor as well as their connectivity. If the vendor requires an OOB communication device along with their router/VPN hardware, this device must be reviewed and approved so that it meets best-practice OOB standards. Discussions will focus on the vendor's willingness to be transparent about the patch management of any hardware they provide, and the contracts should reflect this commitment.

Any red flags or gaps in the security controls discovered in the intake assessment require a risk-rating for either a risk acceptance, mitigation, or denial. As in other areas, there are non-negotiables in this space: The connectivity must be encrypted at a minimum of AES-256, the access management must enforce multi-factor authentication (MFA) for privileged access to the hardware, and transparency must be present on the patch levels. These three items are absolutely required to ensure that the device is hardened and that data leakage risk is reduced.

When this intake assessment process is complete, the implementation can then be planned in coordination with the vendor and any service provider who is scheduled to perform the installation (i.e., if it is not the vendor directly performing the installation). The operations staff at the demarcation point (whether in a data center or a networking closet) must be notified as well to ensure that personnel is available.

Implementation Implementation requires a few assurance checkpoints that the installation and configuration are completed as expected to the HLD. These design documents are referenced by the installation engineers for how the security controls and network configurations are installed and completed. In this case, the engineers use a checklist to validate each design step. This checklist of the items completed successfully must be placed with the vendor's system of record as well as into the asset management system. Because this is a connection from a third party, this checklist also is catalogued in the cybersecurity TPRM system for monitoring and due care for the remainder of the connection's lifecycle (see Figure 13.1).

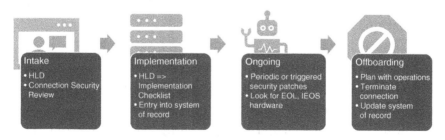

FIGURE 13.1 The Vendor Connection Lifecycle

Ongoing Due Diligence and Due Care As the asset is in the cybersecurity TPRM system for tracking, it will not know what software versions were last updated on the hardware. This system is either automatically tied to a CVE alert for high or critical patches required for the hardware, or it is manually checked at least quarterly for any new critical patches.

The hardware is owned and managed by the vendor, so when it is time to perform a maintenance or security patch, do not rely on said vendor to do it. Notify them of the available critical update and request to know when they plan to perform the maintenance. Ideally, this will go smoothly and be accomplished as quickly as can be planned without any business interruption. If a vendor pushes back or refuses to provide a timely update, then the process instructs that the Cybersecurity Third-Party Risk team escalate the issue with both the vendor manager and business sponsor. Should the delay continue, then there is a termination process where a date is given to turn off the connection (along with the hardware) to stop the risk. This final escalation step should be treated as a last resort and is mostly designed to provide a final push for the uncooperative vendor to complete the necessary upgrade.

Each patch or upgrade is updated in all the required systems internally at the company, and a new date is set for the next check or automatic alert. Pay attention to any end-of-life and end-of-service notices, as they require more runway for a third party to find suitable replacement hardware and schedule the swap and installation.

Offboarding and Termination Whenever a contract is going to be terminated, or a connection is no longer needed, the termination process of the connectivity must follow procedure to ensure that it's completed, and that hardware is returned as requested. The trigger, if automated or manual, should be initiated by the vendor manager and notify both the operations staff and the TPRM teams of the impending cutoff. Much like the intake assessment that needs time to prepare for installation, the same is true of a vendor's removal: Ensure that your operations staff are ready to escort any engineers needed by the vendor and provide physical validation to the Cybersecurity Third-Party Risk team of the step's completion.

The third party's lifecycle for network connectivity should be documented from end to end and track all the relevant information, including the type of hardware involved, OS level, patch levels, type of connectivity, and information on the owner/contact at the vendor in case of emergency. Lastly, it is common to forget the hardware once it is installed (both by vendor and customer). Track them and perform your periodic due care and due diligence as directed according to your process and best practices.

Zero Trust for Third Parties

The *Zero Trust* (ZT) model is not new, but one that many companies struggle to implement internally. Zero Trust is a security model requiring that all users, accounts, and devices (both trusted and untrusted) be authenticated and authorized, and to continuously validate a company's security configuration before any access to applications and data is granted. The way a ZT network is established is similar to the approach of Cybersecurity Third-Party Risk. ZT architecture is based on the principle that nothing can be trusted (i.e., zero). The starting point is that everything is a potential threat that must be authenticated. "Never Trust, Always Verify" is the principle upon which this is based.

Created by John Kindervag, Vice President for Forrester Research, Zero Trust stems from the realization that modern networks operated on the principle that anything and everything within the network was to be trusted, without question. When the ZT model is deployed on a network, the first step is to identify the location of the data and systems or applications that need to be protected. When that area is identified, the users and systems that move across that sensitive area can be analyzed. An accounting of the users who access the systems, the levels of access provided versus required, how the connectivity is occurring, and other factors determine how the policy and controls can be implemented to achieve ZT. The area in which these assets are available to connect on the network is the *surface area* that needs to be segmented in order to limit the access to legitimate traffic. This is accomplished most commonly with Next-Generation Firewalls (NGFWs) using application layer–level inspection to ensure that unauthorized traffic is blocked and logged.

The NGFW set at layer 7 (i.e., application) is granted a level of visibility into traffic to enforce a *Kipling Method* policy. The Kipling Method refers to the early twentieth century stories by Rudyard Kipling, "Just So Stories," and the six questions of Who, What, When, Where, Why, and How. Yes, technically there's actually six questions, but the "How" question is a valuable detail. This level of questions can be very appropriate in accessing a protected surface in ZT. If the connection into the area passes the first five, what about the "How"? Say the VP of Human Resources is attempting to access the HR file of the executives during normal working hours from a U.S. location in order to run a report on a personal device. That covers Who, What, When, Where, and Why. Yet, the "How" is not correct: It was using a non-corporate device and the connection is not allowed by rule on the firewall. In this case, the device used for access is not authorized to access the content. The same person, however, accessing the same information with an authorized device, would be granted access to the data.

Third-party connections can benefit from this ZT model in the prevention of lateral movement, the ease of deployment for connections, and lower due diligence efforts. By definition, these connections are areas of high risk. The surface area for attack is these network connections. It is a network area where connectivity happens with the vendors, and the same principles can be applied, just differently than on an internal network deployment.

Similar to ZT's internal network methodology, the first step is to identify the *protected surface*. The protected surface for vendor connections is lateral movement outside the connection point-to-point. What is meant by this is the expectation that the connectivity between the vendor and customer is only going back and forth to the required data. It must not expand beyond that narrow "beam" of data exchange as required. The transaction flows are the vendor and customer communications, and many of these connection types have similarities, including partners, service organizations, and data processing, among others. ZT architecture is based around these similarities with the policy aligned to match. Let's take a look at how KC Enterprises deployed ZT for third parties.

KC's first step was to establish the protected surface. The protected surface for them was the internal network itself, which enabled the vendor connection's lateral movement through it. The need to prevent communications to and from the vendor from going outside the approved connection was the goal for ZT in this implementation. The challenge was that each vendor connected largely with the same level of controls. They were good controls; however, they did not address the different risk levels among the various types of connection use cases. It led to a transaction flows discussion.

In a third-party context, transaction flows are classified in terms of the types of vendor access and transactions. Not all vendors perform the same activity or service for KC, but commonalities exist among many of them according to the Kipling Method of the six questions. Large, easy buckets were created: Sales Partners, Business Process Outsource, Integrated Support, and Production Support. Each of these vendor connection types had an identifiable pattern of who, what, when, where, why, and how. These data types could be collected and placed into an NGFW to create enclaves for each of them. Identity also plays a critical role in the ZT model, as it ensures only those users who have been properly authenticated and authorized gain access. The ZT concept trusts no one until they've proven they are a "trusted" user.

The Sales Partners enclave (i.e., a distinct bucket or network area) remained reserved for companies and contractors who sold their widgets and e-widgets in bulk. This enclave access looked for a valid sales partner user and ensured they were accessing only the sales database and incentives programs, that this action was performed at an accepted business hour, from an expected location (by IP address) to update their sales numbers and check on their sales bonus from a vendor-controlled laptop.

Business Process Outsource vendors will remain only offshore for KC. This meant the question of "where" was always going to be outside the United States, but it would be specified in their case to originate from a specific offshore IP block to ensure it is not spoofed. Their connectivity restricts them to connecting to the Virtual Desktop Infrastructure (VDI) environment only to ensure they cannot traverse the network. Any logging and monitoring is geared toward data loss prevention on the production data locations.

Integrated support services, such as contractors and professional services, who collaborate directly with departments inside the company are placed in an enclave tailored to their type of connectivity (see Figure 13.2).

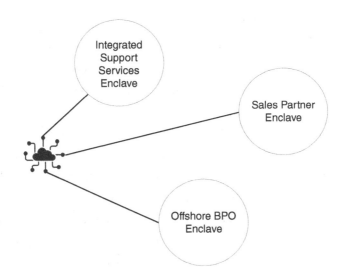

FIGURE 13.2 Vendor Enclaves in ZT for Third Parties

Because they often need direct access to software within the company, their network connectivity allows traversing into specific areas that are separated on a virtual local area network (VLAN). Its monitoring is focused on looking for anomalous traffic and data loss. The connectivity between the VPN and the software it is connecting to is IP address to IP address to each connection, and will only accept connections from whitelisted IP addresses.

As the groups are created with their own security rules, access control lists, logging, and monitoring, the vendors are moved into them and tested to ensure that production is working. When new suppliers are brought on board, their type and access required allows the team to place them in the correct area. Doing so lowers deployment times, ensures consistent baseline security controls, and provides for a repeatable process.

Lastly is the approach to remote access for third parties regarding VPNs and remote access. Many of the vendors require a VPN connection to perform work, but these are difficult to place in the ZT model. However, KC adopted a ZT access model based upon a software-defined perimeter (SDP). See Figure 13.3. A VPN requires customer provisioning and, when connecting to the VPN gateway or concentrator, it meant the vendor had to do almost a v-shaped connection as they go out of the network to connect to their cloud solution. This SDP added ZT principles and permitted the user to connect directly to the cloud or other location without going through KC's network first. Doing so lowers the risk of a traversal if breached.

An SDP connectivity solution entails placing a controller on the control path between the user and the application. The controller is not on the data path, however, so the latency is not impacted. When the controller gets an access request for an application, it sets up an encrypted connection between the user and the software. When the connection is completed, the SDP controller essentially gets out of the way and goes into pass-through mode (traffic flows freely).

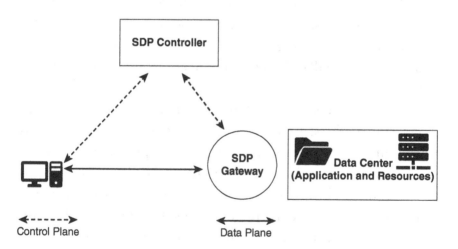

FIGURE 13.3   An SDP Gateway

Internet of Things and Third Parties

First coined by Kevin Ashton of Proctor & Gamble in 1999, The *Internet of Things* (IoT) is a term used to describe physical items such as sensors, software, and other capabilities, which are connected to the internet. The concept of the IoT was discussed as far back as 1982, when a soda machine was connected the internet at Carnegie-Mellon University, as the first known IoT device. At the end of 2025, there are expected to be 21.5 billion IoT devices connected worldwide (according to Research and Markets: `www.researchandmarkets.com/reports/5174853/iot-middleware-market-growth-trends-and?utm_source=GNOM&utm_medium=PressRelease&utm_code=hsm7q8&utm_campaign=1482270+-+Worldwide+Industry+for+IoT+Middleware+to+2025+-+Manufacturing+Expected+to+Have+High+Potential+Growth&utm_exec=jamu273prd`).

Your company will always have vendors who need to place IoT devices for certain services. These solutions can range from IP cameras, point-of-sale systems, medical devices, printers, or industry-control devices. Tremendous security risk is inherent in these devices due to both the ways they are manufactured and configured, and more importantly how they are managed.

Often viewed as the first biggest risk to IoT devices is how manufacturers lack focus on security. Makers of the IoT gadgets will either hardcode the devices (i.e., the code is in an immutable memory that cannot be changed) or provide weak, easily guessed passwords. Many will not have a way to update the devices or patch them securely, leaving the old embedded OSs and unencrypted data transfer and storage. Such weaknesses must be addressed when reviewing the security of any proposed IoT devices that are to be added to a network.

The second biggest weakness is the organizations themselves and their lack of process and management of these IoT devices. Because many of the devices come with weak passwords, security posture, and often are in need of updates and security patching, they must be treated like any other hardware and hardened before connected. (*Hardened* here means the system has undergone the latest security patches and a series of checks are done to lower security risks.) Using unique credentials for each device ensures that each of them is authentic and authorized. Never allow the use of static passwords or shared keys as they can be easily exploited by an attacker. Shared keys do not allow security to validate each device; they must simply accept that any device presenting a shared key is authorized and validated. These key stores, if broken into, are an obvious attack vector.

Using a Trusted Platform Module provides hardware-based security. The TPM chip in the module is a trusted and secure processor that performs cryptographic activities and can do these much more securely than a software-based product. These modules ensure that a product has not been hacked and is running authentic code from boot-to-OS operation. When updating the software, require that the software is digitally signed to verify the package is authentic. Have the devices validate against an internal Private Key Infrastructure (PKI) to ensure that the certificates are valid. All of these are capability requirements for when a vendor is providing an IoT device(s) as part of their service.

Finally, you should establish how the devices will be managed for their lifecycle. Their patches, security updates, and maintenance can be done by the vendor or the internal network teams. If it will be performed by the supplier, any agreement must be specific about the supplier's roles and responsibilities. In addition, there will likely be some concern about the issues of penetration testing, breach notification. and hardware updates. This concern is because the pen testing ensures they are tested for vulnerabilities; breach notification needs to be as fast as possible to lessen the damage or impact; and hardware updates are critical to allow for the ability to adapt to new risks or capabilities.

While some government regulations on IoT devices exist, they are still fairly new in their creation. Outside the United States, the Organization of Economic Co-operation and Development (OECD) Guidelines on the Protection of Privacy and Transborder Flows of Personal Data of 1980, along with the updated 2013 version, deal with the loss of data due to the IoT devices. In the EU, the Directive 95/46/EC of 1995, also known as the Data Protection Directive (DPD), governs the movement of data across boundaries and IoT devices.

In the United States, the U.S. Privacy Act of 1974 is relevant, in addition to the recent three recommendations in 2015 by the Federal Trade Commission (FTC) for data security, data consent, and data minimization. Data security directed that IoT manufacturers design the devices to safeguard data collection, storage, and processing. Data consent directed the makers to enable users to choose which data they want to share or transmit. Data minimization relates to collecting only the minimal data necessary to perform the activity.

IoT devices are inevitability located on a network and can pose a significant risk to an organization if not properly vetted and managed. Your company should draft some minimum standards on what devices can be accepted, including no hardcoded passwords, access management that's fully configurable by the user, requiring a hardware-Trusted Platform Module (TPM), and ensuring the ability to perform patches and updates. Unfortunately, these requirements can pose an issue for many commercially available products, so there will need to be a buy-in that these are almost non-negotiables due to the risks if allowed on the network without these requirements.

Trusted Platform Module and Secure Boot

When purchasing most modern hardware devices (e.g., IoT, routers, firewalls, etc.), a requirement must be included that they contain a TPM or a Secure Boot on them. As previously discussed, a TPM is a processor that provides security-related activities, such as creation and secure storage, certificates, and encryption keys. A Secure Boot is a security standard that ensures when a device boots up, it only loads software from the trusted manufacturer. The firmware on the chip checks the digital signature of all the boot software, firmware, drivers, and the OS for authenticity. TPMs provide a hardware random-number generator, secure generation of cryptographic keys, and remote attestation, and each chip has a unique and secret Endorsement Key (EK) burned into it at production. This key is immutable and used to validate authenticity. See Figure 13.4.

A standard from the Unified Extensible Firmware Interface (UEFI) for Secure Boot is acceptable in lower-risk environments. UEFI Secure Boot is less secure than the TPM because

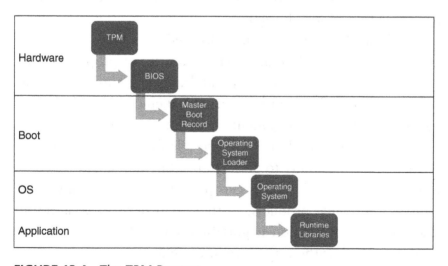

FIGURE 13.4 The TPM Process

it is not hardware-anchored and it does not validate the basic input/output system (BIOS) at boot-up. This makes it vulnerable to a rootkit being inserted.

The process of Secure Boot starts with the verification that the initial bootloader is genuine and not altered. The bootloader then executes and checks that the required subsystems exist and function properly. If those check out, then the system initiates basic logging. The process then checks for any firmware updates; if updates exist, they are then checked to be authentic, are updated, and the system rebooted. Next is the verification that the external services (e.g., power supply, NTP, etc.) are operating as expected, which are then authenticated using the application code.

The initial stage—where the bootloader is verified—is critical. Only when confirmation is complete can the rest of the boot process be completed. This verification is done using public-private keys. When a hardware maker places the TPM module, there is an immutable private key. The device has the public key associated with the maker's private key stored securely in the TPM. The bootloader code has the cryptographic hash of their private key securely stored. As the bootloader starts up, the hash signature is validated against the TPM's embedded public key to ensure that it's an authentic hash. The bootloader coder is then hashed again and compared against the signed hash. Once it is confirmed to be a match (and therefore not tampered with), then the rest of the process is allowed to complete.

Performing this process with a read-only (RO) chip, as compared with the TPM processor, is not an acceptable substitute. Yes, an RO chip can ensure that no tampering has occurred at boot, but it lacks the ability to ever be updated. If the keys are stored in the chip, should they ever become compromised, then all devices with those keys would be at risk for being hacked.

The U.S. Department of Defense (DoD) requires that all new systems (e.g., servers, desktops, laptops, mobile devices, etc.) support TPM version 1.2 or higher. Microsoft announced in June 2020 that it requires TPM 2.0 and secure boot in new Windows Server Hardware effective January 1, 2021. Secure boot must be turned on by default and have the updated TPM version preinstalled. It's further suggested that BitLocker encryption should be leveraged on them to protect against rootkit malware.

Secure boot and TPM technology has been broadly adopted across all hardware types and sizes. Given the risk of some devices (e.g., IoT, servers, and networking equipment), it should be a requirement that the vendors who supply them have secure boot and/or TPMs to lower the risk of security breaches and data loss.

Inside Look: The Target Breach (2013)

A quick reminder of how important OOB devices and vendor connectivity security is to your organization's security is the Target breach that occurred in 2013 (previously mentioned in Chapter 2). According to the state's investigation, the cybercriminals gained access to Target's network by stealing credentials from their air-conditioning company (HVAC) vendor who was sloppy with their access management. The result was the payment accounts of about 41 million customers and personal identifiable information (PII) of nearly 70 million customers. It cost Target $236 million in total expenses and over 140 lawsuits to defend in court. There was a multi-state settlement of $18.5 million to cover government-specific costs for the investigative expenses. In addition, Target promised $10,000 to any customer that could prove their data was compromised.

These connections are a high risk to your company and must be treated as such. The cost of negligence is not just monetary but reputational. The Target breach is still one of the most widely known and not something any company wants to be synonymous with—a confirmed breach. Note that any search of this breach mentions the HVAC provider, but rarely is there a mention of the vendor's actual name nor much attention paid to their lack of sufficient access management.

Conclusion

Connections into your company by a third party are a high-risk endeavor due to them opening up the possibility of an attacker traversing from their third-party network into your enterprise network. Use ZT principles to set up enclaves by vendor type to ensure that minimal access is required and have a repeatable process for them. Beware of IoT devices given by strangers: Have a specific list of non-negotiable requirements for them to be accepted from a vendor. Hardware should all have TPM or Secure Boot at minimum as they are now considered standard practice for critical infrastructure. Keep an eye on all your connections and have a published lifecycle to deal with them from intake to offboarding and termination. Lastly, network connections often can be forgotten by the vendor, and it is not enough to rely on them to perform the necessary updates and maintenance. Establish transparency expectations with these third parties on patch levels and hardware. At the same time, take on some ownership as Cybersecurity Third-Party Risk and monitor them for security risks. This can be done via an arrangement with the vendor to have read-only rights access to the device to check it yourself, or via a periodic (i.e., quarterly) check to the third-party contact to validate that they have installed the required security patch updates.

14

Offshore Third-Party Cybersecurity Risk

Offshore vendors pose a different risk than those who reside within your home country. The majority of the time, the term *offshore* refers to those who are located in countries where business process outsourcing is typical; for example, India, the Philippines, Vietnam, South America, and others outside the United States, Canada, Europe, and other countries where costs can be higher than for the same processes outsourced to a lower-cost location. Challenges exist in performing both due diligence and due care for the location, and differences in standards, practices, regulations, culture, and other risks offshore exist in comparison to a supplier local to your shores.

Distance can present challenges for several reasons. Vendors and their subject-matter experts (SMEs) who participate in the conversations for due diligence are remote, and can be located in different time zones, making scheduling a challenge. Typically, this can be overcome by including a local representative from the offshore vendor, and/or when the remote staff is on your local time or have an agreed schedule that overlaps with the home country's time zones. There can also be issues with holiday coverage and notification risks. Secondly, the third-party's distance makes performing on-site due diligence costly in terms of time and travel. Some countries might require a visa for entry and can take a day of travel, depending on locations and connecting flights.

Local regulations for data privacy and data security are a risk as they can differ greatly from your country or region. It is not hard to see how a U.S.-based company could outsource to Argentina (for Spanish-speaking expertise and a lower-cost support model) where the Ibero-American Data Protection

Network (RIPD is the acronym in Spanish) covers that country. Further, in 2000 the Argentina National Constitution executed the Personal Data Protection Act 25.326 (PDPA) to help protect data privacy. PDPA aligns with the EU data privacy model, and Argentina was the first Latin American country to be able to perform data transfers to the EU with the "adequacy" qualification. How does a firm deal with any differences in how data privacy is treated? It can be said that the data is coming from the United States and only concerns U.S. citizens and residents. However, there could easily be a U.S. resident who is an Argentine citizen, who is also your customer, who could be protected by the PDPA and the RIPD that allows them access to their data. A bigger company could have up to hundreds or more examples of cross-border regulations, which presents risks for how data is handled and stored and needs to be addressed by offshore vendors.

Other risks are as follows: The countries themselves and how work is performed, internet traffic that might be monitored or blocked, areas of the world where internet hackers and criminals operate out of, and regions with potentially armed conflict (including cyber conflict). The following presents a company with an option to determine boundaries where the risk to business, and cyber risk in particular, should be avoided: Some countries are known to block or monitor web traffic, which can present risk for offshore data protection. If the region has a high cybercrime rate, malware/ransomware attacks, and is not prepared to deal with them, it's of particular concern when drawing boundaries on where offshore vendors can and cannot be located. The home government will publish an ever-evolving list of forbidden countries for business. But this list is about the legality of working, not the advisability. When drawing red lines around countries or regions for your business to avoid, it should not be confined to what the regulations are, but to avoid unnecessary risk by performing business in a country or region when less risky options are available.

The lifecycle of an offshore vendor is not different than a local one, but different risk considerations must be addressed at each phase. To make the process more descriptive, we will explore how KC Enterprises performs the lifecycle of a remote or offshore vendor.

Onboarding Offshore Vendors

Onboarding a vendor who is offshore requires that many of the same questions are asked, but the focus on some areas is more pronounced or incorporates different questions due to the different risks. KC Enterprises' IRQ includes questions to ensure that these risks are caught early. The review includes extra risk questions and can trigger other third-party risk domains to become more engaged. If you recall, in Chapter 5, KC's intake questions about potential offshore work included two separate questions about fourth-party risk:

- Will the vendor require other third parties to provide service to KC Enterprises?
- Will any of the vendors or its third parties (i.e., KC's fourth parties) perform work or support services outside the United States?

These two questions are direct and designed to get these vendors the appropriate questionnaires, additional contract language, and other due diligence processes focused on remote suppliers. When they are answered in the affirmative, the next set of formal due diligence questions on the intake assessment includes language and reviews tailored for them. At KC, the same team that performs local vendor due diligence also performs these reviews, as they are trained or already have the experience necessary to perform them. On-site assessment team employees are required to have valid passports, so they can perform these activities in whatever country is required.

The questions for a Request for Proposal (RFP) do not change as there is also a question about the potential for offshore risk: Does the product have any development or support outside the United States?

And as the RFP process uses a grading system, this risk can be graded as the answers are evaluated. Depending on the project, this grading will hinge on the project's scope (e.g., is it designed to be done offshore or is it preferred onshore?), but the risk is then weighed into those results. When the selected vendor is known to be remote, this data is added to the next step (in the IRQ).

This next step is to ensure that the vendor and internal business sponsor are aware of the KC Enterprise non-negotiable where no KC customer or employee data may be stored or processed outside the United States. This means all work must be performed via remote access from the offshore vendor's location to a virtual environment at a KC data center or a U.S.-based co-location or Cloud Service Provider (CSP). Given how solutions could be moved to the cloud and there were existing due diligence workstreams to deal with that risk, this was viewed as providing choices to the business while maintaining a low-risk profile when it comes to entanglements in external data privacy laws such as General Data Protection Regulation (GDPR).

The intake assessment process is designed to provide both a vetting process for vendors that could pose a risk to the company unnecessarily (will not encrypt data or in a country that poses unneeded risk), and to perform due diligence on those that can proceed. For offshore business, the IRG and intake questions focus on the key areas of risk for performing business outside the country. Because these locations are remote, performing the physical security validation with an on-site assessment becomes important and leads into the ongoing due diligence efforts.

Ongoing Due Diligence for Offshore Vendors

Ongoing due diligence for remote vendors requires the same activities—remote and on-site assessments—but the questions and validation included vary slightly. Remote questionnaires can be performed on an annual basis for offshore, but there is a requirement for doing a physical, on-site security evaluation due to the risks. At KC Enterprises, the Cybersecurity Third-Party Risk team plans an on-site assessment annually at each remote vendor. The assessments for KC's offshore vendors in India, the Philippines, and Ireland are all done in one trip to each country but use different personnel for each journey.

Physical Security

The main purpose of a visit to these offshore vendors is to view *in the flesh* that security controls are in place as expected. As the assessment team approaches the Offshore Development Center (ODC), the evaluation has already begun, by noting how the security around the ODC is performing as follows:

Outside:

- **Indication:** There should be no external indication what clients the vendor manages or performs work for at the location.
- **Physical barriers around the building(s):** Is there a wall or fence at least 8 feet high along with closed-circuit

cameras around the perimeter? Walk around the fence or wall to visibly check for any holes or access points and that the cameras are covering all angles. If there is no wall or fence, the visual inspection around the building should look for doors or access points that are not locked or guarded. When a wall or barrier is present, the distance should be sufficient to allow for interception *before* an intruder can get to the building itself.

- **Entry and guards:** As the entry is approached, watch how the guards pay attention to others entering: Are they spending time matching identifications with the faces of the employees or guests? How are bags, purses, and other hiding places (e.g., jackets, fanny packs, etc.) inspected for any recording devices (e.g., cameras, phones, etc.). Is the search cursory with little interest in finding anything, or do they clearly understand the risk and treat it with proper curiosity?

- **Inspection:** When it is your turn (i.e., the assessors) to pass through the security guard checkpoint and inspections, note how the process is handled. Did they have you sign into a guest log and sufficiently check and log your identification? Did they check your baggage for recording devices and require you to give them up, per the policy? Just because you are a customer does not mean the on-site team should receive favorable treatment. If they allow this customer team through without holding them to the policy, then it is likely they are not following the process for others as well.

- **Logs:** Ask to see the log for visitors to see how they manage it. View it with a critical eye for informational consistency on the visitors being logged, including dates, times, where they were from, who they were visiting, and logout dates and times. Ensure the log is filled out with data for each visitor as expected.

- **Any other entry controls:** Note if a metal detector or other devices are used to screen staff and visitors. Are bollards located at the entrance to prevent a smash and grab? Are the entry controls and physical barriers sufficient to stop an unauthorized entry or does it seem possible for someone to circumvent with little effort?

Inside:

- **Production area:** Ask to see the area where sensitive data is accessed first to assess physical separation and the Clean Desk policy. As the ODC's production area is approached, ensure there is no alternate access points into this area that would evade the guarded main entry area. The entry to the production space should have another entry check, such as a badge and/or PIN code. When entering and observing this space, look for unattended desks with computers unlocked and sensitive documentation left out on the desk. Ask to view any break areas or supply rooms to also look for any documentation or devices that could contain sensitive data (e.g., laptops, hard drives, etc.) and are left unattended.

- **Validation of physical separation:** The Offshore Addendum states that production and development areas must have a physical separation. This division must be validated and has some discretion by the on-site team. The preference is for these areas to be separated on separate floors or in another building. There can be cases where the engagement with the vendor is small enough that having this level of separation is not possible without significant cost to the customer. In such cases, these areas can be located on the same floor but must have a barrier (i.e., wall) between the two areas.

- **Paper documentation security and destruction:** If the production area will be managing paper documentation, then it is necessary to have a locked area where these papers can be securely stored when not in use. Also, a locked bin should be used to store such materials prior to their destruction. View the logs for destruction and verify that they are filled out completely.

- **Production workstation:** There are restrictions on what the offshore workers can do on the VDI that need to be validated. Have one or more of them log in and substantiate that they cannot copy and paste out of the virtual desktop or access the internet beyond what they need to perform their job. Look at the desktop software running on the vendor's PC for any communication software that has access outside the supplier's network. Check to ensure that any external drives and media are not accessible physically or logically (i.e., can they plug in a thumb drive and download data to it?). Ensure antivirus and malware software are running and check to see when they were last updated.

These are the high-level key security controls for the physical pieces. If the offshore staff supports other clients, make sure there are specific controls in place to address KC data and that systems access is isolated and separate. More of these can be added, depending on what sort of work a vendor performs and how they perform it for the customer.

Offboarding Due Diligence for Offshore Vendors

Offboarding an offshore vendor is similar to any other supplier, with the exception of the additional steps on the validation of any remote data destruction and connectivity termination. The steps to offboard a vendor start with the notification from the business about the impending change and dates of when the contract is to be finished. At KC Enterprises, the Cybersecurity Third-Party Risk team performs a remote assessment, in addition to planning several conference calls along this timeline with milestones set for the vendor to meet.

Initial work by the team focuses on gathering all the following relevant data for the vendor, noting each item that requires confirmation and due diligence on the offboarding process:

- **Data records:** If the vendor was processing paper records for KC, then there must be a certificate of destruction (COD) from the shredding firm confirming that all final documentation was destroyed. If there is a need to retain the documentation for legal or regulatory reasons, the team works with the vendor to securely transfer those records to the appropriate team for the duration of the retention.

- **Data:** The contracts for offshore vendors at KC require them to wipe any hard drives or memory devices that were used for their services. These devices do not need to be destroyed, but the wiping process must include breaking the link between the hard drive encryption and the keys to ensure that the data cannot be recovered. While no data was stored locally, the links to the VDI and any other risks drop when the data is rendered non-recoverable.

- **Connectivity:** The way offshore vendors connect to perform their services at KC is through a VDI from their onshore partners/company. This ensures that no data ever leaves the country and lowers the risk of data leakage as the desktop environment is controlled by KC's team. If there is a leased line or VPN that is involved in that connectivity, then the termination of it follows the same path as other connections. Whenever a contract is going to be terminated, or a connection is no longer needed, the termination process for the connectivity must follow a process to ensure that it is completed and that the hardware is returned as requested. The trigger, if automated or manual, is done by the vendor manager who notifies both the operations staff and the TPRM teams of the impending cutoff.

Much like the intake process that needs to have some time to prepare for installation, the same is true of the removal. Ensure operations staff are ready to escort vendor's engineers needed from the vendor and provide physical validation to the Cybersecurity Third-Party Risk team of the step's completion.

Inside Look: A Reminder on Country Risk

A reminder on the Vietnam supply-chain attack. As previously mentioned, the Vietnamese government dictates that all documentation must be signed using their digital signature through the Vietnam Government Certification Authority (VCGA). The supply-chain attack was done by compromising the digital signature toolkit that exploited the installers on the VCGAs website "ca.gov.vn" that contained spyware called PhantomNet or Smanager. The toolkit was distributed by the government that provides cryptographic certificates that are required to digitally sign documents in Vietnam.

The attack took place from July 23 to August 16, 2020. The two modified installers "gca01-client-v2-x32-8.3.msi" and "gca01-client-v2-x64-8.3.msi" for 32-bit and 64-bit Microsoft Windows systems were part of the install packages that contained the malware. Because the downloads happened over a secured pathway (HTTPS), this leads investigators to believe it is not a man-in-the-middle attack. This would be where an attacker takes over the back-and-forth traffic between the website and the user, redirecting them to another malicious website. This meant that the attackers had altered the software directly and loaded it into the website for download by unsuspecting victims.

Once the compromised software was downloaded and installed, the application ran the PhantomNet backdoor with a regular file named "eToken.exe," which looked like a legitimate part of the software. The trojan then contacted a command and control server for further instructions.

There have been additional supply-chain attacks that point to Advanced Persistent Threats (APTs) going after sectors or countries as a whole. In the Able Desktop attack, the chat application was exploited to disrupt Mongolian government agencies from a likely Chinese APT. GoldenSpy was an instance of a Chinese bank that had a backdoor tech toolkit that contained an exploit which got sent to international trading firms doing business with it in China. Wizvera VeraPort device, a security software manager popular in South Korea, was compromised by the Lazarus Group, a known North Korean hacking group.

While doing business in Vietnam, Mongolia, or South Korea is not stopped due to these APT supply-chain attacks, they do demonstrate that some countries will carry additional risk depending on adversaries and political climate. The danger of doing business offshore in some countries carries additional cybersecurity risk due to state-sponsored APTs in certain regions.

Country Risk

Part of the risk of a country or region stems from cybersecurity risks. Performing work outside the home country of the company, as described, entails risk due to the distance and differing regulations. It is prudent for a company to examine the risk of working remotely with vendors and establish some guidance for the business to use in making less risky decisions on which nations or regions are considered more acceptable and those that pose undue risk. The way this can be accomplished varies by industry, regulatory guidance, and business operational decisions; cybersecurity risks also must be considered. Does the area or country have an elevated danger of open conflict or is it already at cyberwar with another? For example, the conflict between the Ukraine and Russia has produced some negative impact on business and life in the Ukraine. In some countries, the free flow of data across the internet is not the same as others. If there is known monitoring or the blocking of traffic, it could pose an unnecessary risk to work being performed in those countries.

KC's Country Risk

There were times at KC where the process worked correctly for an offshore vendor. However, along the way, it somehow was "discovered" that they were, in fact, in a county of "concern." These countries were not ones that the U.S. government said that if we did business with them, we could go to jail. These were countries that the cybersecurity teams knew had higher risk than others. When these late discoveries were made, it often led to uncomfortable discussions with the internal business sponsors and the vendor. KC decided that the firm needed a unified explainable definition of which countries weren't acceptable to perform business in and which ones were preferred, and that it was necessary to explain why these decisions were made so they could be shared internally and externally.

The team based these definitions on a list that provided options for business but also set boundaries with some explanations. First, there was the easy list of sanctioned countries, including Cuba, Iran, North Korea, and Syria, resulting in no ambiguity about their exclusion. The policy was listed in several different standards as such:

> No KC Enterprise employee, contractor, agent, or representative will engage in any discussions or business operations with a country currently listed by the U.S. Department of Commerce (DoC). In instances where a country is added to this list that already has a vendor(s) performing services for KC Enterprises, all activity must stop effective the date required by the U.S. Government and regulatory guidance.

The next part of the list contained the preferred countries. The word *preference* meant that if these countries were selected as one of the offshore countries, then standard due diligence would take place. If another country was chosen, then due diligence could require additional questions and did not guarantee approval. Preferred locations were determined to be, in this case, where the company already had an offshore footprint and where other countries were seen as favorable for business operations. Favorable for business operations meant the government had long been friendly to western business operations, did not restrict or were known to monitor internet traffic, and contained capable infrastructure (e.g., technology, air travel, road travel).

The decision on these definitions produced a list for internal business that was easily explained:

- **Countries not permitted due to law or regulation:** Cuba, North Korea, Syria, and Iran. Consult the latest U.S. DoC website for any updates. This can be driven by regulatory or legal limitations.
- **Countries KC Enterprises considers unfavorable for business:** Afghanistan, Somalia, Yemen, Pakistan, Libya, Myanmar, Nigeria, Chad, Ethiopia, and Venezuela.

- **Preferred countries (current operations):** Philippines, India, and Ireland.
- **Other countries:** On a case-by-case basis.

For intake, it not only clarified preference, but stated that additional countries could be considered with the understanding that there would be more due diligence and no guarantee of approval. This had the effect of pointing most options to the three countries currently performing offshore work for the company. The process for the case-by-case basis was established for those times when it was required for a new country to be added to a restricted list or the preferred countries.

Countries not on the preferred list had to be reviewed by Cybersecurity Third-Party Risk with the following criteria:

- Is there a similar provider in an existing "preferred" country?
- What is the state of cybercrime in the country?
- Does the country monitor or block internet traffic?
- Does the country pose an elevated risk to KC's data or network connectivity?

These security assessments for countries not already reviewed and having business operations enabled an open dialogue to occur between business leadership, KC's upper management, and the cybersecurity team about the risks observed and guidance provided. Their process is not designed to be a checklist, but more of a discussion of the findings and risks the Cybersecurity Third-Party Risk team found in relation to the business's operation and benefits the offshore vendor provided. The first question of "Is there a similar provider in a country already on a preferred list?" was one that required the internal business leadership to come ready with an answer. If they were unsure or had not done the required work to find one, then that must be completed to provide a complete picture of a way to avoid the risk.

Conclusion

Performing work offshore to save a company money is not new, but a business can often underappreciate the cybersecurity risks with them. Setting clear boundaries of acceptable and non-acceptable nations or regions in policy or standards provides early guidance to follow. If work is to be done offshore, then the on-site physical validation assessment becomes a key security control itself for due diligence efforts.

Ensure that data controls are in place to address any data exfiltration from the offshore vendors' premises, especially with the pandemic and remote access from homes in those countries that typically would have worked from a controlled corporate location pre-pandemic. The security of offshore—meaning not in your primary company location and market—requires more work and controls because by definition they are very remote. This remoteness means performing regular on-site due diligence, and other validations require an extra level of trust that can be achieved with tighter control language in contracts and due diligence.

CHAPTER

15

Transform
to Predictive

The statistics on the number of firms who do not perform adequate third-party due diligence are astounding. Surveys on this subject by such groups as Ponemon Institute routinely find that fewer than 55 percent of businesses have a vendor risk management program and an even fewer percentage of them perform any cybersecurity risk assessments. These programs are shown to be in desperate need, given the level of security incidents and breaches detailed in the Chapter 1. Those businesses with robust programs that view cybersecurity as a key risk domain have the ability to change the timing of some of their risk reduction.

All the due diligence activities described in the previous chapters have focused on either point-in-time assessments or Continuous Monitoring (CM). The steps outlined in those chapters articulate and describe the actions needed to start programs or improve upon existing ones. Engaging vendors in conversations and building relationships with them increase transparency and enable both businesses and their vendors to collectively work on reducing risk Such activities produce a lot of data, which is often just sitting there unused, unless it is needed for another due diligence or due care activity. This valuable information, however, can provide instructions on where risk really is located when a business is able to look at such data in an aggregate and holistic way.

In addition, engagements with the vendors are largely reactive as vendors arrive and teams perform the intake process assessment. In a year or more, as dictated by the risk policy or regulatory requirements, periodic remote or on-site assessments will occur. Occasionally, the vendor might be engaged if a CM alert crosses the threshold. The only other way a vendor could become occupied with the customer's Cybersecurity Third-Party Risk would be in the event of a breach or security incident notification. All these activities are reactive, and are not predictive or instructive.

Much like other risk domains, the Cybersecurity Third-Party Risk has enough data, and there is evidence that the right tools exist to change this current model. Plan to use the collected data and leverage it through data science to provide insightful analytics to make informed decisions. The ability to take all the risk data relevant to a vendor(s) for a complete picture across the whole company, within business groups, and down to individual suppliers, is not difficult once the required activities have begun as described in the previous chapters. It takes the Cybersecurity Third-Party Risk from one that waits for a timer or breach notification, to one that clearly identifies the vendors at highest risk and in need of more oversight.

The Data

The data is there. Whether your program is small or large, new or well-established, as due diligence and due care activities take place for third parties, data is recorded in systems of record. The following sections give just a few examples of data sources, but it can expand to include external data sources, such as Real Simple Syndication (RSS) feeds, application programming interfaces (API) connections, CVE data, or supplier updates directly, and is not confined to data in-house. See Figure 15.1.

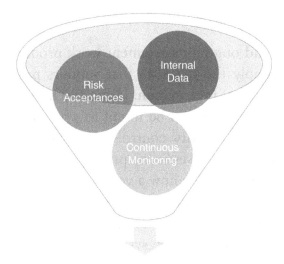

Reporting

FIGURE 15.1 The Data Funnel to Reporting

Vendor Records

One of the most important sets of data is on the third party itself: What type of data and how many records do they manage or process for the company? Is the data in a Cloud Service Provider (CSP), co-location, or the vendor data center, as each of these carries different levels of risk? For example, a CSP has a lower risk of physical access control failures than a vendor data center will, typically. Know what the supplier's history is for adherence to security controls: Is there a history of security gaps and/or incidents that would cause them to be considered risky as a matter of practice, or have they often received a "clean bill of health" from cybersecurity due diligence activities?

Due Diligence Records

IRQ, intake, and ongoing assessment work produces data. This data is not simply the raw data that vendors provide, but the trends of that actual information. Using the Intake and Remote questionnaires, answers can be found to provide more security for gaps or lower security controls than would otherwise be required. The on-site assessment produces some of the largest and most reliable data for how a vendor is performing on their security controls. This data is all entered and updated in the system of record for vendor risk management.

These gaps will be in the system of records most likely as "findings" or an "issue" that are tracked with remediation dates. If no remediation date is present, it is most likely to be a Risk Acceptance (RA). The findings that are tracked during the supplier's lifecycle are used for data in the reporting. Link periodic assessments to find any systemic issues with a vendor. If the same issues persist over a longer period of time, the risk may be increased due to lack of mitigation from the vendor.

Contract Language

All the vendors that are going to be part of the Cybersecurity Third-Party Risk scope must have, by process and policy, an Information Security Addendum or cybersecurity language in the Master Services Agreement (MSA). These security controls, which are listed in contractual language, produce data on a vendor's willingness or capability to meet them. As they are negotiated and language is redlined out or altered, it must be recorded in the system of record as well. If there were RAs on this or a known variance with the standard language, it is noted also in the vendor record.

Risk Acceptances

Along the way in the vendor lifecycle, a vendor may have RAs for an inability or reluctance to meet security control requirements. Organizations for risk management have a process defined for how a company can accept the risk for the missing control(s) to enable business to begin or continue working with the third party. These RAs are clear indicators of a gap in a control, and until there is remediation, they must remain "open" and tracked as such.

These RAs must contain some key information for them to be useful for tracking and reporting purposes. First, the security control gap(s) should be clearly identified along with what the control requirements are at the time of the Risk Acceptance. Documentation must also indicate if the vendor intends to remediate in the future (i.e., whether a specific date or a quarter in a future year for remediation is set) or if it has no plans to fix the gap.

Continuous Monitoring

CM provides valuable near real-time data for how vendors are performing for cybersecurity. This activity gives alerts on suppliers based upon key security controls that can be identified with the vendor security ratings software and the CM process. CM's process and program produces both point-in-time data and trends as the software and procedures output both the alerts and how they move over time for security.

Enhanced Continuous Monitoring

The enhanced CM process (ECM) and data provide a more in-depth data source for the vendors in this program. These vendors are the high-risk and/or systemically critical third parties as identified by a business and its cybersecurity. The data collected as part of enhanced CM is valuable and detailed, and includes fourth parties, software used to provide the service, connectivity data, and where the data is stored (e.g., a CSP, co-location, or vendor data center).

How Data Is Stored

It is important how this data is placed in any software system. This might seem like a simple issue, but many times a system of record or how a process works for the data can produce challenges for data use. For example, an RA process could be valid and effective by having an artifact circulate for the RA as it goes from Cybersecurity Third-Party Risk to the stakeholder(s) who are going to perform the acceptance with a signature. Once the artifact is completed with the appropriate executive's signature, the document goes into the system of record on the vendor's file as an attachment. How the data on the RA is accessed, catalogued, and followed in any reporting tool becomes challenging because most tools cannot dive into an attachment, scrub it for relevant data, then report against it. The RA and the data for what was the gap and its risk-rating must be available in any tracking software for a business intelligence or middleware tool to retrieve it. If the vendor stores the data in a cloud environment, ensure that its properly managed not only during the active engagement with the vendor, but also when the vendor is offboarded.

Level Set

Now that your team has the data as described in the preceding section, there's a process to collect it into a database and/or business intelligence tool. The next step is to consider the data's thresholds, or the levels for triggers, that are relevant for reporting and how the data will be managed.

The data produced can be quite large, depending on the number of vendors servicing your firm, as well as how much data is collected through the third-parties' lifecycles. Thresholds are necessary so that your Cybersecurity Third-Party Risk team recognizes when a limit is reached and needs attention. For this program, *thresholds* are the levels of risk that must be met in order to *trigger* action from that team. Triggers are the prompt for action or attention from the team when a threshold for a vendor has been met. A trigger can be a call to increase monitoring or to directly engage with a vendor, again depending on the thresholds.

It's best that the thresholds are first set and run at a prescribed time to find out what the triggers need to be for this purpose. This needs to be an iterative process as the bars, or levels, for each of these can require adjustment. Once it is determined that the thresholds are correct, then the triggers need to be placed in this "learning" mode to monitor their effectiveness. Lastly, the program documentation will list a periodic review date (at least annually) for the thresholds and triggers to assess their effectiveness and potential need for change based upon this analysis.

Next, the team needs to decide how to weight each data feed. Data from an on-site physical assessment is given a heavier weight than remote ones. Data from the internal systems of record are also given a heftier score than data coming from external feeds. This math must be clear and explainable to the audience. KC's math was published on an internal website, and a link was made available on all dashboards that took the user to that website. This openness led to acceptance of these reports with very little need to convince vendors of their value.

A Mature to Predictive Approach

The data is now in the systems of record, in a format that is available for reporting. In addition, your team has established levels and thresholds. The intended outcome is take all this data, place it in a business intelligence or analytics tool, and go from reactive to a more predictive risk-based approach on engaging vendors. In order to best demonstrate how it will work, let's use KC Enterprises and some of their use cases to illustrate how to move into this predictive model for Cybersecurity Third-Party Risk.

The Predictive Approach at KC Enterprises

All the work accomplished at KC produces the data and ability to provide analytical output for how they can manage their third-party pool in a more deliberate rather than reactive way. The team begins by exploring and cataloging where the relevant data is stored across the enterprise. An overwhelming majority of data is found in the Third-Party Risk Management software, yet some is also located in the purchasing software, threat intelligence systems, and the cybersecurity team's own software and tools used to manage vendor risk and their Cybersecurity Third-Party Risk program.

Thresholds are set based upon the vendor's assigned risk category, which are consistent with the risk-based approach that the program takes and enables for clear explanation of the "how" and "why" each vendor receives an escalation or intervention based upon the data and business intelligence software. A decision is made to use a "stoplight approach" for identifying triggers for action of red, yellow, and green to match the three levels of risk: high, medium, and low. It's also an easy way to clearly identify those that require attention (red), those that need some investigation (yellow), and vendors that are based upon the data available who present no new increased risk (green). See Figure 15.2. The triggers for each level are broken down as follows:

- **Red:** Vendors with red lights (i.e., who are high risk) are those who meet the following thresholds:
  - A breach within the last year
  - A high-Risk Acceptance that is still open
  - A high-risk finding that is not physically validated as remediated
  - A trigger from CM that is risk-rated as High
- **Yellow:** Vendors with yellow lights (i.e., who are medium risk) are those who meet the following thresholds:
  - A breach within the last two years
  - A medium- or low-Risk Acceptance that is still open
  - A medium- or low-risk finding that is not physically validated as remediated
  - A trigger from CM that is risk-rated as Medium
- **Green:** Vendors with green lights (i.e., who are low risk) are those who meet the following thresholds:
  - No breaches within the last three years
  - No open RAs, findings, or other identified risks

KC's team created a separate database for the data from all the identified sources, which are collected and then utilized by the business intelligence software. The links to these data

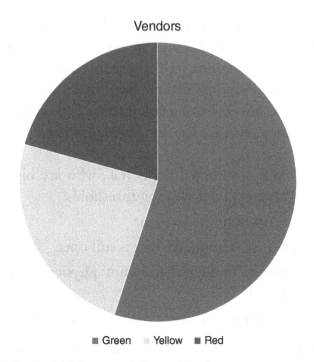

FIGURE 15.2   Red, Yellow, and Green Vendors

sources then are created and managed. For the internal vendor risk management software, the REST API transfers data on a nightly basis when any changes are made to vendors that are part of the security controls reporting. A *REST API* (also known as RESTful API) is an application programming interface (API or web API) that follows to the constraints of REST architectural style and allows for interaction with RESTful web services. The vendor security monitoring tool also contains a REST API, which updates any alerts and data for each vendor. Incident management software tools, threat intelligence applications and feeds, Risk Acceptance data, and the enhanced CM data are all then fed into this database as well using either APIs or an ETL (extract, transform, load) to blend the data from multiple sources into the data store. This database is called the "Vendor DB" for references in documentation.

The business intelligence (BI) tool then uses the Vendor DB for its data, and the triggers and thresholds are programmed into the BI tool. The biggest hurdle is often the variances in vendor names. For example, is ABC Corp. the same as ABC Inc.? This likely means a manual process to account for small differences in names. While the BI had some logic built into it to attempt to resolve such issues, it places any of these discrepancies (or suspected mismatches) into a separate folder for the analysts to manually intervene and update.

Use Case #1: Early Intervention

KC's point-in-time assessments were previously recognized as leaving large gaps of potential risk in between each of their due diligence activities. It was found that it could be a minimum of 364 days before a vendor's security posture was revalidated. As a result, the team created the CM and ECM programs, which created ongoing engagements with their vendors based upon leveraging the vendor security rating tools, threat intelligence products, and existing knowledge about the vendor's risk in the systems of record. These programs produced good results as the team saw risk reduction activity based upon the CM activities. However, the Vendor DB and the BI tool provide the ability to identify risk trends from a vendor(s) that goes a bit further than the CM model.

ABC Corp. is a vendor for KC that processes past due and collections notices for loans from their customers. ABC has access to personal identifiable information (PII) data, which includes names, emails, phone numbers, account information, and in many cases, payment information (i.e., bank account numbers and credit/debit card numbers). While the amount of past due and collections for loans varies month to month, the average is about 10,000 customer PII data records annually. This means ABC is placed in the medium-risk pool. The security reviews at the intake and ongoing assessments produced some findings, but they are closed through remediation and physical validation per their agreements. They have an open RA (listed as medium risk per the analysis by the Cybersecurity Third-Party Risk team) for the lack of a Privileged Access Manager (PAM) tool, which shows up on their vendor profile in the BI tool. Using the methodology described previously, the vendor has a yellow condition or an elevated risk due to the size and type of data plus the open RA at the medium-risk level. This vendor is not a critical vendor and while they are monitored with the CM program, they are not part of the Enhanced CM portfolio.

The BI tool and Vendor DB store and present all this data on a regular basis, while ABC Corp. remains at this Yellow status for a while. One day, however, a trigger originates from the threat intelligence software that someone from the Dark Web is offering to sell some supervisor accounts stolen from ABC Corp. The Vendor DB takes in this data from the API linked to the threat intelligence application. The BI tool then flags it, and based upon the keywords presented (i.e., supervisor, administrator, privileged), marks it as high risk. The vendor then appears in the red high-risk area, so the BI presents it on a dashboard for new high-risk events. A Cybersecurity Third-Party Risk analyst looks at the underlying data to ensure that there's no logic break or some mismatch, then they start the process to proactively engage ABC Corp.'s cybersecurity SMEs with the data to see if they can help investigate if the accounts are active. This can also be a starting point for a conversation about the value of a PAM solution and how this tool can vastly lower the risk of a privileged account being hacked.

Use Case #2: Red Vendors

Like many medium to large companies, KC Enterprises has many vendors and limited resources. Vendors in the Red category are those who meet the following thresholds:

- Have had a breach within the last year
- Have a high RA that is still open
- Have a high-risk finding that is not physically validated as remediated
- Have a CM trigger that is risk-rated as High

When a vendor meets one or more of these conditions, the team knows they require more due care and due diligence. Within this Red Vendors category, as the team calls it, there is additional sorting done for suppliers with more than one of these conditions. As a result, these vendors rise to the top of the category, further directing attention to where the highest known risk is identified. A monthly update is sent to the Business Information Security Officers (BISOs) who are assigned as both liaisons and advocates for building cybersecurity into the business units. Due to how these vendors are presented as the dashboard's Top 10 Red Vendors, they are often referred to as the "Wall of Shame." This nickname effectually draws more discussion around how these vendors can lessen their risk and move down to the Yellow or Green categories in cooperation with the business. (The second driver for such cooperation will be explained in Use Case #3.) Once executives repeatedly viewed this Wall of Shame on their reports, they realized that they were unaware that these particular vendors had such poor cybersecurity controls.

The Vendor DB and BI tool indicates which vendors are in the Red category and focuses attention on them. It does not mean the Yellow and Green vendors are ignored. This categorization provides a single pane of glass (the dashboard) for all vendors pulling in multiple data sources. This dashboard for Red Vendors, sorted by their business unit, is often used at meetings with the business leadership when discussing the overall health of their own vendor pool. When having these discussions, the fact that the criteria can be easily explained (and isn't a complex algorithm or math) enables for a transparent discussion of the risk a vendor poses and how vendor managers can plan to move to the Green category.

Use Case #3: Reporting

There is always going to be a need to report on the results, Key Risk/Performance Indicators (KRI/KPIs), and last-minute requests for individual, line of business, and whole portfolio data and trends. Whether these reports are regular, monthly, or quarterly reports to board risk committees, or ad-hoc requests, the Vendor DB and BI produce a way to clearly present the data in ways tailored for the need, which saves hours of time of gathering data from different systems, or leaving out important risk data because it is not linked or not easy to locate.

KC's Cybersecurity Third-Party Risk team created the following custom dashboards for each purpose or use case: Cybersecurity Leadership View, BISO View, BU View, Connected Vendors View, Enhanced CM View, Third-Party Incident Management (TPIM) View, CISO/CIO View, and so on. It took time to meet with the stakeholders and build requirements for each of the dashboards, and to perform some back-and-forth qualitative assessment (QA) in order to arrive at a final dashboard or view. In many cases, they were able to begin with an existing dashboard and allow it to evolve. Each viewer (user) who received these views could either wait for the regular periodic updates given to each (the Board reports went quarterly, the Enhanced CM work was viewed daily as both work queue and report), or they could look at the BI view assigned to them on demand. Because the data loads mostly stem from the API or ETL that ran nightly, viewers could look up timely risk data to make their decisions or ask questions.

The other data benefit was the transparency of the risk that individual suppliers posed, and how the data looked according to how its business unit or technology stack effectively shaped behavior. When business leadership is able to view the risk and understand third-party risk (post SolarWinds and others), then their support flows down into the culture of the company. It didn't occur overnight for KC, but there were more instances of business sponsors turning a keen eye to the risks of their vendors before consideration. As the data was tracked over months, the discussions taking place during reporting saw the number of Red Vendors slowly decrease. This decrease can take time as many contracts are set multi-year, and in some cases, as we discussed earlier, there are vendors who KC had little choice of as the only worthy vendor in the space. However, more pressure was coming from business leadership that raised the importance of remediating important high-risk findings or Risk Acceptances. That high-risk focus presented a real reduction of risk to the KC Enterprises.

Conclusion

In any organization, from small to large, data exists on how vendors are doing on cybersecurity controls. In a small company, data may be in the spreadsheets and files. In medium to large businesses, there are software packages, workflow tools, purchasing software, Third-Party Risk Management tools, technology tools and software, and often many more tools that contain this information. There are also external sources such as CVE feeds, pushes from RSS feeds, APIs, and more that pull or push information relevant on the same topics. Most companies that have a cybersecurity team almost certainly have a team that is collecting tons of data in Splunk or other tools in order to view and make decisions about their company's security. The same data and more exists for the risk and vulnerabilities that the vendors pose. Tools and software collect and manage this data (in data lakes, databases, and so on), in addition to countless BI and analytics tools that connect to where the data is stored.

The KC example is simple in design but effective for communicating risk. KC's Cybersecurity Third-Party Risk team directly benefited from the ability to create dashboards for their own work. For the on-site assessment team, if there were any new Red Vendors that drew particular concern as the team planned and scheduled each upcoming quarterly physical or virtual visits, these vendors were given close attention. KC's CM team created dashboards that drew attention to particular cases based upon the thresholds they set. Because they were threat hunting for third parties, that team designed a single pane of glass (a view that they were used to seeing in other similar off-the-shelf tools; here, a single pane of glass refers to being able to go to one place, digitally, to view status and reporting instead of going to multiple sources). While the third-party vendor risk management software provided some reporting on open findings, the security analyst team's Findings Dashboard provided additional contextual information about these open findings. This contextual information provides valuable data to the analyst on how to approach the vendor and vendor manager.

CHAPTER

16

Conclusion

In Chapter 1, we covered the cybersecurity risk of working with third parties via reports of various company breaches due to their vendors. In late 2020. the SolarWinds supply-chain attack news broke. Then, the Vietnam and Mongolian supply-chain hacks went public. All of these latest breaches are believed to have been perpetrated by Advanced Persistent Threats (APTs) who spent months performing the reconnaissance and leveraging key components to exploit weaknesses in the third-party due diligence of companies, governments, and individuals.

Advanced Persistent Threats Are the New Danger

The evidence surrounding SolarWinds and how the attackers used sophisticated means to perform the attack is mounting, with the discovery that a third identified malware was used in the attack. Named Sunspot, this malware was used in addition to the Sunburst and Teardrop malware already identified. It is believed that the Sunspot exploit was the first used in the chain. Amazingly, cybersecurity firm CrowdStrike released information that this malware was first deployed way back in September 2019 when the SolarWinds network was first breached.

It appears that the attackers planted the Sunspot on the build server for SolarWinds, which was used to construct the software and build the applications they sold. Sunspot was designed to do one thing: Observe the build server and watch for commands to assemble the Orion software—the one that was ultimately exploited—which was their top product with more than 30,000 customers globally. It's pretty incredible, as it's been implied that the hackers performed research on the top product they wanted to use for a broader attack, because SolarWinds was a means to an end, not the final target. They installed it and let it run for a long time, meaning they were willing to wait for it to achieve their ultimate goal—gaining access to tens of thousands of Solar-Winds customer networks.

It gets even more intriguing as it is observed what the Sunspot malware did: When a build command was sent to the build server for the Orion application, it stealthily pulled out the legitimate code and replaced it with the code the attackers created, which included the Sunburst malware. This meant the source code was altered and not even the developers were aware. The infected code then was uploaded to the official SolarWinds update servers for customers to download, which unwittingly opened their networks up to data theft and damage.

When the malware-infected Orion software was downloaded and installed at the customers' networks (e.g., governments, organizations, companies), it collected data and sent it back to the attackers via command and control servers (C&C). (The technique used was not common but had been previously used by APT teams.) The C&C used DNS communications to hide under the radar of the monitoring tools. Orion used a *domain generation algorithm* (DGA) to create domain names to contact. DGAs are algorithms used in many forms of malware that periodically generate a large number of domain names, which are used as drop-off locations for the C&C servers. The huge number of drop-off locations created by the DGA makes it nearly impossible for any law enforcement or forensics team to determine these locations and shut them down. The attackers even went so far as to use a public-key encryption to impersonate the hackers because C&C servers will only accept commands from properly signed controllers.

Each infected computer receives a unique ID by the Sunburst malware. This ID is comprised of the MAC (hardware) address, the computer's domain name, and the Windows installation Universally Unique Identifiers (UUID). The ID is then encrypted using an MD5 hash (i.e., an encryption algorithm typically used for digital signatures) and other sophisticated encryption methods. Due to how the communication takes place, the infected computer does not contact the C&C servers directly but goes over normal DNS traffic until it lands at the hacker's DNS server. The payload includes the domain name of the infected company and the information found on the compromised computer.

The communications to the C&C also includes information about any security software running on the computer. The malware would look to determine if any of the CrowdStrike, Carbon Black, FireEye, ESET, F-Secure, or Microsoft Defender tools were present, operating, stopped, or disabled. Based upon this information, the software then decides whether to stop the attack or to deploy another communication channel. The attackers then decide, based upon the information collected, whether the victim is worthy of the next step: deployment of the Teardrop backdoor trojan. For those instances where the victim was deemed unimportant or too high a risk, the Sunburst malware was instructed to remove itself from the network.

Further evidence now indicates that the attackers made a test run. From September to November 2019, the Orion product contained changes in it from the hackers, who were just seeing if they could insert malicious code into their builds without detection. As companies and governments continue to admit to being victims of the hack, more revelations will continue. One mystery that still remains is how the hackers gained access to the SolarWinds network in the first place. Was it a phishing campaign, exposed credentials, or some other method?

This detailed explanation of the SolarWinds timeline and methodology of the attackers is a new chapter in Cybersecurity Third-Party Risk. Along with the others previously mentioned (Vietnam, Mongolia, and so on), it shows how patient but focused these attackers are to get to their ultimate victims. These exploits highlight the numerous gaps that can be found in our security for third-party software and our detection capabilities; and they reveal how non-critical software can be exploited, and how even security experts and firms can be hacked as well. The names of those caught up in the SolarWinds attack are not small-time organizations, but ones with good defense-in-depth and security practices.

These advanced threats are not going to dry up when the pandemic is over and life returns to a new normal. The Solar-Winds attackers started well before anyone heard of COVID and are unrelated to the risks that it posed. Similar to the state attacks in Vietnam, Mongolia, and elsewhere, these attacks did not leverage the confusion and fear over the flu, but weaknesses in the supply chain. They will continue and more likely grow in their spread and sophistication. What is amazing right now is that of the 30,000+ customers that used the Orion product, so few have publicly disclosed the hack. The attackers actually tailored their product to avoid detection, to erase copies of unneeded malware, and to avoid targets that were viewed as well protected with popular antivirus or malware solutions.

The APT attackers have already figured out how to exploit the weakness at a time when the Third-Party Risk Management (TPRM) and Cybersecurity Third-Party Risk practices are still unprepared for this new threat. Organizations have an obligation to their customers and employees to protect their data, which can only be accomplished by developing, activating, managing, and testing a Third-Party Risk Management and Cybersecurity Third-Party Risk team that meets this new challenge and the existing threats.

Cybersecurity Third-Party Risk

Cybersecurity Third-Party Risk is not practiced enough, and statistics show that of those who perform it, they are not performing it enough. This gap has increased as organizations continue to ignore, or not pay enough attention to, their supply-chain security, and the cybercriminals and APTs are exploiting them in ever more crafty and dangerous ways. The recent exploits are a "call to arms" for organizations to not only pay attention to their own internal cybersecurity, but to treat supplier security with equal energy and resources.

Organizations lacking a TPRM program should start by creating a program and governance immediately. The frameworks are freely available and can be used as great starting points. In addition, several industry organizations can provide peer guidance and documentation to anyone who joins. Do a quick internet search on TPRM and you will get more than a few results. Start by making an inventory of your vendors, then identify those with sensitive data or a connection to your network. Create policies and standards for how third parties can conduct business with your organization. Identify leaders for each of the risk domains appropriate for your company and have them create questions and requirements for each of them.

Build a mature enterprise-wide TRPM program. Many approach it as a silo, where each business manages its own vendor pool. This compartmentalized approach, however, leads to several increased risks. First, when a single business unit decides to accept a risk, it is oftentimes accepting that risk for the whole company. If a breach occurs on the sales database at the vendor, the news and potential litigants will not blame the sales team or the vendor. It falls on the shoulders of the *whole* company to rectify the bad press and to pay for costs to make customers whole again. Second, the silo approach means the organization likely has multiple standards (if any) for vendor requirements and due diligence efforts. Allowing multiple standards provides zero clarity at the executive leadership level about risk across the entire organization.

Creating an enterprise TPRM reduces this risk of a nonstandard unified approach to third-party risk. A steady well-defined process for a vendor's intake, ongoing, and offboarding assessments benefits both the company and the vendors. The requirement to have suppliers go through a centrally managed process ensures consistency and the ability to provide a holistic view to company leadership of overall risk. TPRM and cybersecurity organizations have a lot in common—they exist to identify and reduce risk. These two teams have a common goal and with that, a singular focus. They just need to bridge the gap between them for a more direct and complete picture of the cybersecurity risks that third parties pose.

If you are a public company with a Board of Directors or a sole proprietorship, the tone of taking vendor risk seriously starts at the top. Senior management in all forms needs to be educated because they are ultimately the ones responsible to shareholders, customers, and employees for third-party risk. There must be a culture of transparency and accountability for how vendor relationships are screened, onboarded, monitored, and offboarded. Leadership must present a policy or standard statement that sets the tone and tenor for taking on vendor relationships as a risk that must be managed and reported. Leadership at a company can change a culture from one of compliance or complacency to an active threat-hunting mode that will lower risk from third parties.

Always take a risk-based approach. Most companies have hundreds or thousands of third parties that pose a risk to them. While the scope of vendors means they all need due diligence, focusing on those with the higher risk means resources know where to focus their energies. Create tiers or levels for suppliers to be placed in according to the risk they present; using a quantitative approach by number of records is an easy way and can lead to discussions about cyberliability coverage levels as well. These risk levels are used to determine how often a vendor should have assessments performed, the level and depth of questions in the assessments, and whether additional steps are needed to validate their security.

A risk-based approach also must to be taken into context when deciding which due diligence activities, monitoring software, staffing, and other resource considerations to consider. Just as in securing the internal corporate network, a cybersecurity team and corporate leadership will not always deploy every solution, software, and infinite resources; this is similar in the third-party risk area. Being risk-based means observing, calculating, and weighing the risk against the countermeasures or costs of mitigation. Not every solution can be deployed or should be used, but the ones that work for your organization at the levels required for your risk appetite are the most appropriate.

Conversations with third parties are crucial to the partnership needed to reduce their cybersecurity risk. Because many organizations view the third-party risk as a compliance or checkbox activity, their efforts are focused on sending out questionnaires and checklists for vendors to fill out attesting to their controls. These remote assessments can be useful, but a checklist will not produce a view of how the vendor's security is implemented holistically. Conversations with vendors, whether via a video-conferencing tool or in person, involves eye-to-eye contact and is valuable as a way to build trust and transparency.

On-site assessments are the best option for determining the actual security controls in production at a vendor. Remote and other assessments are where the supplier describes what they view as their state of infosec controls. It's the equivalent of asking your kids the state of their room's cleanliness. We've all been children or had children and know that their definition of "clean" is almost never the same as the parents' definition. An on-site assessment allows an analyst to perform a physical validation of security controls by looking at a vendor's policies and procedures, then having them demonstrate they are followed in production and practice. When parents go to their kids' rooms in our example, it offers a direct view of the items under the bed and the closet stuffed with all the toys and dirty clothes.

Concentrate your company's attention on closing risks and findings. All the due diligence activities are important in discovering security gaps at third parties. However, the end goal should be focused on remediation and closing up these gaps. A Cybersecurity Third-Party Risk team that takes ownership of these identified gaps and drives them to closure with the vendor is one that is bringing the purpose of their team to fulfillment—reducing risk.

Focus on cybersecurity risk with your vendors. While there are other risk domains in Third-Party Risk Management, the evidence and trends clearly demonstrate a need to "beef up" the security space. The other risk domains are not to be ignored, but the financial, reputational, and physical risks from a cybersecurity incident far outweigh any recent or historical cost of another risk domain being breached. This means having appropriate levels of staffing and expertise in the cybersecurity space assigned to or focused on third parties.

Many cybersecurity organizations have staff focused on the company's internal security. These teams specialize in looking for threats and preventing them from hacking into the network. And while some do have a Cybersecurity Third-Party Risk team, most do not if the polls are accurate. Resources can be a challenge. But in a new TPRM program, it can be as simple as collaborating with cybersecurity leadership to identify the appropriate subject-matter experts (SMEs) to assist with due diligence efforts. In organizations that are further along in the maturity model, having a Cybersecurity Third-Party Risk team does not necessarily guarantee success.

Most of these current teams reside inside Governance, Risk, and Compliance (GRC) teams. In regulated industries, Cybersecurity GRC teams are a necessity and there is nothing wrong with them as a practice. The issue often becomes that a Cybersecurity Third-Party Risk team is viewed as a compliance effort. Compliance and security are not synonymous. Compliance is a checkbox activity to let an auditor or regulator know that your organization obeys the rules. Security is an ongoing activity that never stops and is certainly not a point-in-time compliance effort. These teams need to get out of that mentality and become more akin to their cyber peers in threat operations teams who perform ongoing daily investigations into the security of the vendors.

Fourth parties cannot be ignored in any Cybersecurity Third-Party Risk program either. The processes for intake, ongoing, and offboarding assessments must screen and monitor these critical parts of the supply chain that are too often ignored or not viewed. Require vendors to declare what fourth parties they use to provide the service or product to your company. Place in the legal contracts that they must inform you of any updates or changes to their third-party relationships so new risk assessments can be performed if necessary. If a supplier is offboarded, do not forget to look at any fourth party that has your data and ensure it is properly destroyed or returned.

A smarter way to perform this oversight on fourth parties is also risk-based: Enhanced Continuous Monitoring focuses on the vendors who are viewed by business as systemically critical and the cybersecurity team has labeled as high risk. This pool of suppliers will be asked additional questions to provide more transparency on their third parties—your fourth parties—who are necessary to provide the service. Because each vendor can have dozens or more of their own third parties, managing fourth parties across your whole portfolio can become an exponential problem. Focusing on these high-value, high-risk vendors and what vendors they use provides a focused risk-based group that is small enough for a team to manage.

Cloud deployments with vendors are normal and cannot be avoided for most services or applications. The Shared Responsibility Model for the different deployment models (i.e., IaaS, PaaS, and SaaS—Identity, Platform, or Software as a Service) have distinct duties for the vendor and the CSP. Knowing which model a supplier is using with the CSP should drive the control questions asked as well as determine the responses required. The data's location, whether in a CSP, a co-location, or a vendor data center will require differences in approach as well, as most of the CSPs do not allow a physical security review. Vendor data centers can present some security challenges on the physical side as these are expensive complex environments.

Network connections are a door into your network by a vendor. The lifecycle of a third-party link must be clearly described in a policy and a process that is automated, lowers the chance of something being missed. Define clear guidance on both the hardware and any out-of-band (OOB) communications services that are allowed to be deployed. There are Zero-Trust (ZT) options for these third parties based upon their type of business or access pattern. Sales partners, integrated support services, and offshore business process outsourcing (BPOs) are some of the examples that were presented. These can be given their own enclaves with the benefit of a repeatable process that provides the correct access limits based upon the use case.

Legal requirements on security controls are critical mechanisms to clarify what your organization holds third parties to and often focuses the vendor on what is important to your security. If the language is in the Master Services Agreement (MSA) or in a separate addendum, the cybersecurity team can provide the specific controls for information security, hosting/cloud, privacy, and offshore controls. Create a list of non-negotiables that the company views as immutable requirements that protect your data and network. The obvious ones are ensuring data is encrypted at all stages, enforcing multi-factor authentication (MFA) for privileged accounts, and the ability to perform on-site assessments for vendors meeting this criteria.

Offshore third parties can bring cost savings and productivity gains to organizations, but they do require special contractual language and due diligence to monitor and control their particular security concerns. Vendors who are remote from the home country can increase challenges for travel and scheduling on-site assessments; however, these in-person due diligence efforts are almost obligatory for them. If possible, reduce or prevent the ability for data to move offshore to lower the risk of it becoming subject to another regulatory body. Plan the on-site assessments and be ready to perform them with an eye toward the physical security controls.

Use technology to your advantage. Lots of options exist to manage the TPRM program and its information through software and technology solutions. These applications can play a critical role in assessments, Continuous Monitoring, management, and reporting of risk. Centralizing the information in a database offers streamlined improvements for due diligence efforts, audits, compliance reporting, and ongoing performance oversight. Leverage workflow automation to ensure that people do not drop the ball. Either the TPRM software can contain this automation, or another tool that can interface via API to perform the workflow.

Some more advanced tools also exist that can consolidate and manage the third-party risk information and intelligence for risk-based decision-making. This reporting can be created on your own with a database and a business intelligence or analytics tool, or the software can be bought and customized from one of the makers of these more advanced software applications. These solutions can identify high-risk vendors and provide risk impact and likelihood, risk rankings, and vendor controls that are found insufficient or suspect. Leverage these tools to open communications about "Red Vendors" and ways to shape their behavior by lowering their risk with the help of business sponsors.

Test and validate your program periodically. There should be at least an annual validation of the program by another internal independent team or an outside entity. These assessments of the effectiveness of the program should start with looking at the policies, standards, and procedures that are published and followed by the internal teams. These audits then take random samples from the due diligence, monitoring, third-party incidents, and other activities to ensure that the steps are followed and provide the value expected. When gaps are found between policy and practice, they need to be documented, discussed, and remediated as soon as possible. This feedback into the program helps build a more mature and effective TRPM program.

Develop a reporting program and provide updates to the stakeholders and executive leadership to foster more transparency of vendor risk and ownership within the business and to help lower that risk by making different choices or pressuring current vendors to remediate gaps. The data from due diligence efforts, ongoing monitoring, Continuous Monitoring, connectivity, and other items can be rolled up in a database or with TPRM software tools. Teams can then create Key Performance/Risk Indicators (KPI/KRIs) to track the risk appetite using the data being produced. The number of third-party breaches, amount of past-due high-risk findings awaiting remediation, and other

KPI/KRIs are important for the Cybersecurity Third-Party Risk team to drive vendors to remediation and as a flag for executive leadership indicating potential high risks as the triggers surpass preset thresholds.

More mature programs can expand their abilities by leveraging all the data collected (internally and externally) to start a more predictive, risk-based focus on their third parties. Most of the TPRM programs—in particular, the cybersecurity teams—are fairly reactive in their work. A third party notifies them of a breach, a security assessment finds a gap or two or more, or the CM program throws an alert. The next step is to use all this data to begin making more deliberative decisions based upon all available information for those vendor(s).

Create some thresholds and triggers, along with how to provide a weight to each of the inputs. Not all data is created equally: An on-site assessment is more reliable than a remote one, and information retrieved from internal systems of record can be more dependable than external feeds. The dashboards that these systems can create will provide more transparency to executives but also can give the cybersecurity team a chance to become more predictive in their approach to vendors. When a third party has been trending toward a more "Red" category, it's different than waiting for an alert. Analytics and BI software offer an opportunity to get out of the current reflexive response into a model where third parties that are on a negative trajectory can be engaged with earlier.

Cybersecurity Third-Party Risk and Third-Party Risk Management are both professions and practices with solid frameworks, industry best-practices published, and adequate certification paths for adherents, in addition to all the other software, tools, and technology available to produce successful programs. There has been a lack of attention in some cybersecurity teams to the risks posed by third parties, and some TPRM groups have not sufficiently paid attention to the risks of cybersecurity. Much of the focus in regulated industries has been on compliance and not on treating them as a security activity. While TPRM and Cybersecurity need to grow their maturity individually, they need to increase their collaboration to mature cybersecurity third party risk as a whole. This collaboration will lower the risk posed by Advanced Persistent Threat actors to your data and networks.

Index